THE NEW PUBLIC MANAGEMENT OF SCOTLAND: LOCAL GOVERNMENT AND THE NATIONAL HEALTH SERVICE

AUSTRALIA
Law Book Co.
Sydney

CANADA and USA
Carswell
Toronto

HONG KONG
Sweet & Maxwell Asia

NEW ZEALAND
Brookers
Wellington

SINGAPORE and MALAYSIA
Sweet & Maxwell Asia
Singapore and Kuala Lumpur

THE NEW PUBLIC MANAGEMENT OF SCOTLAND: LOCAL GOVERNMENT AND THE NATIONAL HEALTH SERVICE

By

Dr. Bobby Mackie BA MSc DPA PhD FCIPD

Associate Dean
Caledonian Business School
Glasgow Caledonian University

Published in 2005 by
W. Green & Son Ltd
21 Alva Street
Edinburgh EH2 4PS

www.thomson.wgreen.com

Typeset by LBJ Typesetting Ltd of Kingsclere
Printed and bound in Great Britain by TJ International Ltd, Cornwall

No natural forests were destroyed to make this product; only farmed timber was used and replanted

A CIP catalogue record for this book is available from the British Library.

ISBN 0414 01600 9

Dedication

This book is dedicated to my wife Jean and our children
Elizabeth and Craig

Acknowledgements

I would like to take this opportunity to thank those who have supported this scholarly activity and those who have helped my academic development over my career. These include my colleagues past and present at Bell College, Hamilton and Glasgow Caledonian University as well as those I have worked with at the University of Strathclyde, the Open University and Unison. I would particularly like to thank Emeritus Professor Lewis Gunn of the University of Strathclyde and Colin Mair of the Scottish Local Government Improvement Service for their guidance on public management in Scotland and Dr. John Stanhagen for academic encouragement over the last 25 years.

I would also like to thank staff in the Division of Management and in the Centre for Public Policy and Management at Glasgow Caledonian University for their support and George Russell for reading the draft text. I would also like to acknowledge the support I have received from the publishers Thomson W. Green, particularly Valerie Malloch, Duncan Black and Alan Bett.

Finally, I would like to thank my wife Jean and our children Elizabeth and Craig for putting up with my academic endeavours over many years.

CONTENTS

CHAPTER 5: DEMOCRACY AND PUBLIC INVOLVEMENT

CHAPTER 6: MANAGEMENT AND DECISION MAKING

CHAPTER 7: ACCOUNTABILITY, REDRESS AND RESPONSIVENESS

CHAPTER 8: BEST VALUE, COMMUNITY PLANNING AND PARTNERSHIPS

CHAPTER 9: DELIVERING PUBLIC SERVICES: POLICY IMPLEMENTATION, PERFORMANCE MANAGEMENT AND QUALITY

PREFACE

Overview

This book was written to help students and practitioners gain a better understanding of the changing nature of Scottish local government and the NHS in Scotland taking into account the experience of devolved government since 1999. There are no other books that deal with management in Scottish local government and the NHS in Scotland in such a comprehensive manner and no other books that deal with the New Public Management of Scotland in the post-devolution period. The book is substantially a product of the author's research and consultancy activities in local government and the NHS over a 25-year period. In particular the author worked in and with Hamilton District Council and Strathclyde Regional Council from 1975–96. During that period the author was the Chief Examiner in Local Government Services for the Scottish Vocational Education Council and an author and consultant to Unison Education and Training. This book has been designed to meet the needs of undergraduate and post-graduate students as well as the needs of practitioners in both local government and the NHS in Scotland. It will be of particular use to local government officers and NHS employees wishing to know more about their own organisation and the ways in which it interacts with other areas of Scottish public administration and management.

Guide to Chapters

Chapter 1 sets the context of the New Public Management of Scotland by considering the key features of contemporary public management. In Chapter 2 there is a review of the development of Scottish governance and an explanation of the current structure and responsibilities of the Scottish Executive. Chapter 3 brings the reader up to date with a consideration of structures, contemporary mandates and the purposes of local government and the National Health Service in Scotland. Chapter 4 focuses on the finance of both systems and reviews the diversity of their services provision. Chapter 5 examines the ways in which the public can influence and participate in local government and the NHS. In Chapter 6 the book moves into a detailed analysis of public policy and management and its current status in both systems. Chapter 7 considers the accountability of local authorities and health boards and Chapter 8 reviews the implications of Best Value, Community Planning and Partnerships. Chapter 9 analyses the key features of contemporary public services delivery including policy implementation, performance management, performance indicators and quality systems. Chapter 10 presents a summative assessment of the future of local government and the NHS in Scotland in the devolved Scottish governance.

A Responsive Text

The purpose of the text is to respond to an identified need for more comprehensive information on contemporary developments in Scottish local government and the NHS in Scotland. The book brings together information from a diverse range of resources published by the Scottish Executive, the Scottish Parliament, NHS Scotland, the Convention of Scottish Local Authorities and Audit Scotland and adds commentary based on academic writings and personal experiences. The overall effect is a flexible contemporary resource focusing on Scottish local government and the NHS in Scotland.

Chapter 1

NEW PUBLIC MANAGEMENT

Introduction

This chapter establishes the context of the New Public Management (NPM) of Scotland by defining what NPM is and by reviewing its characteristics and development. The chapter begins by looking at the changing nature of management in the public sector before considering Public Choice Theory. The key features of New Public Management are then considered before moving on to a review of environmental influences on Scottish governance. Subsequent chapters look at the key features, past and present, of the two systems drawing conclusions on the ways in which NPM has impacted on local government and the NHS in Scotland. Chapters 6 and 9 pick up on the public management theme by considering management (Ch.6) and performance management (Ch.9).

The Changing Context of Public Services Delivery

The ways in which public services are delivered to client groups have changed radically over the past 25 years. The changes began with the privatisation policies of the Thatcher Government in the early 1980s. In addition, legislation forced public sector organisations to put increasing amounts of service provision out to competitive tender. Following the 1987 general election, the Conservative Government advocated far-reaching reforms in the organisation of the Civil Service through the creation of "Next Steps" agencies. Under these reforms, Civil Service Departments were disaggregated into distinct agencies, each responsible for delivering a particular public service. These agencies remain responsible to a government minister. Currently some two-thirds of the Civil Service are employed in executive agencies that deliver the bulk of services previously provided by central government departments. Public services are also provided increasingly through Non-Governmental Organisations (NGOs) and through Public Private Partnerships (PPPs) and the Public Finance Initiative (PFI). The

PFI was launched in 1992 as one of the main mechanisms through which the public sector can improve value for money in partnerships with the private sector. Recent changes have encouraged more widespread use of Design Build Finance Operate (DBFO) schemes whereby the responsibilities and risks relating to the procurement and operation of a capital asset are transferred to the private sector and the asset is then rented back to the public service provider. Examples are new schools, libraries, police stations and residential homes, and the refurbishment of existing property. The levels of payment by the public sector for use of the capital asset are based on the performance of the private sector against agreed levels of service.

The Scottish Executive has also become involved. The White Paper, *Modernising Government,* published in March 1999 (Scottish Executive, 1999), identifies a challenging agenda for improving public services and commits the Scottish Executive to improvements in policy making, increasing service responsiveness, enhancing service quality and to more effective use of new technology. In May 2003, the Scottish Executive set out in *A Partnership for a Better Scotland* (Scottish Executive, 2003) its continued commitment to improving public services in Scotland.

Public Management Trends

Before beginning this study of Scottish local government and the NHS in Scotland, it is necessary to review some of the key developments in UK public management over the last 50 years. A key influence on the relevance of management in the public sector was the work of the Plowden Committee (1961–1963) on the Control of Public Expenditure. The recommendations of this committee heralded a series of reforms in public expenditure, planning and control and general economic management. Keeling (1973), argues that these post-Plowden changes were a necessary, if not sufficient, condition of any significant improvement in management in the public service. In 1968, the Fulton Report (1968) gave a further description of "management" which was wider than any given previously and which was much more consistent with the use of the word in business. Thus, Fulton states that there are four aspects that make up the total management task of the Civil Service:

(a) formulation of policy under political direction;
(b) creating the machinery for implementation of policy;
(c) operation of the administrative machine; and
(d) accountability to Parliament and the public.

Policy in this context means a series of patterns of related decisions to which many circumstances, as well as personal, group and organisational influences, have contributed. For a policy to be regarded as a "public policy" it must to some degree have been generated or at least processed within the framework of governmental procedures, influences and organisations (Hogwood and Gunn, 1984, p.24). Keeling (1973) defines public administration as:

> "The review, in an area of public life, of law, its enforcement and revision; and decision-making on cases in that area submitted to the public service."

Management was traditionally considered to be a lower-level activity than policy and administration. Keeling (1973) views administration as the link between policy and management. Thus the traditional public sector model was of a continuum from policy through administration to management. This contrasts with the private sector interpretation as policy (in the form of strategies) followed by management and then administration (routine support). Dunsire (1975) considered that in industry it is management and direction that does the assigning of weights to decision factors, not administration.

Management has been well defined by Mintzberg (1975), as having the following basic purposes:

(a) to ensure the efficient production of goods and services;
(b) to design and maintain the stability of organisational operations;
(c) to adapt the organisation, in a controlled way, to the changing environment;
(d) to ensure that the organisation serves the ends of those persons who control it;
(e) to serve as the key information link between the organisation and its environment; and
(f) to operate the organisation's status system (see Chapter 6).

Managers carry out the above purposes through the management process. Each manager will be responsible for different types of decisions and will therefore place a different emphasis on the managerial activities he or she is involved in. The different elements in the management process include: planning; organising; directing; co-ordinating; controlling; communicating; and motivating. This list is by no means exhaustive, but it embraces the core elements identified by Fayol (1949) and Brech (1975).

Perry and Kraemer (1983) argue that between 1900 and 1970, American administrative theory alternated and was torn between the claims that public administration is unique (essentially a political science perspective) and that public and business administration are both part of generic management. Since 1970, the emerging and integrative paradigm is public management. Rainey *et al.* (1976) dispute this conclusion and suggest that public administration is different from management, if not wholly unique. Alison (1993) concludes that public and private managers are at least as different as they are similar, and that the differences are more important than the similarities. Gunn (1987), drawing on the aforementioned writings, considers that there are two positions on public management. The first is that public management involves learning from the generic management but maintaining a distinctiveness, because the public sector is much more dissimilar than similar to the business sector. The second position is that public management is management and the claims to uniqueness are overstated. Gunn (*ibid.*) concludes that there should be major inputs from "public policy" to public management teaching and research, as well as from "business management" and "generic management". But we should not forget what is relevant from the older "public administration" tradition, since there remain several important respects in which management of the public sector is necessarily and properly different from management of the business concern.

Public choice theory

Public choice theory uses the methods of neo-classical market economics to analyse politics and this approach, according to Carter (1998, p.184), has encouraged the use of marketplace surrogates to improve public service provision. Public choice theory has developed from the theoretical arguments made by conservative market economists such as Hayek (1944) and Friedman (1980). The basic argument supporting public choice theory is that government bureaucracy restricts the freedom of choice and power of the individual, and in addition, the traditional bureaucratic model does not provide an equivalent structure of incentives and rewards to those of the market (Hughes, 1998, pp.46–50). Government "contracts" with providers of public services, and in this quasi-contractual relationship requires information about the inputs, processes, outputs and outcomes of the contracted service provider. In a monopoly supply situation, there is a lack of information available on the extent to which the public service organisation is delivering value for money.

Public choice theory argues against "big" government and its key assumption is a comprehensive view of rationality. The "best" outcome will involve a maximum role for the market forces and a minimal role for government. If the role of government in supplying goods and services could be reduced, the economy as a whole would benefit. Markets, it is argued, have better mechanisms for accountability as opposed to a bureaucracy accountable to no one (Hughes, 1998, pp.10–11).

One means by which governments can improve their understanding of the public service providers' performance is to create competition in service provision. This involves the use of competitive tendering processes to ensure that the service contract is awarded to the contractor that convinces the public sector organisation that it provides the best value for money of those organisations tendering.

Theory assumes that by introducing the competitive dimension into the tendering process and following this up with performance monitoring, review and evaluation, government can enhance the value for money demonstrated by public service providers. In reality, government determines the public expenditure committed to a particular service and using this theory derives the optimum output for a given level of input, thereby maximising the value for money gained from public expenditure. Public choice theory advocates the maximisation of choice by individuals for both individual freedom and efficiency reasons. Dunleavy (1986, p.3) argues that the "rational actor" model assumes that people have the capability and the desire to rationalise their public service consumption choices to maximise their benefits net of costs. Niskanen (1973, p.23) argues that individual ambition leads to budget maximisation by the agency and to sub-optimisation within a public sector organisation as principal sub-divisions protect their own position at the expense of the well-being of the organisation as a whole.

Public choice arguments have been challenged by academics on the basis of a lack of evidence of bureaucrats maximising budgets to achieve their personal ends (Lane, 1995, pp.64–65). Hughes (1998, p.50) argues that public choice theory exaggerates the power of bureaucracy and disregards its public purpose. The results of the application of public choice theory to governmental activity over a 30-year period have been mixed according to Walsh (1995, pp.16–20). Markets do not work better under all circumstances, but there is evidence that using rational choice methods to design public policy may allow better targeting of expenditure. Public choice theory when translated into managerial action implies the use of private sector management techniques within the public sector.

New Public Management

New Public Management (NPM), according to Hood (1995, p.48), is a term used to describe the changes in public management that have taken place since the election of the Thatcher Conservative Government in 1979. The essence of NPM is a movement on the part of the public sector to become more like private business coupled with greater accountability to funders, stakeholders and clients for results achieved. There are several explanations of why

NPM emerged in the 1980s in many developed countries (see Taylor and Williams, 1991, p.172 and Osborne and Gaebler, 1992, pp.322–330). Hood (1995) concludes that the internationalisation of NPM contains important variations but there are also common themes. He argues that, in spite of allegations of internationalisation and the adoption of a new paradigm in public management, there was considerable variation in the extent to which different OECD countries adopted NPM during the 1980s. Four key conclusions are derived from the available evidence on the rise of the NPM. First, the pace of change has differed between countries. Secondly, there are clear variations between countries in the form that NPM has taken. Thirdly, there is no simple relationship between macro-economic performance levels and the degree of emphasis laid on NPM. Fourthly, there also seems to be no simple relationship between the dominant political party in government and the degree of emphasis placed on NPM. Dunsire (1990) identifies that much of NPM is built on the concept of homeostatic control and this necessitates the clarification of mission and goals in advance, and then developing accountability systems in relation to those pre-set goals. Many countries accepted the logic of this homeostatic control process and applied it to governmental activity. Most writers agree on the key elements of NPM and each of these is worthy of more detailed consideration.

According to Aucoin (1990), NPM has a hybrid theoretical background that combines economic organisation theory, emphasising centralisation and contractualism, with management theory emphasising devolution and managerialism. NPM thus includes management methods, devolution, deregulation, market reforms and customer/client service. Ferlie *et al.* (1996) distinguish between four different NPM models: the efficiency drive; downsizing and decentralisation; in search of excellence; and the public service orientation. NPM focuses on a number of issues but particularly on the role of government in society. Pollitt (1986, p.45) identifies several strands to the critique of this role. There was an assumption of public sector inefficiency; the recourse to private sector expertise; the value of performance-related pay; and the emphasis on new accounting procedures. There were also attempts to distinguish the policy role from the activity of management and to upgrade the importance of management.

The underpinning ideology informing NPM was conservatism and this resulted in a belief in the merits of the private sector. Public sector bureaucracies had become overstaffed and inefficient. The private sector knew how to engage in "turnaround management" the objectives of which are to cut costs, eliminate waste and return to competitiveness (Peters and Donald, 1994). Politicians came to accept that management was superior in the private sector and whenever possible the public sector should emulate the private sector or simply privatise the function (Peters, 1989, p.9). NPM involves a different conception of public accountability that requires the lessening or removing of differences between the public and private sector and shifting the emphasis from process accounting towards a greater element of accountability in terms of results. This approach reflected high trust in the market and private business methods, and low trust in public servants. The ideas of NPM according to Hood (1995) were couched in the language of economic rationalism.

There have been few independent evaluations of public management reforms. Broad-scope evaluations of the UK experience, according to Pollitt (2000), were notable by their absence during the Thatcher/Major administrations. The Blair administration appears to be more committed to the idea that evaluation should be a regular part of the reform process. Pollitt (2000) comments of the evaluations using a framework based on the potential gains from NPM reforms that these are: savings; improved processes; improved efficiency; greater effectiveness; and an increase in overall capacity. One conclusion of the evaluations in relation to savings is that the hypothesis that bureaucratic regimes would perform less well in macro-economic terms than regimes which had modernised themselves according to the NPM prescription cannot be proven or disproven. Movement in macro-economic aggregates simply will not provide sufficient evidence on the effects of management reform. In relation to specific savings attributable to local management reform initiatives, it is clear that many reforms have resulted in savings. Pollitt (2000) comments that savings on one dimension may have been offset by increases in expenditure elsewhere, or by quality reductions, or by scope of service reductions, or by shifting costs elsewhere in the public sector. Some governments have clearly reduced the number of public employees.

In relation to improved processes, there is no doubt that enhanced management competence has resulted in clear and lasting improvement in the way some public sector organisations operate. However, in some cases, improvement in one area has been at the expense of reductions in service effectiveness in other areas. High profile successful changes often disguise a shift in resource allocation that adversely affects the client's experience of a public service. As far as efficiency is concerned, this has been the key objective of many UK NPM reforms in the Civil Service, the NHS and in local government. Yet "evaluation" studies have often been flawed and present very subjective findings of efficiency gains. Talbot's research (1996, 1997) into the performance indicator systems used by UK "Next Steps" executive agencies showed that measurements of their efficiency were not robust. Reliability and validity in measures of performance efficiency were not widespread in UK public management.

Assessing public sector effectiveness is a difficult task. Management reforms do not in themselves address the multiple problems of public policy implementation and indeed are themselves subject to implementation difficulties. The UK Labour Government declared that there was a need to focus on outcomes rather than just on inputs, functions or value for money (Prime Minister and Minister for the Cabinet Office 1999, pp.15–18). Pollitt (1990) concludes that there is some evidence of improvements as a consequence of NPM but the evidence is limited and there are often alternative perspectives on the value of the NPM reforms. There is little doubt that NPM is a consequence of a variety of influencing factors but public choice theory underpins most, if not all, of the following NPM elements.

Disaggregation of public organisations

There has been a movement to break down large-scale public organisations into smaller units each having a high degree of autonomy and commonly providing a single service or servicing a single client group. Careers Scotland provides free careers information, advice and guidance to the people of Scotland—whatever their age, background or circumstances (youth careers advice was formerly a local authority service); the Scottish Prison Service (formerly part of the Scottish Office) provides custodial services and Highlands and Islands Enterprise provides business development support to the North of Scotland and to the Islands with Scottish Enterprise providing these services to the rest of Scotland. This disaggregation implies each smaller-scale organisation having its own corporate identity, greater autonomy in resource management, devolved strategic planning and operational management while retaining accountability and funding links to government and funding bodies.

Competition

NPM implies the creation of competitive and quasi-competitive markets to replace monopolistic public service provision. The trend towards greater competition began in the United Kingdom with the introduction in the early 1980s of Compulsory Competitive Tendering (CCT). CCT required certain public sector organisation to award contracts for specified services such as cleaning, roads maintenance and catering (the direct services) following a tendering process which was open to private sector organisations. CCT has been replaced by Best Value principles and practices but its legacy remains in the "business-like" management of public sector direct services.

Private sector styles of management

There is much greater use of private sector management tools and techniques in the public sector than there was 25 years ago.

Even the language of public management has changed to incorporate terms such as "performance management", "strategic management" and "total quality management". An illustration of this trend is the changing titles of programmes of formal qualifications for public sector employees. Gone are the days of the HNC in Public Administration and the Diploma in Public Administration (DPA) as these have been replaced by named awards in "Public Management" and by public management options within business studies and management programmes such as the Master of Business Administration (MBA) degree.

Resource management

There is a much greater emphasis in public management organisations on value for money and the growing trend to account for the ways in which resources are used through external audit and the publication of performance data in the form of performance indicators (PIs). Within organisations there is extensive devolved budgeting where managers at different levels in the organisation control their own budgets. Audit Scotland works closely with the Scottish Executive to monitor the ways in which Scottish public sector organisations manage their resources (see Ch.4).

"Hands-on management"

Managers, particularly at executive levels, in public sector organisations are much more directly involved in both the strategic management of the organisation and the operationalisation of strategy. A common approach in the public sector is for the government and/or funders to set out what they would like the public sector organisation to achieve, but thereafter the organisation formulates its own strategic plan, submits it for approval and, following approval by the Scottish Executive or an agency acting on behalf of the Scottish Executive, implements the plan. A good example of this is the Development Planning process followed by the Scottish colleges of further education. Colleges submit plans to the Funding Council and when approved the Development Plan becomes the responsibility of the college executive and its management team who implement the plan to the best of their ability.

Performance expectations

Government, under NPM, is much more "hands-off" but nevertheless has to retain control of public spending and at a more micro-level has to ensure that its public policy objectives are met. Government and funders tend to set out explicit standards of expected performance which must be built into the strategic plans of the public sector organisations. The public sector organisations are assessed on the extent to which they have achieved the desired performance levels (see Ch.9).

Performance results

This is linked to the previous element and relates to the ongoing monitoring of performance by government and funders. This emphasis on output controls requires much more comprehensive systems of performance indicators, inspection and audit. Future levels of funding are, in part, determined by the levels of performance achieved.

Collectively, these elements create radically different public management organisations with radically different operating systems and accountability processes from those of the 1970s. For the purpose of comprehensive analysis, the NPM changes can be considered at three distinct levels. The first is at the level of "performance governance". This focuses on the changing nature of the relationships between public sector organisations and government, and between public sector organisations and funders acting on behalf of government. The emphasis in performance governance is on effective public policy implementation, accountability and value for money. The second level is "performance management". This concerns the strategic and operational management of the organisation by its executive and its managers at all levels. The emphasis here is on the effective operationalisation of strategy through managerial decision-making which recognises the significance of economy, efficiency, effectiveness, quality and equality in public service provision. The third level of analysis is "consumerism" that is the extent to which public sector organisations develop and build relationships with their stakeholders and their clients and customers. These three elements provide an excellent framework for analysing the New Public Management of Scotland.

Having considered the generic features of NPM and its underlying theory, it would beneficial to now consider the ways in which the public management environment has impacted on public management and public managers in Scotland. With the setting up of the devolved Scottish Parliament in 1999, the Scottish dimension of change has emerged. Prior to this there were particular Scottish responses to environmental influences but Scottish public management tended to follow UK influences.

Environmental influences on the New Public Management of Scotland

PEST analysis, as a technique has been used extensively by public and private sector organisations as part of their strategic management processes. PEST analysis, in this context, involves examining political, economic, social, technological and other influences and their impacts on public management and the management of local government and the NHS. Fahey and Narayanan's model of the macro-environment (1986, pp.28–34) stresses that the environment can be understood only as a system, in which each factor is related to and affects every other factor. This section will therefore be divided on the basis of the sub-elements of the PEST analysis to better understand the factors affecting the public management of Scotland.

Political influences

The Labour Government elected in 1945 promoted nationalisation, the creation of the NHS and the consolidation of the welfare state. Successive governments, Conservative and Labour, remained committed to this broad-based policy direction between 1945 and 1970. The post-war consensus thus involved a change in the relationship between citizens and the state as government became more active in the social and economic fields than it ever had been before the Second World War. The Wilson Governments (1964–70) sought to expand the system of further and higher education and in this period education replaced defence as the biggest item of public expenditure after social services.

The Heath Conservative Government (1970–74) was initially committed to challenge some of the core elements of the post-war consensus. There was to be no government support for "lame duck" industries that could not survive the rigours of the marketplace. Central government was rationalised and local government reformed and re-organised. This challenge to the post-war consensus was blown off course by a series of "U-turns". Such events included major industrial disputes, the nationalisation of Rolls Royce and the "oil crises".

The Labour Government (1974–79), under Wilson then Callaghan, attempted to return to the post-war consensus policies but was unable to do so because of an economic crisis. Britain sought and obtained a loan from the International Monetary Fund (IMF) on the condition that there was to be a reduction in public expenditure. This was a watershed in British politics as it marks the end of the post-war consensus and the associated role of the state. The Government was forced to cut public expenditure, reduce the money supply and abandon the commitment to full employment policies. The Government also decided to sell off some of the state-owned shares in British Petroleum thus setting a precedent for the privatisation policies of the Thatcher Governments. In the 1978–79 "Winter of Discontent", the "social contract" between the Government, the trade unions and employers finally collapsed. Margaret Thatcher and the Conservatives were elected in May 1979.

The consensus on the mixed economy and the welfare state disintegrated in the period from 1979. Particularly significant influences were the liberal views of the Government on the role of the state and the management of the economy. Margaret Thatcher associated the public sector with bureaucracy, inefficiency, absence of choice and the generation of a welfare dependency culture. The term the "New Right" was used to describe this mixture of liberalism and conservatism that influenced the ideology of the Thatcher Governments. The post-war consensus was fundamentally challenged and the values of the free market promoted as the basis of efficiency in the allocation of resources. The New Right policies were targeted at reducing the scale of the public sector, reducing the scope of government and changing the way in which public sector organisations operated. The key aims being to maximise the role of the market forces and minimise the role of government. The rise of New Right thinking within the Conservative Party was facilitated by linking free market ideas with a "more congenial conservative emphasis on a stronger state in the fields of defence, and law and order, and a strengthened family" (Gamble, 1985, p.139). This coupled with a stress on community, the preservation of national sovereignty, and a reassertion of traditional morals, discipline and respect for authority amounted to the core of New Right thinking.

In the early 1990s, internal disagreements emerged within the ranks of the Conservative Government and the Labour Party sustained its shift to the centre ground on such issues as the free enterprise economy, public spending, unilateral nuclear disarmament and Europe. By 1992, a new consensus, further to the right than its post-war predecessor, had emerged (Jones and Kavanagh, 1998, p.7). John Major became leader of the Conservative Party and the Conservatives gained a slender majority at the 1992 general election. The Major Government repealed the Poll Tax, concentrated on curbing inflation, improving the delivery of public services and reforming the Civil Service.

In the 1997 general election, the Conservative Party was faced by a formidable and much reformed Labour Party. Tony Blair's New Labour was elected with a substantial majority and accepted existing rates of income tax and levels of public spending, set tough targets for inflation and promised to reduce public borrowing. New Labour also accepted many of the trade union reforms, privatisation and a more selective approach to welfare. There was therefore considerable convergence between the policies of the New Right and the policies of New Labour. However, Tony Blair argues that the ideology of New Labour is a "third way" between the New Right and the "Old Left".

The devolution debate in Scotland and Wales has concerned the extent to which powers could be appropriately delegated to the new Scottish Parliament and to the Welsh Assembly. The Labour Government has fulfilled its election commitment to the Scottish and Welsh peoples and elections for the Parliament and the Assembly were held on May 6, 1999. The Scottish Parliament extends democratic control over the responsibilities previously exercised administratively by the Scottish Office.

Economic influences

Post-war governments in the United Kingdom have been heavily involved in the management of the economy. Both Labour and Conservative governments after 1945 accepted that it was their responsibility to achieve popularly-supported economic objectives. For over 30 years after the Second World War, governments of both parties accepted that it was part of their job to do at least four things:

(a) to maintain a high and stable level of employment;
(b) to achieve economic growth (and rising standards of living);
(c) to keep prices stable; and
(d) to avoid deficits in the balance of payments.

These aims were influenced by John Maynard Keynes (1936), hence Keynesianism. From 1945 to 1970, every government put their faith in Keynesian "demand management" and set up a variety of prices and incomes controls plus measures to stimulate investment and plan future growth. In 1970, Heath's Conservative Government experimented briefly with a monetarist approach but reverted to Keynesianism. By the mid-1970s, Keynesianism seemed inadequate as Britain was experiencing high inflation, stagnant growth and high unemployment, resulting in an economic crisis. In 1976, the Labour Government adopted policies on monetary control as required by the terms of the International Monetary Fund (IMF) loan. Public expenditure cuts and increased unemployment coupled with Keynesian intervention through incomes restraint and government cash for ailing industries resulted in economic improvements, but this was insufficient to convince the electorate. A Conservative Government was elected in 1979 committed to monetarist economic policies.

This owes much to pre-Keynesian classical economists such as Adam Smith and its chief contemporary protagonist has been Milton Friedman. Governments must, according to Friedman, concentrate on strict control of the money supply and withdraw from substantial economic intervention thus giving the market forces free reign. Inflation will dampen down and the economy will return to healthy growth.

The periods of Conservative government have left long-term growth prospects in Britain better than would have seemed possible in 1979. Macro-economic management was the weakness of the Conservative's economic policies, with major errors responsible for excessive economic fluctuations and the eventual loss of the government's reputation for economic competence, while at the same time their record on inflation comparing favourably with that of other OECD countries. Micro-economic management was much better through privatisation, improved industrial relations and reduced public expenditure. Opportunities were missed, according to Craft (1998, p.35) in the areas of welfare and tax reforms.

"Old Labour's" attachment to state ownership, protectionism, high taxation, subsidies to physical investment and Keynesian demand management together with an unwillingness to accept reforms to industrial relations and welfare benefits, were, according to Craft (1998, p.36), most unfortunate. New Labour appears to have radically different economic policies from Old Labour with the establishment of an independent central bank, no interest in reversing privatisation and continued public expenditure restraint. The intentions to raise standards of education and promote fundamental reform of welfare provision also indicate that there is an implicit acceptance of many of the supply-side reforms of the Conservative years. Indeed, the Labour Government gave a commitment to accept, for the first two years of its office, the income tax and spending levels inherited from the previous Government. Hutton (1996 and 1997) argues that it is possible to achieve the social reformist goal of a balance of economic growth and social welfare and retain a more liberal approach in creating a prosperous market economy with long-term investment, a commitment to community and political reform to modernise the state.

Social influences

The occupational structure of Britain has changed considerably over the past 50 years. Traditional, labour-intensive industries have declined to be replaced by highly automated light manufacturing and service industries. There has been an exponential growth in part-time employment and in the number of women in the labour force. Public sector employment peaked at 7.2 million in 1981 but has reduced to less than 6 million. The occupational pattern has changed from a pyramid shape to a pear shape largely due to an expanded middle class and a smaller working class.

Wealth and income differentials have narrowed marginally in recent years. During the 1980s, the Thatcher Government's tax reductions combined with benefit cuts caused a substantial increase in the differences between high and low earners. A substantial amount of wealth is owned by individuals in the form of bank deposits, savings accounts, property and stocks and shares. The pattern of distribution is much more unequal than that of income: the ownership of wealth is highly concentrated with the wealthiest 50per cent of the population owning over 90per cent of the country's wealth.

Over 65 per cent of the population own their own home, this figure was greatly boosted by the sale of over 1 million council houses since 1979, yet there are still over 30,000 people homeless in the United Kingdom.

One in three children live in poverty and almost four in ten adults earn less than the Council of Europe's decency threshold. Sixty-five per cent of disabled people live below the poverty line. The poorest groups in society are the old, the disabled, the unemployed, immigrants and families with young children.

There remains considerable movement between the different social groupings in Britain. Goldthorpe (1987) identified that the least socially mobile in society are the upper class and the working class. Adonis and Pollard (1997) perceive what they call the emergent "super class". They argue that we have a new elite of top professionals and managers divorced from the rest of society by wealth, education, values, residence and lifestyle. These authors maintain that the new class was born out of the financial services industry based in the City of London that expanded hugely in the 1980s. The emergence of this "super class" has resulted in Oxbridge graduates changing career aspirations and career directions away from public service towards the City and the law. Moreover many who opted for the public sector have since left it. Education is a vital factor in determining social mobility. Access to higher education is particularly important in determining life chances. About 7 per cent of children are privately educated, yet over 80 per cent of senior judges in the mid-1970s were privately educated. The replacement of grammar schools by comprehensives has not altered this elitism. The proportions of those entering higher education from manual working class families has scarcely shifted by comparison with those from the professional and managerial classes.

Many groups in our society continue to suffer from inequality of opportunity. There are regional variations in earnings and other socio-economic indicators. Socio-economic indicators also confirm the multiple disadvantages suffered by people as a consequence of gender, race, disability, ethnicity and sexual orientation in British society. There is evidence of an "underclass" in Britain comprising the long-term unemployed, single parent families and pensioners living solely on state benefits. Dahrendorf (1985) has commented that the problems caused by the "underclass" are "the greatest single challenge to civilised existence in Britain".

Technological influences

Global competition, technological innovation, and a shift away from the mass production of standardised goods and services, according to Piore and Sable (1984), led to a sustained attack on the bureaucratic paradigm of organisational efficiency and its replacement by the flexible or adaptive paradigm. The progressive features of this flexible paradigm include greater workplace democracy, job satisfaction and social justice. However, according to Halsey *et al.* (1997), the potential of the flexible paradigm has not been realised because of the adverse effects on people of the transition from bureaucracy to flexibility. The demise of mass long-term employment has led to the public sector employees having to come to terms with uncertain occupational futures (Butler and Savage, 1995).

Bureaucracy, as the form of organisation that delivered mass education and industrial efficiency, is now considered outmoded and inefficient; while the notion of a common culture promoted through multi-cultural educational provision is being challenged. Various cultural groups have asserted their rights to educate their children according to their specific religious and cultural values.

The impact of technological change is everywhere. In particular, changes relating to the creation, transmission, manipulation and presentation of data have impacted on all organisations and all of our lives. Rowe and Thompson (1996) summarise the diverse ways in which technology has influenced the world in which we live under six principal headings:

(a) size;
(b) cost;
(c) reliability;
(d) capacity;
(e) speed; and
(f) flexibility.

In effect, information technology has resulted in smaller components, lower costs of equipment, increased reliability, improved capacity, enhanced speed of processing and much greater flexibility. The range of applications of information technology is enormous as it can serve as the basis for new products, replace conventional circuiting in existing products, change production and service delivery processes and affect information systems.

In relation to public management, it is the influence of technology on information systems that has had the greatest impact. The first computer to be used for administrative work in government in the United Kingdom was installed in January 1958 to process payrolls (Fulton, 1968, Vol.4, p.634). From the early 1970s onwards, the use of mainframe computers spread from central functions of government to service delivery departments thus making it possible to cope with the growing scale, scope and complexity of public services. According to Taylor and Williams (1991), the increasing synergy of computing and telecommunications created the possibility for distributing computing power and computerised information to front-line staff and, therefore, for decentralised or flexible administrative arrangements.

The Fulton Committee (1968) advocated accountable management and recognised that this necessitated informational resources and methods of measuring performance. However, in the 1970s progress on comprehensive management information systems (MIS) was haphazard and it was not until the 1980s that MIS in the public sector developed. According to Taylor and Williams (1991), central government departments have been asked to deliver a variety of not entirely compatible information reflecting the plurality of stakeholding in MIS. The National Audit Office (1986, p.4) identified that there was inflexibility and fragmentation in government MIS. In the 1990s, there was a shift from a focus on outmoded technologies to an emphasis on the quality of information that can be generated by a good MIS. There has been recognition of the need for bespoke systems, designed and developed through systems analysis techniques, to ensure that systems meet MIS stakeholders' requirements.

It is against this background of environmental influences that the governance of Scotland has been re-shaped.

Conclusion

This chapter has considered New Public Management (NPM) and its influences. To gain a better understanding of the impact of NPM on Scottish local government and the NHS in Scotland, it will necessitate a comprehensive analysis of key features of local government and the NHS in Scotland within an analytical framework based on the key elements of NPM coupled with the framework of performance governance, performance management and consumerism.

According to Scott (2003) organisations are systems of elements, each of which affects and is affected by, the others. Goals are not the key to understanding the nature and functioning of organisations, no more than are the organisations' origins, stakeholders, structure, technology and environmental forces. To fully understand organisations you have to consider all of these elements. Chapter 2 begins this process by looking at the governance of Scotland.

Chapter 2

THE GOVERNANCE OF SCOTLAND

Introduction

This chapter picks up on the assertion by Scott (2003) that in order to understand organisations you have to consider, among other things, their origins and goals. The chapter begins by considering the historical development of government in Scotland before going on to establish the distinctive characteristics of local government and the NHS in Scotland. It therefore establishes the context of the relationships between the Scottish Executive, local government and the NHS in Scotland. Chapter 3 then focuses on the structures (past and present) of local government and the NHS.

Government in Scotland

Devolution has not removed Scotland from the United Kingdom. The Westminster Parliament remains sovereign over all of the United Kingdom. Scotland is represented by 59 Westminster MPs and some government policy matters remain "reserved" for Westminster decision-making, others are devolved for the Scottish Parliament at Holyrood in Edinburgh. To fully appreciate the dynamic nature of Scottish governance, it is necessary to review the pre- and post-devolution arrangements for the governance of Scottish affairs.

Scottish Governance prior to July 1, 1999: Westminster and the Scottish Office

The kingdoms of Scotland and England were united under one crown in 1603 when James VI of Scotland ascended the English throne, however, separate Parliaments continued to meet in Edinburgh and London. In 1707, the Scottish and English Parliaments passed the Act of Union which joined the two nations under one Parliament of Great Britain meeting at Westminster in London. The settlement provided for a number of seats for Scottish representatives in the House of Commons and the House of Lords and for a Secretary of State for Scotland in Parliament.

New arrangements were made in 1709 when responsibility for Scotland was given to the Secretary of State for Great Britain, but as the post was often vacant, the Lord Advocate, the principal law officer in Scotland, managed Scottish affairs. Parliament appointed separate Secretaries of State for home and foreign affairs in 1782, and the Home Secretary, advised by the Lord Advocate, became responsible for domestic affairs in Scotland as in England and Wales. In 1885, a Secretary for Scotland was appointed, and the Scottish Office was established at Dover House, Whitehall. The Secretary for Scotland took responsibility for administering Scotland's separate legal system and the Scottish Boards for agriculture, education, local government and health.

The increasing responsibilities of the Secretary for Scotland saw the post upgraded to Secretary of State in 1926, and in 1928, the Scottish Boards became departments of the Scottish Office. Further re-organisation in 1939 brought about the establishment of departments of the Scottish Office: home affairs (including prisons), fisheries, education, agriculture, health and housing. St Andrews House in Edinburgh became the headquarters of the Scottish Office and Dover House was retained as a liaison office in Whitehall. Between 1945 and 1999 the responsibilities of the Secretary of State for Scotland widened considerably to include economic and industrial affairs, the environment, roads and transport, and town and country planning but excluded responsibility for defence, foreign policy and social security.

The Secretary of State for Scotland prior to July 1, 1999 was responsible to Parliament for the operations of the Scottish Office and for Scottish legislation. Westminster Parliament utilised the Scottish Grand Committee, consisting of all Scottish MPs, to consider proposed legislation concerned exclusively with Scotland, and debated the financial estimates of the Scottish Departments and wider aspects of Scottish affairs. The Scottish Grand Committee met occasionally in Edinburgh. There were also two Scottish Standing Committees, each of at least 16 Scottish MPs whose role was to examine in detail legislation affecting Scotland, and a Scottish Select Committee of 11 Scottish MPs which examined the financial estimates, administration and policy of the Scottish Office and other public bodies.

Scottish peers are still entitled to sit in the House of Lords, and the 59 parliamentary constituencies in Scotland continue to elect Members of the House of Commons. The number of Scottish MPs at Westminster was reduced from 72 to 59 from the 2005 General Election onwards.

The Secretary of State for Scotland was a member of the UK Cabinet, and directly responsible to Parliament for those functions of government which were separately administered in Scotland. The Secretary of State for Scotland had to ensure that the UK Cabinet and other ministers with responsibilities in Scotland were kept fully aware of Scottish needs and circumstances.

The Secretary of State for Scotland was advised on legal matters by the Scottish Law Officers (the Lord Advocate and the Solicitor General for Scotland), who were Ministers of the Crown, and was supported by a Minister of State and the Parliamentary Under-Secretaries of State who took day-to-day responsibility for Departments of the Scottish Office. The Secretary of State for Scotland appointed members to the boards of various public bodies, including Scottish Enterprise and Health Boards.

Prior to July 1, 1999, the Scottish Office consisted of five principal departments: agriculture and fisheries; education; environment; home and health; and industry. The responsibilities of the principal departments are clear from their titles, but for the purpose of this review it is worth stating that housing policy, local government, land-use planning and environmental issues were within the remit of the Scottish Office Environment Department and the Scottish Office Home and Health Department had responsibility for police, prison and fire services; health policy and the management of the NHS in Scotland; social work services; and electoral procedures. The Scottish Office Industry Department had responsibility for industrial development and the construction, improvement and maintenance of the trunk road network in Scotland. The Scottish Office had several other departments including Scottish Office Central Services Divisions, the Scottish Courts Administration and the General Register Office for Scotland.

Devolution and the Scottish Parliament

The 1973 Royal Commission on the Constitution (the Kilbrandon Commission) recommended a form of legislative devolution for Scotland. The Labour Government 1974–79 put forward legislative proposals to establish a Scottish Assembly, and the Scotland Act 1978 was passed, requiring that 40 per cent of the Scottish electorate had to support the Act in a referendum before the it was implemented. In the March 1, 1979 referendum, the legislative proposal to support the devolution scheme was supported by 52 per cent of those voting, but this only constituted 33 per cent of the electorate and as a consequence the devolution proposals contained in the Scotland Act 1978 could not be implemented.

The Conservative Governments 1979–97 did not support the concept of devolved government for Scotland, but pressure was growing in the 1980s for some governmental response to the demands of the devolutionaries. Various pressure groups formed the Scottish Constitutional Convention in the late 1980s, and in 1989 it published its policy aims incorporating the demand for a Scottish Parliament with law-making powers. The Scottish Constitutional Convention continued to lobby for devolved government in the 1990s and produced a final report in 1995 entitled "Scotland's Parliament, Scotland's Right". This report strongly influenced the Labour Party's devolution policy and was incorporated into its manifesto for the 1997 general election.

Following the election of the Blair Government in 1997, legislative proposals on devolution were produced which included plans for a referendum in advance (unlike the 1978 arrangements). The referendum held on September 11, 1997 contained two questions: the first related to the desirability of setting up a Scottish Parliament, 74.3 per cent of turnout (44.87 per cent of electorate) supported this proposal; the second question was on the desirability of a Scottish Parliament having tax-raising powers, 63.5 per cent of turnout (38.24 per cent of electorate) supported this proposal. The Scotland Bill was placed before Parliament in early 1998 and received Royal Assent in November of that year.

The Secretary of State for Scotland, Donald Dewar, had meanwhile established a Consultative Steering Group to develop proposals for the implementation of the Scotland Act 1998. Following consultation, the Consultative Steering Group produced a report in January 1999 entitled "Shaping Scotland's Parliament" which was used to develop the operationalisation of the Scottish Parliament. There would continue to be a Secretary of State for Scotland who would be a member of the Westminster Parliament and Scotland would continue to elect MPs to the Westminster Parliament.

Elections were held on May 6, 1999 for the 129 representatives known as Members of the Scottish Parliament (MSPs). The electoral process used is a form of proportional representation known as the Additional Member System. Each voter has two votes. The first vote is for a constituency member who will be the candidate winning the largest number of votes in a constituency (a total of 73 MSPs). The second vote is for a political party (who provide a list of nominations) or for a candidate standing as an individual, within a larger electoral area called a Scottish Parliament region. There are eight regions and each region has seven seats in the Scottish Parliament (a total of 56). MSPs are elected for a term of office of four years. On July 1, 1999, the Scottish Parliament held its first meeting since 1707 in Edinburgh. The Scottish Parliament has powers to pass legislation on devolved matters and to alter the rate of taxation by up to three pence in the pound. The first First Minister was Donald Dewar.

The Scottish Executive from 1999

The Scotland Act 1998 provides for the transfer of ministerial functions relating to devolved matters in or regarding Scotland, subject to the constraints set out in the Act. Ministerial functions relating to matters reserved for Westminster Parliament continue to be exercised by the appropriate Secretary of State. The Scottish Executive comprises the First Minister, the Lord Advocate, the Solicitor General and other Ministers appointed by the First Minister and is the devolved government of Scotland. It is responsible for devolved and reserved matters.

The first Scottish Executive was formed by the first First Minister, Donald Dewar, and comprised a Cabinet of 11 ministers supported by a further 11 deputy ministers (Pyper, 2000). At present, the First Minister is aided by a Deputy First Minister who is also a minister with portfolio plus a further nine ministers and eight deputy ministers plus the two Law Officers giving a total Cabinet of 21.

The Scottish Executive operates on the basis of collective responsibility. This means that all decisions reached by ministers, individually or collectively, are binding on all members of the Executive. It follows from this that every effort must normally be made to ensure that every minister with an interest in an issue has a chance to have his or her say—in an appropriate forum or manner—before a decision is taken. It also means that all ministers should have access to all the information held by the Executive which they require in connection with their duties either as a minister with specific functional responsibilities or as a member of an executive which accepts collective responsibility for the actions of all its members. Some decisions taken by Ministers—for example, decisions taken by them in a quasi-judicial capacity, such as decisions on planning appeals—may, however, require to be handled differently from other decisions in order to ensure that the process through which the decision is made does not provide grounds which might support an action challenging the decision in the courts. In some cases this may impose constraints on the extent to which the Minister to whom the function of taking the decision has been allocated can engage in collective discussion of the issue in question before the decision is made, although collective responsibility will of course apply to the decision once it is announced. The key objective of the arrangements for supporting collective decision-making within the Scottish Executive is to enable ministers to reach clear, defensible and consistent decisions on the matters which they need to settle collectively in order to achieve their political objectives and fulfil their statutory and legal obligations.

The Scottish Executive is accountable to the Scottish Parliament and manages an annual budget in excess of £20 billion. The Scottish Executive is also the term used for the civil service administration in Scotland and there are currently seven principal departments of the Scottish Executive:

(a) Development
(b) Education

(c) Enterprise, Transport and Lifelong Learning
(d) Environment and Rural Affairs
(e) Health
(f) Justice, and
(g) Finance and Central Services

The Scottish Executive Development Department (SEDD) is responsible for social justice, housing, land use planning and building control. SEDD sponsors Communities Scotland, the national housing agency, whose mission is to assist owner-occupation and to promote the development of a comprehensive rented sector. SEDD also provides advice and guidance to local authorities and other housing agencies on the supply of housing for community care groups and for homeless people. SEDD is also responsible for policies promoting social justice such as regeneration and is responsible for managing Social Inclusion Partnerships. The Department advises the Scottish Ministers on national planning guidance and advice, local authority structure plans, development proposals of national importance, and deals with planning appeals. The SEDD is responsible for policies on building control and also provides economic advice and statistical information to the Scottish Executive.

The Scottish Executive Education Department (SEED) is responsible for administering government policy in relation to pre-school and school education, children and young people, and tourism, culture and sport. The Children and Young Peoples Group has the responsibility of ensuring the co-ordination and integration, across the Scottish Executive, of policies and associated resources affecting children and young people. The Social Work Services Inspectorate is responsible for ensuring the quality and effectiveness of social work services throughout Scotland, and is also responsible for social work education and training. The Schools Group has responsibility for the administration of policy in relation to education, teachers and schools, New Community Schools, social justice, school ethos and pupil welfare, health education, special education needs, support and inclusion, new educational developments and qualifications, assessment and curriculum. The Tourism, Culture and Sports Group has responsibility for the administration of policy on tourism, the arts, film, architecture, cultural heritage, sport, Gaelic and liaison with the UK Government on broadcasting and the lottery. There are two Executive Agencies linked to the SEED, Her Majesty's Inspectorate of Education and Historic Scotland.

The main partners of the SEED are the local authorities, and the Department also supports a range of non-departmental public bodies including:

(a) Learning and Teaching Scotland

(b) The General Teaching Council for Scotland
(c) The Scottish Qualifications Authority
(d) The Scottish Children's Reporters Administration
(e) Visit Scotland
(f) The Scottish Arts Council
(g) Scottish Screen
(h) The National Museums of Scotland
(i) The National Galleries of Scotland
(j) The National Libraries of Scotland
(k) The Royal Commission on Ancient and Historical Monuments of Scotland
(l) The Royal Fine Art Commission, and
(m) sportscotland.

The Scottish Executive Enterprise, Transport and Lifelong Learning Department (SEETLLD) is responsible for supporting business, encouraging enterprise, improving skills and employability and developing an efficient and effective transport and communications infrastructure. The key objectives of SEETLLD cover economic growth, industrial development, further and higher education, skills, lifelong learning, energy, transport and digital connectivity. The Executive Non-Departmental Public Bodies working with SEETLLD are Highlands and Islands Enterprise, Scottish Enterprise and the Funding Councils for Further and Higher Education. The Department also has an Executive Agency, the Student Awards Agency for Scotland (SAAS). Interestingly, there are two Nationalised Industries associated with SEETLLD. These are Highlands and Islands Airports Ltd, and Caledonian Macbrayne Ltd. Careers Scotland is part of Scottish Enterprise and Highlands and Islands Enterprise as is Business Gateway.

The Scottish Executive Environment and Rural Affairs Department (SEERAD) is responsible for agriculture, rural development, food, the environment and fisheries. The Department is charged with promoting the improvement of the economic performance of Scotland's agriculture, aquaculture, fishing and food industries within the context of sustainable development. SEERAD also has to secure a clean, healthy and safe environment, and is responsible for ensuring a safe and effective water industry. The Department also aims to promote the development of rural Scotland, and to ensure that the interests of rural communities are taken into account in policy development.

SEERAD works with Forestry Commission Scotland to manage Scotland's national forests and sponsors the Scottish Environmental Protection Agency (SEPA) which is the regulatory and enforcement authority for environmental protection and pollution control in Scotland. SEERAD also sponsors Scottish Water which has responsibility for the provision of water and sewerage services in Scotland. SEERAD is furthermore responsible for the natural heritage of Scotland and exercises this responsibility through Scottish Natural Heritage. SEERAD is assisted by three executive agencies: Scottish Agricultural Science Agency; Fisheries Research Services; and Scottish Fisheries Protection Agency. The Department is also responsible for several scientific research establishments in Scotland and sponsors some non-departmental public bodies including the Royal Botanic Gardens, the Crofters Commission and the Deer Commission for Scotland.

The Scottish Executive Health Department (SEHD) is responsible for NHS Scotland and the development and implementation of health and community care policy. SEHD also has responsibility for the Scottish Ambulance Service; NHS 24; the State Hospital; NHS Health Scotland; and NHS Quality Improvement Scotland. The Department is also responsible for social work policy, and for community care and voluntary issues.

The Scottish Executive Justice Department (SEJD) is responsible for the police and fire services in Scotland, and criminal justice including criminal justice social work. SEJD is also responsible for aspects of criminal and civil justice and civil law, for courts administration, for legal aid and liaison with the legal profession. The Department also deals with electoral procedures, including registration of electors, and with royal and ceremonial matters. SEJD is responsible for aspects of the work of district courts and supports a number of courts and tribunals including the Scottish Land Court and the VAT and Duties Tribunal. There are several agencies and associated departments working with SEJD such as: the Scottish Prison Service; the Scottish Court Service; the Association in Bankruptcy; the Registers of Scotland; and the General Register Office for Scotland.

The Scottish Executive Finance and Central Services Department (SEFCSD) comprises a number of groups that provide common services to the Scottish Executive departments including human resources (personnel), finance, information and support services. SEFCSD is also responsible for co-ordinating relations with the UK Government and the European Community as well as local government relations. The Department also provides support to the Scottish Cabinet. The Finance Group within the Department advises ministers on the allocation of the Scottish Budget and accounts for the budget including the issue of payments and recording of receipts. It also advises other Scottish Executive departments on financial matters, and issues guidance to the Executive, NDPBs and other public bodies on propriety and regularity in financial affairs. SEFCSD is responsible for policy development and policy administration in relation to local government. The Department sponsors the Local Government Boundary Commission and the Accounts Commission for Scotland.

The work of the Scottish Executive is also carried out by agencies established by ministers, task forces and by public bodies.

Public bodies have roles and responsibilities for aspect of government but are not in themselves a part of a government department. Public bodies are referred to as Non-Departmental Public Bodies (NDPBs). The NHS Boards in Scotland are NDPBs, local authorities are not. This is a fundamental distinction between local government and the NHS. This distinction was not always the case.

Local government and the NHS in Scotland comprise social units deliberately constructed and reconstructed to seek specific goals. According to Hall (2002, p.31), an organisation is a collectivity with a relatively identifiable boundary, rules, hierarchy, communication systems and procedures; this exists on a relatively continuous basis, in an environment, and engages in activities that are usually related to a set of goals. The activities have outputs and outcomes for the members, the organisation itself, and for society.

Local authorities and NHSScotland health boards clearly meet this definition and can also be considered to be open systems. All open systems have inputs, transformation processes, outputs and outcomes. Scottish local government is a system and each local authority is a sub-system. NHS Scotland is a system and each health board a sub-system. Each sub-system also has inputs, transformation processes, outputs and outcomes. According to Katz and Kahn (1978) open systems interact with their environments and can therefore influence and be influenced by environmental forces. Every system has a boundary which clarifies the limits of the organisation's activities. In the case of a local authority, a system boundary would be the physical boundary between one local authority and another. In the case of a health board, its remit would extend to its geographical boundaries. A further system boundary would be between the services provided by a local authority and the services provided by a health board.

Open systems continuously receive feedback, in a variety of forms, from their environment and this feedback allows the system to adjust to changing environmental demands such as a declining and ageing population. Such changes will require the local authority to make adjustments to the service provision in areas such as number of school places required (declining population of school age) and to increase social work provision to the elderly (ageing population). Open systems often operate in a cyclical manner by obtaining inputs, transforming the inputs and then delivering outputs to client groups in the form of local government services which impact (outcome) on the communities served by the local authority. Inputs can take a variety of forms including money, people, premises, equipment and machinery. Each financial year, local authorities and health boards obtain financial resources from the Scottish Executive, and other sources, to fund their transformation processes for another year. Open systems have a capacity for negative entropy, that is, they can increase their inputs over time and use the additional resources to expand the level of its tranformation processes and its outputs. Open systems can achieve the same outputs and outcomes through a variety of different inputs and different tranformation processes. This is known as the concept of equifinality. Therefore, local authorities and health boards can provide the same services to their clients by using different levels and combinations of resources and by transforming the resources in a different manner.

Fundamental characteristics of Scottish local government

Deoxyribonucleic acid or DNA is the substance of heredity, because it passes on genetic characteristics from one generation to the next. Scottish local government has a number of key features which are akin to the human DNA in that they determine many aspects of the system of local government administration in Scotland. Local government enables local communities to take decisions about the delivery of public services in their area. It is a creation of statute and has no right to exist independent of statute. Thus, central government has ultimate control over local authorities. However, the essence of local government lies in the word "local". The principal characteristics of modern authorities can be traced to the origins of elected local government in the nineteenth century. Although there have been many changes since then, the system has retained its basic genetic characteristics.

Local authorities are, therefore, the product of legislation and, within this legislative framework, the system displays certain distinctive characteristics, which may be summarised as follows:

(a) local authorities are directly elected;
(b) local authorities are multi-purpose;
(c) local authorities cover specified geographic areas;
(d) local authorities have substantial responsibilities for delivery of services;
(e) local authorities may only act within the powers specified by Parliament;
(f) local authorities may raise their own revenue;
(g) local authorities are corporate bodies and can, therefore, do those things that any corporate body may, *i.e.* enter into contracts, own property, sue and be sued.

The Widdicombe Committee (1986) stated that the character of local government in Great Britain is determined by the fact that it is the creation of Parliament; and the particular legislative form that Parliament has given to it.

Scottish local government involves the local administration of diverse services and functions predetermined or approved by

Parliament. It ensures that a wide range of interests and needs, both current and future, of the community are considered and evaluated, and that local services and functions are shaped and organised to meet these particular interests and needs.

Local government has an important part to play in the state provision of services through a democratically representative local authority which provides a range of services to a particular geographic area.

Local government implies the idea of independence. Without this independence we would have no more than local administration, with local authorities acting only as administrative agencies for the Scottish Executive. This independence is of course relative, which is why we talk of semi-independence, and it is indicated through six elements:

(a) accountability
(b) the doctrine of *ultra vires*
(c) responsibility
(d) autonomy
(e) staff, and
(f) finance.

Getting these six elements in the right balance and in balance with the Scottish Executive to suit societal needs constitutes the fundamental problem facing Scottish local government. Not only is the balance a matter of deep controversy and political judgment, but the needs of society are not constant and the solutions evolved to match particular circumstances may become dated and could be counter-productive to the aim of providing effective local government services.

Local government objectives: The Wheatley Commission 1966–69

In order to fully consider the key features of Scottish local government, it is necessary to review the findings of the most comprehenisve study of Scottish local government ever undertaken: the Wheatley Commission 1966–69.

In 1963, the Scottish Office proposed, in a White Paper (Cmnd.2067), a two-tier local government structure for Scotland. The Scottish Office was motivated by its conviction that large-scale economic planning for Scotland could be implemented only within a framework of larger and more powerful units of local government than those established in 1929.

The White Paper, however, came to nothing since, with the return to power in 1964 of a Labour Government, a Royal Commission was established to inquire into local government in Scotland (with a separate Royal Commission for England and Wales, Redcliffe-Maud). The Scottish Royal Commission was known as the Wheatley Commission, after the Chairman Lord Wheatley, and it operated from 1966 to 1969, submitting its report to Parliament in September 1969.

The Wheatley Commission not only criticised the local government structure, but also specified certain broad objectives for a reorganised structure of local government. The Commssion saw four main objectives for local government.

(a) *Power*: Local government should be enabled to play a more important, responsible and positive part in the running of the country—to bring the reality of government nearer to the people.
(b) *Effectiveness*: Local government should be equipped to provide services in the most satisfactory manner, particularly from the point of view of the people receiving the services.
(c) *Local democracy*: Local government should constitute a system in which power is exercised through the elected representatives of the people who should be locally accountable for their actions.
(d) *Local involvement*: Local government should bring the people into the process of reaching decisions as much as possible and enable those decisions to be made intelligible to the people.

Each of the four objectives must be examined in more detail.

Power

This objective relates to a shift in the balance of power and responsibility between central and local government. Local government had lost its standinding over a number of years, but it was in the interests of everyone that local authorities should be strong and vigorous. There were various aspects of power examined by the Wheatley Commission:

Control

Although many of the central government controls over local authorities were necessary, other controls needlessly constrained their independence and initiative.

Structure

In order to enable local authorities to exercise more power and responsibility, steps had to be taken to ensure that local government was exercised at the right *levels* and over the right *areas.*

Functions

Following the changes in the structure, the next step must be to ensure that local government carried out as wide a range of functions as possible. This proposal involved the take-over of some of the functions of the ad hoc boards, at least those which could be provided on a local basis.

Finance

Local authorities, if they were to increase their power, had to gain more financial support from *local* resources and be less dependent on central government. The Commission also criticised the rating system, but did not suggest an alternative system of local taxation.

Co-ordination

The revised structure had to promote concerted action. It was necessary for local authorities to be strong and self-reliant, but they also had to be prepared to work together on many issues.

Effectiveness

A new structure cannot in itself produce effectiveness. Only the people operating the structure can do that and the conditions for effectiveness involve assigning functions for discharge at the appropriate levels, so as to enable certain specific benefits to be gained. These benefits are outlined below:

High standards of service

The highest standards are only attainable at a correspondingly high financial cost. Local authorities must try to achieve such high standards and the structure of local government must not inhibit the attainment of the standards of service required by the community.

Coherent decision-making

Difficulties arise because one set of decisions within local government is reached in isolation from others, with consequent muddle, frustration, waste and ultimately a lower standard of service. Some of the difficulties are due to the *internal* organisation of local authorities and others to *inter-authority* decision-making.

Value for money

Effective administration of a service is a difficult concept to measure. An alternative proposed by the Commission was the concept of "value for money", in which resources must be utilised in the manner which gives the rate-payer the best return for his money. This was recognised as an imperfect measure, but was an improvement.

Adaptability to meet local conditions

Local government should attempt to provide services over the appropriate areas, so that the service can adapt to meet the local needs.

Flexibility to cope with future changes

The recommended changes in structure and functions were only fully appropriate at one point in time. Therefore, local government must *continuously* adapt itself to the changes in its environment in order to remain effective.

Local democracy

The term describes the situation in local government insofar as the effective power of decision rests with the local elected representatives of the people. The essential point is that there must be an elected local council, genuinely in charge of the local situation and answerable for its handling thereof. The structure of local government must, therefore, ensure that:

(a) Councillors and councils should possess power and responsibility and should be constrained by accountability to *some other body* than the electors.
(b) Local authority members must be put in a position to exercise their power and responsibility without practical hindrances.

Local involvement

It was agreed that decisions were being taken at a level too far removed from the comprehension of the man in the street. True local government has the advantage that it can encourage and promote participation, involvement and communication more easily than other forms of public administration.

Effective local participation has three elements:

(a) The structure should offer means of expressing the *voice of the community,* at whatever level that communicy may be found.
(b) Where decisions cannot be taken locally, the structure must make it possible for the advice of local people to be brought to bear on the local application of policy.
(c) The structure should allow the administration of large-scale functions to be decentralised, so that local officers have as much discretion as possible, and are in a position to adapt the service to the needs of local inhabitants.

Fundamental characteristics of the NHS in Scotland

The NHS in Scotland is primarily concerned with the maintenance of health, the treatment of illness and the care of the frail.

Governments have tended to emphasise one or other of two fundamental approaches to addressing illness and health in society by enhancing the health of society or by increasing the provision of access to health treatments for those suffering from ill-health or ailments (Allsop, 1984, p.6). The Committee on Scottish Health Services Report, The Cathcart Report, (Cmd.5208, 1936) contains a range of proposals that collectively identify the fundamental characteristics of health service for Scotland. Professor Cathcart recognised that the health of the nation was dependent on government intervention on behalf of the whole population and the development of a more enlightened society (McCrae, 2003, p.55). The Committee was asked to carry out an urgent review of health services in Scotland and to make recommendations in policy and organisation that may be considered necessary (*ibid.*, p.57). Personal medical services would be comprehensive and available to all and the state's primary role was to attend to those factors which made a healthy life possible and which could be addressed by governmental activity including the promotion of healthier living environments (housing, water and sewerage), the extension of medical services (including maternity services), improved nutrition, reorganised hospital services, the extension of general practitioner services and health education.

The National Health Service (Scotland) Act 1947 took effect on July 5, 1948. The Act, like its counterpart for England and Wales, established a responsibility on the part of central government to fund a health service which rested on the principles of:

(a) collectivism
(b) comprehensiveness
(c) equality
(d) universality, and
(e) professional autonomy.

Each principle is worthy of further explanation.

Collectivism

This principle implies a responsibility on the state to provide health care free at the point of service for those in need, reflecting the social welfare commitment of the post-War Labour Government. Thus financial responsibility for health policy and health services rested with central government. There was to be no elected tier in the NHS. Power lay with ministers and their administrators to make policy decisions and allocate resources to health services.

Comprehensiveness

Central government has a general duty to promote the improvement of the physical and mental health of the people and for the prevention, diagnosis and treatment of illness.

Equality

This principle focuses on the creation of a health service that promoted the attainment of a uniform standard of service for all.

Universality

The NHS provides a range of health services for the entire population, free at the point of use.

Professional autonomy

The NHS endorses and supports the importance of the medical professions in both the decision-making and the running of the service, thus, by implication, medical professionals can operate with a high degree of professional autonomy in the NHS.

Conclusion

This chapter has considered the fundamental characteristics of Scottish governance. There are clearly similarities between local government and the NHS. An emerging theme in this chapter is the extent to which decision-makers in public services are held accountable for their actions. Local government is a democratic system with accountability, at a local level, to the local electorate. In addition, there are various regimes of accountability to funders, central government agencies and central government. While the NHS in Scotland has the latter regimes of accountability, there is no democratic accountability to local electorates. Is the NHS in Scotland therefore undemocratic and less accountable than local government? This chapter has established the context of the relationships between the Scottish Executive, local government and the NHS, and these relationships are considered further in Ch.10.

The post-1979 environmental changes led to a consistency of approach in the relationships between central government and the providers of public services. Policy objectives were increasingly clarified and communicated, and the expectation was that the providers of local government and NHS services would be responsible for incorporating policy objectives into strategic plans and promoting the effective implementation of strategy. Central government, in order to clarify and monitor performance, introduced performance indicators in both local government and the NHS. Initially, the performance indicators related to performance results but as PI systems developed during the 1980s, they began to incorporate PIs as targets for system and organisational performance.

The monitoring of the performance of local authorities and the NHS in Scotland also developed during the 1980s and involved the annual reporting of performance to government and their agencies and for the data to be made available, in many cases, to the general public. By the latter half of the 1990s, the New Public Management of Scottish local government and the NHS in Scotland was embedded in the practices of government and their agencies as well as in local authority and NHS management. It is against this background of development that we can now move on to consider structures, mandates and purposes.

CHAPTER 3

LOCAL GOVERNMENT AND THE NHS IN SCOTLAND: STRUCTURES, MANDATES AND PURPOSES

INTRODUCTION

This chapter brings our review of developments in Scottish local government and the NHS in Scotland up to date by considering structures and the key elements contained in their mandates. Mandates being that which Scottish local authorities and the NHS in Scotland are empowered and required to do on behalf of the Scottish Executive. Mandates therefore relate to government objectives and the efficient and effective implementation of public policy. The purposes dimension of this chapter considers the response by local government and NHSScotland to the pressures exerted on them by the Scottish Executive. The response incorporates both structural and strategic changes designed to enhance the effectiveness of local government and the NHS in Scotland.

LOCAL GOVERNMENT STRUCTURES BEFORE 1975

Scotland and England have different systems of local government because each country has developed its own self-governing local communities and institutions from medieval times. The origins of the Scottish local government structure are ancient and, to understand contemporary developments in structures and functions, it is necessary to begin by reviewing the historical development of Scottish local government from the late eighteenth century to 1975.

Structural Reforms Prior to 1929

During the late eighteenth and nineteenth centuries, existing systems of local government were increasingly unable to cope. The Industrial Revolution had produced many problems, such as rapid population increases, the growth of factories and the growth of industrial towns; and the consequent need for the provision of houses, factories, clean water, sewerage, drainage, public health and hygiene. In addition, it became necessary to make better provision for services like education, police and fire services, and roads. Scottish local affairs in the late eighteenth and early nineteenth centuries suffered from the twin defects of corruption, due to the closed, self-appointing system of selecting councillors, and of impotence in the face of the problems arising from industrialisation, population growth and urbanisation. A consequence of this was that the larger, mainly royal, burghs were reformed by the Burgh Reform Acts 1833 making these burghs subject to open elections. Burghs outwith the scope of this legislation remained unreformed until 1900. Thus, central government activity gradually increased and the old concept of *laissez-faire* became outmoded. As a result, a variety of reorganisational reforms took place.

Industrialisation also resulted in the creation of numerous ad hoc bodies to provide police, sanitation, lighting and water services. The Police Acts of 1850 and 1862 allowed new towns (non-burghal) to establish similar multi-purpose police commissioners, and by the end of the nineteenth century, there were about 100 such "police" burghs. In 1845, following a Royal Commission report, elected parochial boards were established to take over responsibility for the relief of the non-ablebodied poor. Subsequently, these boards became responsible for certain aspects of public health. In 1857, local boards were set up to take care of the mentally disordered. Under the Education Act 1872, locally elected school boards were formed to administer the new system of popular education.

It was not until 1889, however, that a systematic attempt was made to rationalise the system of local government in Scotland by the Local Government (Scotland) Act 1889. The 1889 Act established the principle that each local government service was to be administered by an elected authority over an area appropriate to the service. The legislators made use of the areas that were to hand, namely, the burghs, counties and parishes, and the Act introduced popularly-elected county councils and allocated various local responsibilities to them. It also distributed powers to district committees, local sub-committees, burgh councils within counties and parish councils.

Similarly, under the Burgh Police Act 1892, the functions and relationships between the police commissioners and the burgh councils were clarified and rationalised. The reforms continued with the Town Councils (Scotland) Act 1900, when all burghs were required to have regularly elected councils, each headed by a "provost" and "bailies". At a lower level, elected parish councils were created in 1894 and given responsibility for poor relief.

Prior to 1929, there existed in Scotland:

Burgh councils	200
County councils	33
Parish councils	869
Total	1102

In addition to these authorities, there remained at various stages between 1889 and 1929:

(a) Commissioners of supply;
(b) various standing joint committees;
(c) district boards of control;
(d) parish school boards; and after the Education (Scotland) Act 1881, there were:
(e) ad hoc education authorities.

The structure was simplified by the Education (Scotland) Act 1881, which replaced school boards with 38 education authorities based on the counties and large burghs.

Local government, by the early twentieth century, was, therefore, in a very confused state and it was this confusion which the Local Government (Scotland) Act 1929 sought to resolve.

The Local Government (Scotland) Act 1929

Structure and functions

The Act established five kinds of authority, each with an elected Council.

Table 3.1 : Local Authorities Established in 1929

Type of Authority	**Number**
Counties of Cities	4
Large Burghs	21
Small Burghs	176
Counties	33
Districts (sub-divisions of Counties)	196
Total	430

Each authority was entitled to exercise the functions assigned to it by statute, together with, in the case of the districts and small burghs, any functions that might be delegated to it by the county council.

The functions of each type of authority were as follows:

(a) Counties of Cities
Aberdeen, Dundee, Edinburgh and Glasgow.
All functions.
(b) Large Burghs
All functions, except education and valuation.
(c) Small Burghs
Housing; minor roads; street lighting; cleansing and refuse collection; sewerage; assistance to industry; regulation of shops, markets, etc.; burial and cremation; libraries and museums; places of entertainment; parks and recreation.
(d) County Councils
   (i) In the landward area, that is, outside burghs, all functions.
   (ii) Within large burghs, education and valuation.
   (iii) Within small burghs, education; health: valuation; police; fire; planning; classified roads; public health: registration; weights and measures.
(e) District Councils

Maintenance of public ways and footpaths; concurrent powers with the county council in relation to community centres; places of entertainment; parks and recreation; allotments; rights of way.

Failings of the Post-1929 Structure

Despite the rationalisation of the structure, a variety of separate and independent authorities continued in existence, many having jurisdiction over very small areas, serving small populations and carrying out limited functions. Also, as existing areas had largely been observed, boundaries bore little relevance to modern governmental needs. This meant that certain problems could not be tackled within the structure.

These failings tended to arouse, foster and institutionalise conflicts of interest between members from different areas and their authorities, placing unnecessary and obviously undesirable obstacles in the way of the efficient and expeditious discharge of the work of local government. These weaknesses were underlined by the Wheatley Commission established in 1966 to inquire into local government in Scotland (see Ch.2 and below). The Commission listed a series of weaknesses in the existing system.

Functions and size of authorities

Authorities were generally too small in size, so that the scale on which functions were discharged was not always appropriate. The system also separated functions which ought to have been discharged together and did not recognise that needs varied greatly between one area and another. The system was, therefore, wasteful, in terms of staff and resources.

Finance

The fragmented character of local government resulted in a very unequal spread of rateable resources, leaving local government too dependent on central government financial support. A further problem was the allocation of costs between authorities where one authority provided a service for another authority.

Membership

Due to apathy among the population, it was difficult to find good candidates to stand for local government elections. Of course, this is not a failing confined to any particular structure, but was exacerbated as a problem because of the large number of authorities requiring elected members, very often with limited powers and duties.

Internal organisation

As a result of the internal organisation of authorities, the business of the authorities was being transacted in a cumbersome, time-wasting, uninteresting and inefficient manner.

Central-local relations

Central government had assumed a greater degree of control of local authorities over a long period of time. Some functions had been removed from local government to ad hoc agencies, while others had been reorganised. There was constant administrative interference in the work of local government and too detailed financial control was exercised by central government. This situation was far removed from the original concept of local government and local democracy.

Reorganising the Structure

The Wheatley Commission

The Royal Commission on Local Government in Scotland was known as the Wheatley Commission after its Chairman, Lord Wheatley, and it operated from 1966 to 1969. The Commission specified certain broad objectives for a reorganised structure of local government as a prelude to its recommendations. The Commission found that decisions were generally being taken at a level too far removed from the people affected.

(a) It is acceptable to devolve more power to local government only because it is a democratic institution.

(b) Local democracy has implications for the exercise of power and is closely linked to participation.
(c) Local involvement is essential to the working of democracy and the correct exercise of power.
(d) Perhaps the most important objective is effectiveness, which is the ultimate goal of local government and to which all the other objectives contribute.

The Commission's recommendations were recognised as only being fully appropriate at one point in time, so the need for continuous adaptation of the structure and functions of the system was emphasised. Thus, the system also needed to be flexible.

Main recommendations

The Wheatley Commission did not discover anything fundamentally new, but its research added depth to the discussion. The Commission recommended a two-tier system of local government for Scotland, involving seven regions (the top tier) and 37 districts (the lower tier).

Each authority would be independently elected and levy its own rates. Nearly all important functions would go to the top tier, but, minor aspects of local planning and of housing and amenities, as well as libraries, licensing and administration of justice would be for the lower tier.

The Commission's proposals intensified the debate about whether one tier or two tiers of local government was most appropriate. The relative merits of the two systems have been expressed at different times and in different ways (see Table 3.2 below).

Table 3.2

SINGLE-TIER SYSTEM	TWO-TIER SYSTEM
ADVANTAGES	
(a) Simple to understand and operate	(a) More realistic
(b) Only one set of elections required	(b) Areas not too large as to be remote
(c) Only one body levies rates	(c) Areas not too small as to be starved of resources
(d) Co-ordination between services greatly improved	(d) Strategic services can be provided over appropriate populations
(e) No wasteful competition or repetition of staff	

DISADVANTAGES	
(a) Unworkable	(a) Difficult to apportion responsibility between authorities
(b) Different services require different scales of administration	(b) Two sets of elections required
(c) Internal discussion becomes more complex	(c) Two authorities levy rates
(d) A compromise not fully acceptable to anyone	(d) Co-ordination between levels can be difficult
	(e) Wasteful competition and duplication of staff

Map 3.1

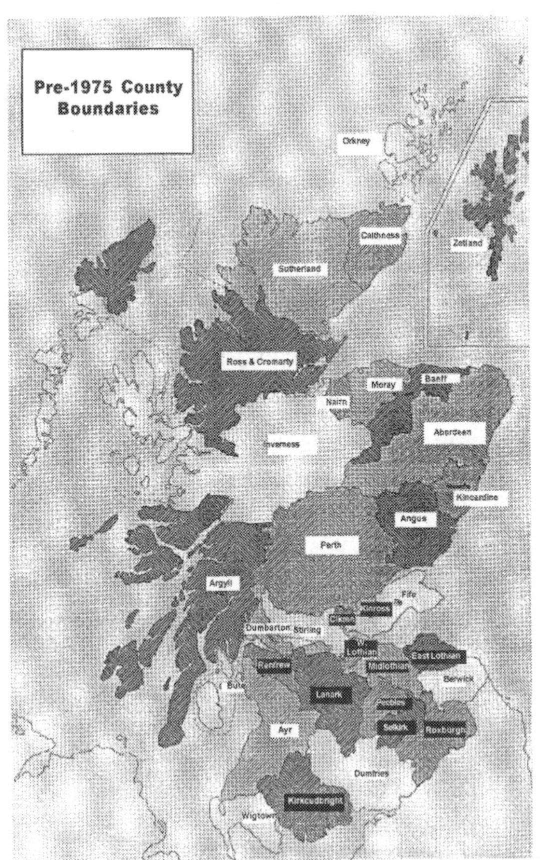

Source: HMSO, Crown Copyright

The general principles of the Wheatley Commission's proposals were accepted by the Conservative Government, as indicated by the overall tenor of the White Paper, *Reform of Local Government in Scotland* (Cmnd.4583, 1971). As a result, many of the recommendations of the Commission were later introduced, although many were also altered by pressures from various sources. The number of elected councils was reduced from 430 to 65 and the number of elected councillors reduced from 3,450 to 1,550 when reform did take place.

Prior to the 1975 reform, the county boundaries in Scotland were as depicted on **Map 3.1** above.

Local Government Structures 1975–1996

The Local Government (Scotland) Act 1973

The long debate on local government reform culminated in the Local Government (Scotland) Act 1973 which was implemented on May 16, 1975. It completely reorganised the structure of local government in Scotland.

The basis of the structure

The structure specified in the 1973 Act was based on (a) a territorial division of the country, and (b) a tier structure.

The territorial division of Scotland into a number of areas produced a system in which individual authorities provided services. The powers and duties assigned to local authorities in general called for their application to different sizes of population and area, so that the services could be carried out efficiently and effectively. The tier structure provided the answer to this problem of organisation and resulted in an interlocking structure of large and small authorities providing different services at different levels.

The 1973 Act created three types of local authority:

Regional councils: There were nine regional councils, which between them covered the whole Scottish mainland: Borders, Central, Dumfries and Galloway, Fife, Grampian, Highland, Lothian, Strathclyde, and Tayside.

District councils: There were 53 district councils in Scotland. Each region was divided into districts. For example, the Grampian Region was divided into five districts: Moray, Banff and Buchan; Gordon; City of Aberdeen; Kincardine; and Deeside.

Island councils: There were, as there are still, three islands councils: the Shetlands; the Orkneys; and the Western Isles.

Community councils: There was, however, another element in the local government structure. Community councils were not authorities in any real sense of the term. They were created with the general function of ascertaining, co-ordinating and expressing to the appropriate local authorities the views of the communities which they represent. Other functions included the safeguarding of local regalia and the organisation of traditional local events.

The structure can perhaps be better understood with reference to **Map 3.2** below.

Map 3.2: Scottish Local Government: The Regions and Islands

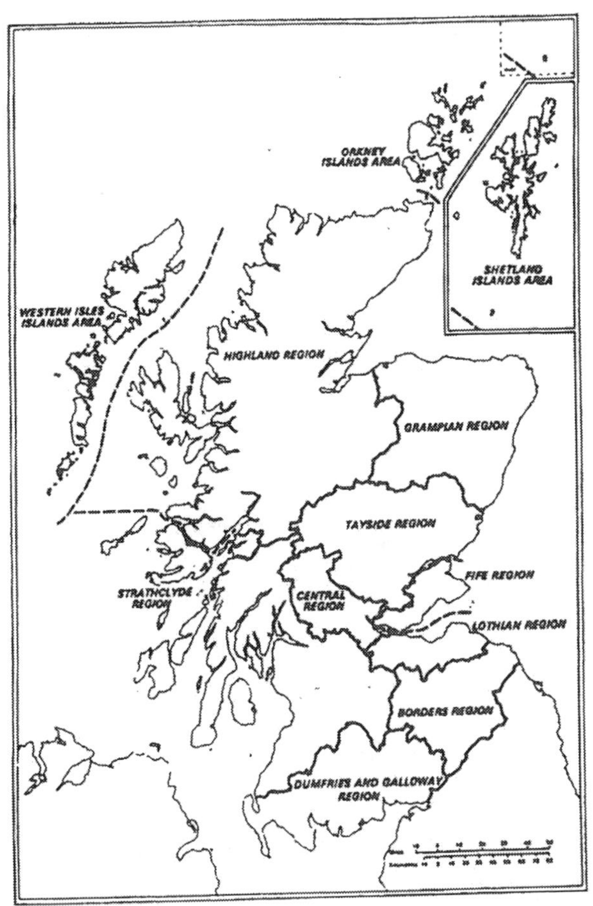

Source: Unison Education and Training (distance learning) Unit, © Unison.

The distribution of functions

The Local Government (Scotland) Act 1973 put into operation the general principle that strategic services needing to be provided and administered over large areas and to large populations should be allocated to the regional councils. Such services included education, social work, and the police and fire services. Services which were essentially local, such as housing or refuse collection, should, however, be dealt with by the district councils.

The powers and duties of local authorities are many, varied, detailed and complex. Despite the two-tier system, a number of functions were administered concurrently. This was the major criticism of the 1975 structure, as it was alleged to cause friction, delay and duplication.

Table 3.3: The allocation of functions following the Local Government (Scotland) Act 1973 (effective from May 16, 1975)

A. Regional Council Functions	B. District Council Functions	C. Concurrent Functions
Strategic Planning	Local Planning	Industrial Development
Roads	Housing	Tourism
Highways' Lighting	Other Public Lighting	Leisure & Recreation
Public Transport	Development Control*	Countryside
Aerodromes	Building Control*	Nature Conservation
Ferries	Urban Redevelopment	Museums
Harbours	Listed Buildings	Art Galleries
Water	Conservation Areas*	Community Centres
Sewerage	Ancient Monuments	Caravan Sites
Flood Prevention	Libraries*	Parks
Coast Protection	Environmental Health	Derelict Land
Diseases of Animals	Refuse Collection and Disposal	War Memorials
Police	Cleansing	
Fire	Slaughterhouses	
Civil Defence	Health and Safety at Work	
Education	Licensing (Liquor, Betting, Gaming,Theatres and Taxis)	
Careers Service	Allotments	
Social Work	Civic Restaurants	
Consumer Protection	Employment of Young Persons	
Electoral Registration	District Courts	
Valuation	Food Hygiene	
Registrars Service (Births, Deaths and Marriages)	Shop Hours	
Food Standards and Labelling	Public Conveniences	

*Except in Highland, Borders and Dumfries and Galloway Regions where the function was regional.

Modifying the 1975 structure

The Stodart Committee

The Scottish Office monitored the effectiveness of the 1975 structure and, in 1979, established a formal group, the Committee of Inquiry into Local Government in Scotland (the Stodart Committee) to consider perceived problem areas.

This Committee, chaired by Anthony Stodart, was appointed in December 1979 with the following terms of reference:

> "With a view to improving the effective discharge of functions by Regional, Islands and District Authorities
>
> (i) to review the working relationships among the new authorities since 15th May 1975;

(ii) to recommend whether any transfer or rationalisation of functions between them is desirable and consistent with fully maintaining the viability of existing authorities;
(iii) to report by December 1980."

The Committee's Report contained 72 conclusions and recommendations, although, after much investigation, many of them were negative, in that no change was proposed. The Committee considered a redistribution of functions and rejected it in the case of the following services:

(a) infrastructural services
(b) housing
(c) education
(d) social work
(e) environmental services
(f) transport, and
(g) protective services.

Many minor recommendations for change were made, but the main ones concerned:

Planning

The Committee did not recommend any change in the existing allocation of responsibilities, but identified that it would like to see greater co-operation and liaison between regional and district planning functions.

Industrial development

The Committee recommended that regional councils alone should have powers to assist industry, but argued that they should be required to establish industrial development committees on which district councils could, if they so wished, be represented.

Leisure and recreation

The Committee recommended that district councils alone should have a comprehensive responsibility to provide and manage leisure and recreation facilities. They contended that such responsibility should extend to museums, art galleries, theatres, parks and free-standing community centres. Regional councils, they suggested, should no longer maintain leisure and recreation departments. Their interest should be limited to a power to contribute to the capital and running costs of facilities where the catchment area was wider than that of the district involved.

Tourism

District councils should have powers to provide tourist-related facilities and literature, and to promote tourism within the United Kingdom.

The Committee also considered the idea of having the four City District Councils (Aberdeen, Dundee, Edinburgh and Glasgow) as most-purpose authorities, combining district and regional functions, but this concept was rejected as it would have undermined the corporate identity of the encompassing regions and would have had to run counter to the concept of the two-tier system.

The Local Government and Planning (Scotland) Act 1982

The Government rejected any notion of a change to a single-tier system of local government. The 1982 Act, therefore, concentrated on tidying up the structure of local government and, in so doing, gave effect to a number of the recommendations of the Stodart Committee.

The Act's main objective in relation to local government functions, was to end certain areas of concurrency, whereby two different tiers of authority exercised responsibility for the same function. The two main areas of change concerned:

Leisure and recreation

Following Stodart, leisure and recreation became the comprehensive responsibility of district councils, along with responsibility for countryside matters and tourism. Regional councils have scope to make financial contributions towards the cost of provision of these facilities where they serve a larger area than that covered by the single district.

Industrial development

Industrial development became mainly a regional responsibility, but the government did not deprive the districts of their existing powers to provide factories and mortgages for industrial purposes. Thus, an element of concurrency remained. Industrial promotion outwith the area of the local authority concerned became the sole prerogative of regional councils.

Thus, with regard to the distribution of functions, all the responsibilities which were concurrent functions became the responsibility of the district councils, except in the case of industrial development. This became mainly a regional function, although the districts retained some responsibilities in this area. Planning, in relation to the countryside, caravan sites and development control, was to be carried out by regional councils in the Highlands, Borders and Dumfries and Galloway Regions.

The Montgomery Report on the Islands Councils

The Committee of Inquiry established by the Secretary of State for Scotland in 1982 and chaired by Sir David Montgomery was set up to consider the functions and powers of the Islands Councils. The Report (Cmnd.9216) was published in April 1984 and provided a clear analysis of work and the problems that faced the three Islands Councils.

The main conclusions were as follows:

(a) A proposal for the creation of a new consultative body—the Council of the Islands—was not supported, but changes in the procedure for consulting local authorities were recommended.
(b) The Islands Councils should have greater local discretion in decisions on their capital spending plans, through the allocation of a single block grant.
(c) The Shetland Islands Council should be allowed to make full use of its income from oil development.
(d) Closer co-operation with the Highlands and Island Development Board was considered desirable, but no transfer of responsibilities to the Islands Councils was recommended.
(e) The Committee expressed support for an element of local control over local fisheries' management schemes.
(f) The Councils should be given powers to run air services and to assume the management of the principal airports in the Islands from the Civil Aviation Authority and, particularly in Orkney, the Council should take over responsibility for the internal ferry services.
(g) Improved liaison between the Councils and the Health Boards was recommended, but the Committee did not agree that the Councils should assume the responsibility for the NHS in the Islands.

The Report was criticised for focusing too narrowly on specific problems, rather than on general questions of democratic control and governance of the islands. For example, the Committee could have backed the case for democratic control of the health service, but chose not to do so.

Further education

The Further and Higher Education (Scotland) Act 1992 removed the 46 further education colleges, which provide a wide range of post-school education and training opportunities from local government control. They became independent bodies funded directly by the Scottish Office.

In 1995, local authority involvement in FE was further reduced when the Secretary of State for Scotland transferred responsibility for the administration of the statutory FE bursary scheme from LEAs to the FE colleges themselves.

National Health Service Structures

Health services in Scotland before 1947

The Scottish Board of Health was set up in 1919 to bring together the various elements of health administration in Scotland. The Local Government Board for Scotland was established in 1894 with local government services and public health as its focus. The Scottish Insurance Commissioners were set up in 1911 and the Highlands and Islands (Medical Services) Board created in 1913. Under the Scottish Board of Health, four Consultative Councils were created as channels of communication between individuals and organisations on the role and responsibilities of the Scottish Board of Health. One of these Consultative Committees was the Consultative Council on Medical and Allied Services which represented the interests of the medical profession. According to Jenkinson (2000, p.3), a report from this Consultative Council in 1920 recommended that the health service should be based on the family as the normal unit of healthcare and the family doctor (general practitioner). The new co-ordinated medical service should function under the control of local authorities (Scottish Board of Health, 1920 pp.6–7). These recommendations were not immediately implemented but there continued to be recommendations eminating from the Consultative Councils on administrative reform. The Local Government Act 1929 incorporated some of these recommendations as part of the overall reduction in the number of local authorities in Scotland (see above). Prior to this, in 1928, the Scottish Board of Health became a Department more directly under the control of the Secretary of State for Scotland and in 1929 it was replaced by a Department of Health for Scotland.

In 1933, the Scottish Health Services Committee was established and it reported in 1936. The report (the Cathcart Report) proposed a National Health Service for Scotland with a comprehensive and co-ordinated structure of medical and allied services and an extension of the general practitioner services to the whole population. There was limited response to these recommendations apart from the passing of the Maternity Services Scotland Act 1937, but there is no doubt that both the MacAlister Report 1920 and the Cathcart Report 1936 greatly influenced the National Health Service White Paper of 1944. It is interesting to note that in this White Paper there were recommendations to model the extended public medical services on the Highlands and Islands Medical Service which incorporated both local and central government control (Jenkinson, 2000, p.8). These proposals were never implemented as the 1947 Act set up a centrally administered medical service.

The NHS in Scotland 1947–74

The National Health Service was established in 1948 to operate a comprehansive system of healthcare throughout the United Kingdom. In Scotland, the Secretatry of State was responsible to Parliament at Westminster for the administration of the NHS, under the terms of the National Health Service (Scotland) Act 1947. The original service, established by this Act, was administered in four separate parts:

(a) Executive Councils
(b) Regional Hospital Boards
(c) Boards of Management
(d) Local Health Authorities

Twenty-five executive councils were responsible for the pharmaceutical and general medical, dental and opthalmic services. Five Regional Hospital Boards were responsible for the planning and development of hospital services. Eighty-six Boards of Management were responsible for the day-to-day management of hospitals. Fifty-six Local Health Authorities provided preventative services, services for mothers and young children and other services to support the sick and elderly in their own homes. Although similar in content to the legislation for England and Wales, the 1947 Act recognised the traditions of independent Scottish health policy (Jenkinson, 2000, p.14). Features of the distinctiveness of the Scottish legislation include the creation of the Hospital Management Boards which had greater powers than their English counterparts, and the fact that administrative control was the responsibility of the Scottish Secretary and the Scottish Office not the local authorities as was the case in England (*ibid*., p.15). For over 25 years, this four-element administrative structure remained substantially unchanged, but, eventually, pressure for reform built up.

In 1967, the Secretary of State for Scotland called for an examination of the structure of the NHS in Scotland and, after lengthy consultations with medical and other professions as well as a range of Scottish and National organisations, a White Paper entitled, *The Re-organisation of the Scottish Health Service* (Cmnd.4734, 1971) set out the Government's conclusions and plans for the NHS in Scotland. This led to the National Health Service (Scotland) Act 1972, which provided the legislative basis for a new administrative structure. The objective of the legislation was to provide better healthcare through a fully integrated service and the reorganisation establishing the revised structure took effect on April 1, 1974.

The NHS in Scotland 1974–91

Health services were primarily the responsibility of the 15 Health Boards and these were based on geographical sub-divisions of the country. The Boards had responsibility for the provision, planning, administration and co-ordination of all health services within a specified area. Health services were provided by the employees of the Board or independent practitioners under contract.

Boards were managed by chairs and members appointed by the Secretary of State, after consultation with interested bodies. Board general managers and unit managers were appointed by the Health Boards. Each Board appointed Chief Administrative Medical Officers, Chief Area Nursing Officers and a Treasurer to report to the General Manager, but provide professional and financial advice to the Board.

The Scottish Health Service Planning Council was set up to advise the Secretary of State for Scotland on the planning and development of the health service in Scotland. The chair and vice-chair of the Council and seven of its members were appointed by the Secretary of State for Scotland. One member was appointed by each health board and each Scottish university with a medical school.

There were also a range of National Consultative Committees composed of the various professions in the Health Service, *i.e.* doctors, dentists, nurses, midwives, pharmacists, opticians, scientists and the professional allied to medicine (physiotherapy, speech and language therapy, dietiticians, podiatrists, radiographers and occupational therapists). The National Consultative Committees advised the Scottish Health Service Planning Council on the development of the services with which each committee was concerned. The chairs of the consultative committees attended the meeting of the Planning Council as assessors. There were also advisory groups to the Scottish Health Service Planning Council offering specialist advice, and Area Consultative Committees advising health boards about the provision of services in their areas. Boards had to consult these consultative committees on matters appropriate to their interests.

The Common Services Agency for the Scottish Health Service undertook a number of important functions such as:

- (a) the ambulance service,
- (b) the blood transfusion service,
- (c) building and legal advice,
- (d) certain aspects of supplies purchasing,
- (e) health statistical services,
- (f) information and computer services,
- (g) management development,
- (h) some work on the approval and pricing of prescriptions and dental treatment,
- (i) studies on the patterns of communicable diseases.

Responsibility for the efficient administration of the agency rested with a management committee, appointed by the Secretary of State and the agency's general manager. A key division of the Common Services Agency was the Scottish Health Education Group which had responsibility for the promotion of health and healthy lifestyle.

In 1980, the Scottish Health Service Planning Council produced a report entitled, *Scottish Health Authorities: Priorities for the Eighties* (or SHAPE) (HMSO, 1980). There was particular emphasis in this document on the importance of care in providing better care in the community. The drive for efficiency as part of the Thatcher Government thinking was evident in the policy, in 1983, to abolish the districts set up under the 1974 reorganisation and to replace them with "Units of Management". This is clearly a move to dis-aggregate in order to promote greater accountability for performance. In addition, in the mid-1980s all local health bodies had to appoint a general manager with clear executive authority (Woods, 2003, p.14).

In 1985, the Health Service Policy Board was established to assess the performance of the service in implementing agreed policy and to identify management action required to improve that performance. The board consisted of senior officials and professional advisers from the Scottish Office Home and Health Department as well as eminent figures from outwith the public sector. The board remit was to give advice to the Secretary of State on the policy decisions required in the health services in Scotland and on their effective and efficient management.

By the end of the 1980s, it was becoming apparent that the 1974 structural and managerial changes were becoming inadequate for the requirements of the New Public Management, and more fundamental managerial changes had to take place to promote enhanced "performance" from the NHS in Scotland.

The NHS in Scotland 1992–97

The Chief Executive of the NHS in Scotland in the publication *Framework for Action* (Scottish Office, 1991) identified a range of changes designed to promote the concept of managed competition and public choice. The cornerstones of the proposals were the setting up of NHS Trusts and the creation of General Practitioner Fundholders. The first National Health Trusts were created in Scotland in 1992. By the end of 1996, there were 47 NHS Trusts in Scotland and 43 per cent of the population were registered with a GP fundholding practice (Woods, 2003, p.16). The underlying philosophy associated with these changes was that of the internal market where NHS Trusts (providers) would compete to win contracts from the Health Boards (purchasers), in the belief that competition and quasi-competition maximises value for money. This systems remained in force until after the 1997 general election when, in December 1997, the Government published the White Paper, *Designed to Care* which advocated fundamental changes in the organisation of the NHS in Scotland with a particular emphais on the replacement of the internal market in healthcare. The Government sought to maintain the improvements in the management of the NHS and advocated the retention of distinctive roles for those responsible for the development and implementation of strategy and for those who deliver services directly to patients: the strategic role and the service role. This White Paper and subsequent changes will be considered in more detail in subsequent chapters.

Local government contemporary mandates and roles

Local authorities in Scotland are statutory bodies, created and given powers and duties by Acts of Parliament. The predominant Act, at present, in this respect, is the Local Government (Scotland) Act 1973, as amended by the Local Government (Scotland) Act 1994. The structure and functions of local government, however, can be, and frequently are, modified by legislation passed by central government. Indeed, the whole system of local government could be lawfully abolished by an Act of Parliament.

The powers and duties of local authorities are directly conferred upon them by Acts of Parliament and delegated legislation, mainly in the form of Statutory Instruments (SIs). Local authorities may only incur expenditure and provide services within the statutory framework. Should a local authority provide services outside the current statutes it would be acting *ultra vires,* literally beyond its powers, and may be subject to legal challenge in the courts. The core legislative framework for local government is listed below.

- Local Government (Scotland) Act 1973
- Local Government and Housing Act 1989
- Local Government Finance Act 1992
- Local Government etc. (Scotland) Act 1994
- The Local Government in Scotland Act 2003
- The Local Governance (Scotland) Act 2004

Local government's powers and duties to provide particular services such as education or social work are contained in separate legislation. In addition, local government is increasingly subject to European Community law and, as an employer of 260,000 people, general legislation on employment.

The powers and duties designation by statute can be divided into three broad categories:

(a) **Mandatory** services which **must** be provided (*e.g.* education for school-age children).

(b) **Permissive** services which **may** be provided (*e.g.* economic development).
(c) **Discretionary:** a general power to spend a limited amount of money which will bring direct benefit to the council area.

The place of local governments in the political system is not, however, derived solely from its former constitutional relationship with a sovereign parliament. Sovereignty of Parliament is underpinned by a body of custom and convention as to the manner in which that sovereignty should be exercised.

The position of local government in the political system is, therefore, governed by constitutional convention as well as by the simple fact that it derives its existence and its powers from the Scottish Parliament (this is further discussed in Ch.10).

There is, in fact, no validity in the assertion that local authorities have a "local mandate" by which they derive authority from their own electorate, thus seeking to place themselves above the law. The electoral basis of local government merely lends added authority to actions that are taken within the law and to any proposals made for changes to the law, but does not provide the right to act outside or above the law.

Through the legislative process, Scottish local authorities have, over the years, been given responsibility for administering a wide range of public services. Many of these services are diverse and seemingly have little in common; nevertheless local government ensures that the wide range of interests and needs, both current and future, of the community are considered and evaluated and that the services and functions are shaped and organised to meet these particular interests and needs.

Recent legislation impacting on local government

There are two recent Acts of the Scottish Parliament that have a major impact on Scottish local government: the Local Government in Scotland Act 2003 and the Local Governance (Scotland) Act 2004. The Local Government in Scotland Act 2003 promotes the duty on local authorities to secure best value and repeals all existing legislation relating to CCT. The Act also provides a statutory basis for community planning and the power of well-being to enable local authorities to work in a more innovative and responsive manner. The Local Governance (Scotland) Act 2004 contains provisions on local government elections, membership of local authorities and the pay and pensions of councillors.

Contemporary roles of local government

Local government has a variety of roles and functions. These can be summarised under four headings.

Provision of services

Local authorities have a long tradition of planning, resourcing and direct provision of a wide range of services. These include education, housing, social work, economic development, public protection, planning, leisure and recreation. Additional methods of service provision which have emerged in recent years include working in partnership with other public agencies and commissioning services from the voluntary and private sectors.

Strategic planning

Local authorities provide a longer-term strategic planning framework setting objectives based on the needs and priorities of their constituents, to direct both the policies and activities of internal functions and to influence the priorities of external organisations within their areas.

Regulation

Local authorities also have regulatory functions such as the granting of certain licences (*e.g.* taxi drivers and public houses), and registration and inspection functions (*e.g.* private residential homes).

Community leadership

A relatively new role for local authorities is that of community leadership, addressing issues which do not fit neatly with any single agency's responsibility.

Such cross-cutting issues include promoting social inclusion, drugs-related issues, ensuring community safety and dealing with environmental concerns. A key objective for local authorities is to facilitate multi-agency responses to these issues. Councils are also seeking ways of developing links with geographical communities and communities of interest through methods such as citizens' juries, consumer panels and focus groups. These methods aim to identify the priorities and opinions of different groups within communities and encourage greater participation and involvement in service design and delivery. Local authorities are also major employers.

NHS Scotland: contemporary mandates and roles

Contemporary mandates for the NHS in Scotland are substantially contained in post-1997 White Papers and Acts of the Scottish Parliament. Following the election of the Labour Government in 1997, there was immediate action on the part of the then Secretary of State for Scotland, Donald Dewar, to introduce changes to the way the NHS in Scotland was run. The White Paper, *Designed to Care—Renewing the National Health Service in Scotland* was published in December 1997 and put an end to the internal market, General Practitioner (GP) Fundholding and contracting for services. There was no longer to be a purchaser/provider split and this was replaced by the strategic/service divide. Health boards were required to produce five-year rolling Health Improvement Programmes and were given the responsibility for their implementation through the NHS Trusts. Trust chairpersons became non-executive directors of health boards. Primary Care Trusts were introduced to manage General Practice and Community Health Services with GPs being given approval to form voluntary Local Healthcare Co-operatives. Health boards were to have the lead role in developing and implementing a Health Improvement Programme working with local authorities. NHS Trusts were initially retained but had to re-focus on improving the quality of service provision by increasing the involvement of clinicians, patients and clients in hospital management. The number of trusts would be reduced and the trusts would take two forms; Acute Hospital Trusts and Primary Care Trusts. Primary Care Trusts would have responsibility for all primary healthcare and comprised community hospitals and mental health services as well as networks of general practices in Local Healthcare Co-operatives. These Co-operatives replaced the GP fundholding system.

The White Paper, *Towards a Healthier Scotland* (1999) focused on public health inequalities by identifying three areas for health improvement: life circumstances; lifestyles; and health topics including cancer and coronary heart disease. This was followed by *Our National Health: A Plan for Action, A Plan for Change* (2000), which introduced unified NHS Boards from September 2001. Membership and the role of health boards were changed with specific provision for local authority representation in the health boards, for NHS staff representation. Trust Chief Executives also had the right of representation. There is a strategic management thrust to these changes with the NHS boards having responsibility for the longer-term direction of the organisation while the trusts (acute and primary care) were charged with the operationalisation of the strategy. The health boards have accountability to the Scottish Executive and are required to produce a single health plan for their area. The health plan became a key tool in the Performance Assessment Framework (PAF) which the Scottish Executive uses to monitor achieved performance against planned performance levels with particular emphasis on health improvement outputs within each NHS Board area (see Ch.9).

Partnership for Care (2003) incorporated proposals for unified NHS Boards, the abolition of NHS Trusts and the creation of Community Health Partnerships to replace Local Healthcare Co-

operatives. These changes were enacted in the National Health Service Reform (Scotland) Act 2004. This Act also places a duty on Health Boards to co-operate with each other, with Special Health Boards and with the Common Services Agency to promote more effective regional planning of health services. There are also provisions extending ministerial powers to intervene to secure the quality of healthcare services. The Act also places a duty on Health Boards and Special Health Boards to involve the public in the planning, development and operation of health services and a duty on the Scottish Ministers and Health Boards to take action to promote health improvement.
The main Acts governing the NHS in Scotland are currently:

(a) The National Health Service (Scotland) Act 1947
(b) The National Health Service (Scotland) Act 1972
(c) The National Health Service (Scotland) Act 1978
(d) The National Health Service and Community Care Act 1990
(e) The National Health Service (Primary Care) Act 1997
(f) The Health Act 1999
(g) The Community Care and Health (Scotland) Act 2002
(h) The Mental Health (Care and Treatment) (Scotland) Act 2003
(i) The National Health Service Reform (Scotland) Act 2004

Contemporary roles of NHS Boards in Scotland

The aim of the NHS in Scotland according to the Scottish Executive is:

> "To improve the health and quality of life of the people of Scotland and deliver integrated health and community care services, making sure there is support and protection for those members of society who are in greatest need." (The Scottish Executive Draft Budget 2004–2005, September 2003)

In promoting this aim the NHS in Scotland has four key objectives:

1. To work towards a step change in the life expectancy for Scots, particularly disadvantaged members of the community, including children and old people;
2. To ensure that healthcare providers provide swift and appropriate access to integrated healthcare, covering primary, community and acute care;
3. To improve the patient's experience of services provided by the NHS;

4. To improve services for older people, at home and in care settings.

Each of these objectives is linked to SMART (specific, measurable, achievable, realistic, time-scaled) targets which collectively set out the NHS in Scotland mandate.

Unified NHS Boards have to adopt a managerial role in relation to the provision of health services to the population resident in their areas. This involves strategy development through health planning processes which take into account the health priorities and healthcare requirements of the population. The health plan, once approved, is then implemented through systems of resource allocation and performance management. NHS Boards are empowered to monitor and assess the population's health and well-being and to respond to identified current and future health requirements by developing healthy public policy; detecting and preventing disease and disability; maximising the health impact of services; protecting the population from health hazards; promoting personal skills development for health and well-being; strengthening community action for health; and carrying out research to develop health improvement.

Following the publication in December 2000 of "Our National Health: A Plan for Action, A Plan for Change", which outlined the Government's plan for the future of the NHS in Scotland, changes were made to the responsibilities and accountabilities of the local health system. In September 2001, unified NHS Boards were established in all 15 health board areas to replace the existing separate board and trust structures. Each unified board was to be responsible for local health planning. Unified boards are accountable to Ministers and the Scottish Executive Health Department and the chief executives of health boards and trusts are members of the unified boards.

There are three types of board accountable to the Scottish Executive Health Department. The first type is the NHS board of which there are 15 and each has its Operating Divisions and its Community Health Partnerships. The second type is the NHS National Services Scotland (special health board) which includes: National Services Division; Practitioner Services Division; Information and Statistics Division; Scottish Centre for Infection and Environmental Health; Scottish National Blood Transfusion Service; Scottish Healthcare Supplies; Central Legal Office; and Scottish Health Service Centre. The third type of board is the Special Health boards of which there are seven: NHS Quality Improvement Scotland; NHS Health Scotland; Scottish Ambulance Service; State Hospital Board for Scotland; NHS Education Scotland; NHS 24; and National Waiting Times Centre.

There are currently 12 National Priorities for NHS Scotland:

(a) Service redesign
(b) Health improvement
(c) Delayed discharges
(d) 48-hour access to a member of the primary care team
(e) Cancer
(f) Coronary heart disease and stroke
(g) Mental health
(h) Waiting times
(i) Public involvement
(j) Workforce development and staff governance
(k) Healthcare acquired infection and hygiene
(l) Financial break-even

The current system of NHS provision

There are 12 mainland and three Islands NHS Boards (see Map 3.4 below). These are corporate bodies whose members are appointed by the Scottish Ministers. The 15 NHS Boards are responsible for the protection and improvement of the health of the population who reside in their geographical area and to that end manage health service provision without detailed oversight from the Scottish Executive. The NHS Boards are responsible for two categories of NHS provision: acute care and primary care.

Primary care involves the delivery of primary, community and mental health services including General Practitioner services, community pharmacists and opticians, community nurses, midwives and other professions allied to medicine such as speech and language therapy, occupational therapy, physiotherapy and podiatry. Primary care provision aims to provide healthcare to people in their home and in their communities and to promote this through Community Health Partnerships which are being established throughout Scotland.

Acute care provision involves the provision of health services largely in hospital settings and therefore includes hospitalisation, surgery, diagnostic services, accidents and emergency services, and longer-term patient rehabilitation. Acute care provision also supports the education and training of health service staff as well as research and knowledge transfer as applied to medicine and related disciplines. As a consequence of this research and knowledge transfer remit, there has to be effective partnerships between Scottish universities and the acute sector of NHSScotland.

Map 3.3: NHS Current Structure

The current structure of the NHS in Scotland is illustrated by the map below.

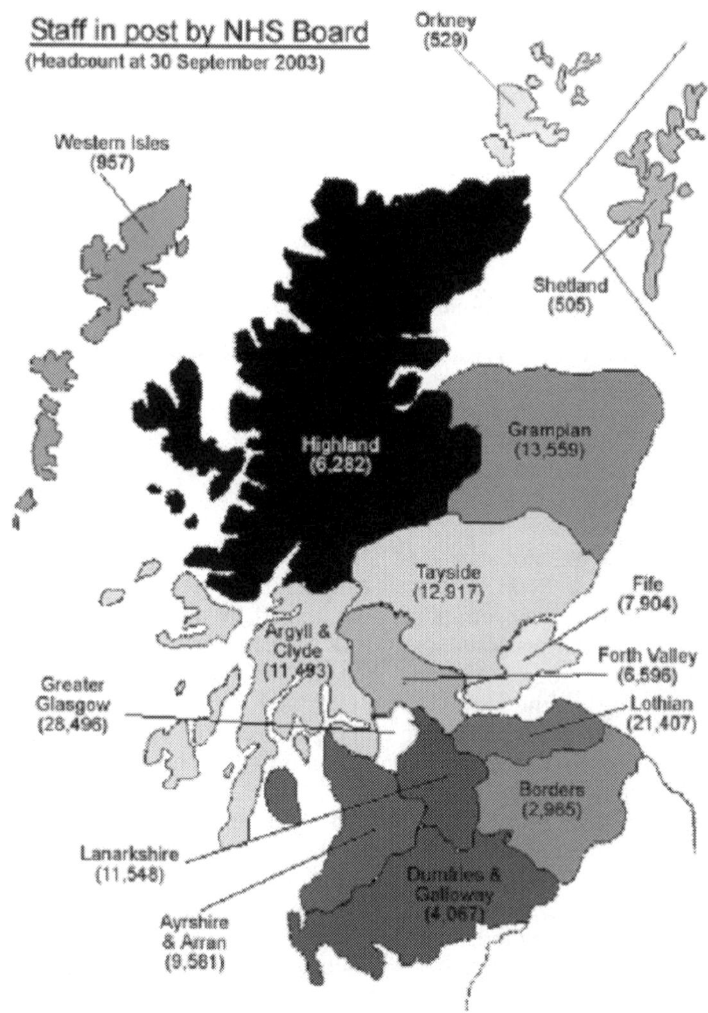

Source: ISD Scotland, © ISD Scotland.

In 2005, the Scottish Executive commenced a consultation process about the proposed dissolution of NHS Argyll and Clyde. If ratified, this would reduce the number of Health Boards to 14.

The 1996 Local Government Structure

In the early 1990s, the issue of further local government reform remained firmly on the political agenda. The then Secretary of State for Scotland, Ian Lang, in a statement to the House of Commons on March 21, 1991 said:

> "The present two-tier system has some advantages, but it also has some clear disadvantages. It blurs the lines of accountability, and it can lead to duplication, conflict and delay. It is often perceived as unnecessarily bureaucratic and remote from local needs. The traditional role of local government is changing, from provider to enabler. The structure must keep up that change. I believe we should now prepare to move to single tier local authorities throughout Scotland. This will strengthen local accountability and I believe it will deliver local services more effectively."

Along with local government reform, the community charge was replaced by the council tax.

The Scottish Secretary had already said that he did not see the need—as in England and Wales—for an independent commission to report on the most appropriate structure, as he believed there to be a broad consensus on the desirability to move to single-tier local government.

That view was not shared by all. Many authorities, including the Convention of Scottish Local Authorities ("COSLA"), did not believe that the consultation paper issued by the Government in 1991 provided a sustained analysis of the case for change. A further criticism and regret of many bodies was that the Government considered that the issues which occupied the Wheatley Commission for three years producing a 300-page report were now capable of reduction to a nine-page consultation paper, and that there was to be no independent review.

The Scottish Secretary published a consultative paper in June 1991, *The Structure of Local Government in Scotland: The Case for Change*. The Government's consultation paper was based on its belief that there should be a move towards a single tier of local government throughout Scotland. The paper argued a number of reasons to support the change to single-tier local government, the principal ones being:

(a) a lack of public understanding of and confusion about, the two tiers of regional and district councils;
(b) old allegiances to former councils live on;
(c) some regional councils are considered to be remote;
(d) a measure of duplication and waste between the two tiers of local government, particularly with regard to common

functions such as personnel or legal services and also in the field of industrial development and urban renewal;

(e) delay and friction with regard to programmes requiring joint actions by the two tiers;

(f) the move since the last round of reorganisation in 1975 away from local authorities directly providing services to a position where services are being provided on its behalf through other bodies or agencies or arrangements, for example, the introduction of School Boards and the impact of compulsory competitive tendering (CCT). Allied to this has been the establishment by the government of a range of appointed bodies responsible for a number of areas which traditionally had been undertaken by local government, *e.g.* Scottish Homes in housing, and the local enterprise companies (LECs) in economic development and training.

This led the Government to conclude

> "that the present two tier system now represents real obstacles to local government in meeting the challenge of change successfully and acts as a brake on desirable and necessary initiatives".

The Government wanted to extend single-tier local government, as found in the three Islands Councils, to the mainland of Scotland and its arguments in favour of single-tier local government were that:

(a) it is simple to understand and removes confusion;
(b) it clarifies accountability.
(c) it removes the potential for duplication, waste, delay and friction;
(d) it allows better co-ordination;
(e) it makes a better use of scarce financial and human resources.

However, the Government also said that, if convincing arguments emerged in a particular area for a structure other than single tier, these would be given careful consideration.

The Government argued that the new system of single-tier local government should be based on the following principles that:

- the new councils should be democratically elected and should not be created simply by the abolition of either regions or districts, nor should they necessarily be of the same size throughout Scotland;
- the new councils must reflect and represent local loyalties and allegiances—geography, natural boundaries and travel to work patterns being taken into account;

- at the same time, the new councils must be strong, cost-effectively resourced and capable of discharging their responsibilities;
- the new councils must be clearly accountable to their electorate, be capable of effective management of services and resources, be demonstrably providing value for money and be able to recruit sufficient staff of appropriate calibre.

The Government put considerable emphasis in the paper on the fact that restructuring necessarily involves initial disruption and transitional costs. It asserted that it would require to be satisfied that these costs could be contained and minimised and that the new system, once in place, would be no more expensive to operate than the present system. Consequently, any proposals for change needed to be justified in terms of cost effectiveness in providing staff savings, increased efficiency and improvements in service delivery.

The Government was concerned (as part of its underlying philosophy) to promote and encourage alternative ways of councils undertaking their responsibilities—other than by doing it directly themselves. These include more use of compulsory competitive tendering and the extension of the principle of council functions being discharged on their behalf by other bodies or agencies. The paper also suggests that some services, for example police and fire, might require to be organised on a larger scale which might require joint arrangements between the new councils. Further, it was suggested that water and sewerage might best be handled by organisations separate from the new councils.

Shaping the new councils

The Secretary of State produced a second consultation document in October 1992 entitled, *The Structure of Local Government in Scotland: Shaping the New Councils*. As well as the consultation document, videos and leaflets were also made available to the public to help them to understand the proposals and to encourage them to take part in the consultation process.

The Government still held the position that there was a strong case for unitary authorities and that, whatever structure emerged, it should be single-tier. They claimed that there has been confusion in the two-tier structure, increasingly seen as a serious weakness. They also believed that people have found it difficult to identify with some of the larger authorities.

The consultation document provided four illustrative structures of possible reorganisation, consisting of 15, 24, 35 and 51 units. These illustrations were not options as such, but were produced to assist respondents to the consultation process.

The Secretary of State also asked consultants to provide estimates of costs over the transitional period of moving to a single-tier structure. These estimates were based on the four illustrations provided in the consultation document. The consultants concluded that the 51–unit option was the only one which would cost more and that any re-structuring which resulted in more than about 40 units would be more expensive. There was, however, a great deal of controversy surrounding the management consultants' estimates of costs and eventual savings.

This second consultation paper described the Government's views in relation to the provision of the various local government services in the various options. The whole question of joint board/committees was a constant feature throughout the document. Clearly, if the option for a larger number of smaller authorities was favoured, then more joint arrangements for more strategic services would be needed.

On July 8, 1993, the Government published their White Paper, *Local Government Reform in Scotland*. The Secretary of State announced in Parliament that he had decided to establish a single-tier structure of 28 local authorities, indicating that savings of up to £65 million per annum might be expected from the new structure and that these savings were likely to pay back the transitional costs within four or five years.

Following the Government's consultative exercise, a Bill was prepared for Parliament and, as the Local Government etc. (Scotland) Act 1994, received Royal Assent on November 3.

Structural changes

The unitary principle

The 1994 Act made radical changes to the Scottish local government system. The Act abolished 62 of the 65 local authorities; only the three all-purpose Islands Councils of Orkney, Shetland and the Western Isles continue in the reformed structure.

From April 1, 1996, mainland Scotland had 29 councils (one more than the Scottish Secretary initially planned). Each locality has now a single council responsible for all local government functions—this is the unitary authority principle.

The unitary principle reduced the number of councils and, indeed, councillors whilst, at the same time, increased the number of smaller councils. The reason is that the new authorities, although fewer in number, are generally smaller than the former regional councils.

Continuity in structure

Amongst the 32 Scottish Unitary Authorities (UAs), some continuity will be evident to the public. Thus, 12 of the new UAs correspond in area to prior district councils (although in two instances —denoted thus*—with a new name:

(a) Aberdeen
(b) Clackmannan
(c) East Lothian
(d) Edinburgh
(e) Falkirk
(f) Inverclyde
(g) Midlothian
(h) Moray
(i) North Ayrshire*
(j) South Ayrshire*
(k) Stirling, and
(l) West Lothian.

Additionally, seven UAs correspond to the area of prior regional and islands councils:

(a) Borders
(b) Dumfries & Galloway
(c) Fife
(d) Highland
(e) Orkney
(f) Shetland,
(g) Western Isles.

No new UA has been created by splitting prior districts council across former regional council borders, *i.e.* all change has been at the level of sub-divisions within the prior regional level.

The structure can be better understood by reference to **Map 3.3** and **Table 3.3**.

Map 3.4

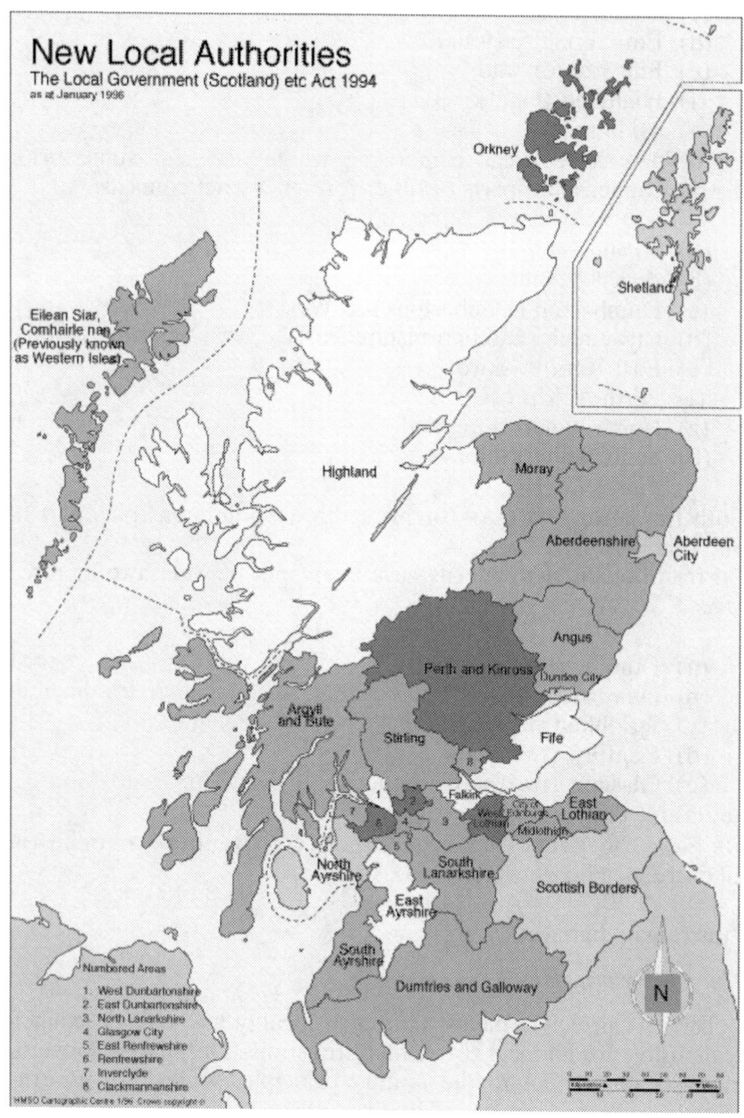

Source: Scottish Executive website *www.scotland.gov.uk*

Change in structure

Six of the UA's areas correspond to amalgamations of whole areas of two or more prior district councils:

(a) Aberdeenshire (three councils)
(b) Borders (four)
(c) Dumfries & Galloway (four)
(d) East Ayrshire (four)
(e) Fife (three), and
(f) Highland (eight).

Eight UAs have areas comprising whole areas of some prior district councils and parts of other former district councils:

(a) Angus
(b) Argyll & Bute
(c) Dumbarton (Dunbartonshire West)
(d) Clydebank (Dunbartonshire East)
(e) East Renfrewshire
(f) Perth & Kinross
(g) North Lanarkshire, and
(h) South Lanarkshire.

Both the latter two UAs comprise three whole areas plus part of one other.

Five prior district councils have been split between two or three UAs:

(a) Dundee (three)
(b) Dumbarton (two)
(c) Strathkelvin (two)
(d) Renfrew (two), and
(e) Glasgow (two)

Of these, however, Dundee, Glasgow and Renfrew continue (in albeit reduced coverage) as a UA area.

Functional changes

The unitary principle

The UA principle means that each locality has a single council responsible for all local government functions. Despite the Government's commitment to the unitary principle, some local government services are not provided, and others not wholly provided by each of the new UAs. Instead, joint arrangements may be necessary to ensure delivery in some locality.

Service provision

The main services provided by Scottish UAs are identified in Table 3.3 below.

Table 3.3: Local Government Service Provision (post-1996)

Administration of Housing Benefit	Industrial and Economic Development
Airports	Industrial Promotion
Animal Health and Welfare	Leisure and Recreation
Archaeology	Libraries
Arts (incl. Museums and Art Galleries)	Licensing of Betting and Gaming, Theatres and Cinemas and Liquor
Building Control	Licensing of Taxis
Burial and Cremation	Listed Buildings and Ancient Monuments
Caravan Sites	Local Air Pollution Control
Cleansing	Local Planning
Coastal Protection	Markets
Community Centres	Nature Conservation
Community Councils	Parks
Conservation Areas	Private Water Supply Monitoring
Consumer Protection	Public Conveniences
Council Tax	Public Transport #
Countryside	Registration of Births, Deaths and Marriages
Development Control	Road Lighting
Diseases of Animals	Roads and Road Safety
District Courts	School Crossing Patrols
Education	Shop Hours
Electoral Registration	Slaughterhouses
Emergency Planning	Social Work
Employment of Young Persons	Strategic Planning
Environmental Health	Tourism
European Community Relations	Trading Standards
Ferries	Traffic Wardens
Flood Prevention	Urban Development
Food Hygiene, Standards and Labelling	Valuation and Rating
Grants to Voluntary Bodies	Waste Collection and Disposal
Harbours	Waste Regulation
Health and Safety at Work	
Housing and Rents	

Note: # Except Glasgow (special PTE)

Relocated functions

Three notable services are no longer provided by local authorities:

Scottish Children's Reporter Administration

The Government considered that the Children's Reporter Service would be more effectively provided as a national service, with a chief reporter responsible for the service's administration and accountable to a board of management.

Water and sewerage

The Government initially established three public water authorities (North of Scotland; East of Scotland; West of Scotland).

These water authorities assumed ownership of the existing authorities' water and sewerage assets and responsibility for maintenance, development and day-to-day operations. However, the Water Industry (Scotland) Act 2002 establishes Scottish Water as the successor to the three water and sewerage authorities.

Careers Service

The Careers Service moved from local government in April 2002 and is now part of Scottish Enterprise and Highlands and Islands Enterprise.

Special provision

Police and fire

The Government decided that there was no need to change the number of forces/brigades in areas covered by existing forces/brigades. Where a force or brigade covered, at reorganisation, more than one UA area, joint committees were established.

Glasgow Passenger Transport Executive

The Glasgow Passenger Transport Executive (PTE) was retained at re-organisation, the continuing responsibility of the Passenger Transport Authority (PTA), whose membership comprises councillors from the constituent UAs in its area.

Joint arrangements

Councils may adopt some form of joint working to provide certain services. This may be because the service operates across the boundaries of two or more authorities (*e.g.* the Glasgow PTA) or because the size and resources of UAs are such that it is more effective to rely on a joint arrangement.

The normal approach may be the joint committee or joint board, but contracting is also possible.

Joint boards

Joint boards, formed to provide a service by the participation of two or more councils such as the Assessor and Electoral Registration Service.

Joint committees

Joint committees, similarly organised, are formed in contrast to boards by councils themselves, and each UA retains its own responsibility for the service.

The 1994 Act permits councils to apply to the Scottish Secretary for a joint committee to be incorporated as a joint board.

Contracting

Contracting is where one council (or a UA consortium) agrees to provide a service for one or more other councils. The possibilities range from bilateral purchase to consortia arrangements.

Conclusion

Local government was reorganised in 1996, but the NHS in Scotland had no similar large-scale reorganisation to contend with during this period. From time to time there has been talk of "joined up public services" where there would be a more comprehensive joint working arrangements but there was no major breakthrough in this area until the Community Care and Health (Scotland) Act 2002 (see Ch.4).

This chapter has considered the structures, mandates and purposes of local government and the NHS in Scotland. Local government and the NHS in Scotland had grown apart particularly since the reorganisations of the 1970s but the Scottish Executive are committed to "join up" public service provision wherever possible. Both local government and the NHS provide services to people in their own homes and in their communities, these "primary care" services are the obvious targets for improving co-ordination and promoting more efficient and effective public services. The *Joint Future Initiative* involves Social Work Services working with NHS Primary Care providers, and Community Health Partnerships will build on this joint approach to service provision. Both local government and the NHS in Scotland have a mandate to support community well-being in the widest sense of that term.

Many need and wants in Scottish society cannot be fully met by a single public service agency. Complex social problems such as social exclusion and drug abuse require multi-agency responses including partnership working within the public sector, and between the public sector and the private sector. The mandates of local government and the NHS in Scotland are dynamic and as a consequence the roles and structural responses of local authorities and NHS Boards to these mandates must likewise be flexible and fluid. For long periods of time, local authorities and NHS Boards were, in the terminology of Burns and Stalker (1966), mechanistic organisations but in their contemporary environments they must be much more organic if they are to respond effectively to client, stakeholder and Government demands on them. Both systems had similar accountability links to central government via the Scottish Office. But there are clearly differences.

This chapter has also considered the structures, mandates and fundamental purposes of Scottish local government and the NHS in Scotland in relation to government policy. Local government can be better understood as an open system and Scottish local authorities can be considered as sub-systems each with their own inputs, transformation processes, outputs and boundaries. NHS provision is Scotland is a system and the Boards are sub-systems each with their *own* inputs, transformation processes, outputs and boundaries.

The essence of local government lies in the word "local". Local government empowers local communities and therefore enhances them. These benefits will only accrue to communities where local authorities retain their semi-independence of central government. Local authorities cannot act in an autonomous manner; they must operate within the legislative framework which enables them to provide certain services to their communities. Local authorities are accountable for their roles, functions and are accountable for their actions to a variety of stakeholders (see Ch.7).

The essence of local government may lie in the word "local" but it does not follow that the essence of the NHS in Scotland is national. The essence of the NHS in Scotland is health services provision, some of which are national, some are local, some are primary and others are acute.

The major problem associated with the current structures is that they were not created by the Scottish Executive and therefore structure has pre-dated strategic direction through public policy. Ideally structure should follow strategy.

Chapter 4 considers the finance of local government and the NHS in Scotland as well as the range of services provided and Ch.10 considers possible changes to mandates, purposes and structures.

CHAPTER 4

LOCAL GOVERNMENT AND NHS SCOTLAND: FINANCE AND SERVICES

INTRODUCTION

This chapter considers the ways in which local authorities and the NHS in Scotland are financed. The chapter develops by discussing the range of services provided by local authorities and NHS Boards. In the current political and economic climate the cost of public services is more and more the subject of scrutiny by Audit Scotland and the Scottish Parliament and this chapter reviews contemporary analyses of the financial performance of local government and the NHS in Scotland.

THE BARNETT FORMULA

The Barnett Formula (named after its author, Treasury Minister Joel Barnett) was developed in the late 1970s and provides that any increase or cut in government expenditure would be allocated in the ratio 10:5:85 among Scotland, Wales and England respectively. The coverage of the Barnett Formula has been expanded over the years and is currently applied to most of the expenditure of the Scottish Executive making up the Assigned Budget or Block Grant (Keating, 2005, p.142). The Scottish Executive and the Scottish Parliament then determine how the Assigned Budget is to be spent. The Assigned Budget represents about 60 per cent of all government expenditure in Scotland. Since 1999, the UK Government has taken the view that Scotland cannot have devolution and an expenditure advantage, and as a consequence the Scottish share of public expenditure has increased at a slower rate than expenditure in England (*ibid.*, p.145).

FINANCING LOCAL GOVERNMENT

Local government in Scotland comprises 32 councils and 35 related organisations, such as police, fire and road bridge joint boards. In

2003–04, total expenditure on services was £13.8 billion. This was offset by service-specific government grants, and fees and charges from service users. The net cost of services of £8.6 billion was financed by central government grants in the form of revenue support grants (RSGs) of £5 billion, redistributed non-domestic rate income (NDRI) of £1.8 billion and by council tax of £1.8 billion. According to Audit Scotland (2005), local authority expenditure and government funding has increased steadily over the last five years. Overall, expenditure has increased by 20 per cent over the past five years. The largest increase is in social work (43 per cent), reflecting pressures from an ageing population and growing concern about child protection and youth justice.

Expenditure on housing fell because of housing stock transfers. Total general fund capital expenditure in 2003–04 was £881 million. This was funded mainly from borrowing, which allows costs to be spread over future years. Housing capital expenditure amounted to £322 million, most of which was funded from the sale of council houses.

Scottish ministers have a statutory duty to consult local authorities on local government finance matters but local authorities determine their expenditure priorities and their council tax levels.

From 2001–02 local authorities have been advised of their individual revenue and capital grant allocations for three years. Local authorities receive their revenue grant on a weekly basis from the Scottish Executive. Although councils are advised of their grant allocations for a three-year period, approval is required from the Scottish Parliament each year for the annual Local Government Finance (Scotland) Order.

The Scottish local government finance system has several objectives including:

- to provide a stable and equitable allocation of revenue grant and capital consents between the 32 Scottish local authorities;
- to reflect the diversity of Scottish local authorities in their expenditure requirements;
- to provide councils with predictable futures to plan expenditure and investment;
- to reflect on new financial burdens on councils as they arise; and finally
- to recognise the impact of local authority expenditure on public expenditure.

Council tax

Since 1989, the system of raising local taxes in Scotland has changed three fold. In April 1989, the domestic rating system was replaced by the community charge or "poll tax", which had the effect of moving from a property-based tax to a personal charge. This was replaced in April 1993 with the council tax.

The council tax is not a personal tax but is rather a property tax with personal factors taken into account in calculating the amount of liability. The principal feature of the council tax is based on placing properties within valuation bands and fixing the tax ratios between bands, which has the effect of creating an amount people are required to pay. In determining the amount of council tax payable in respect of a particular dwelling, the key test is whether the property is someone's sole or main residence, and, if it is, the circumstances of the adults whose sole or main residence it is. There are a range of discounts available for single adult households and other groups, in addition to special provisions for particular categories of property, which has the effect of reducing the liability.

Taxing of non-domestic property

Part of the Government's support for local expenditure is financed by a tax, known as non-domestic rates, on non-domestic or business property which is collected by local authorities. The rates bill is the product of the rateable value of the property as measured by its assessed rental and the rate poundage which is set annually.

Since April 1, 1995, a national non-domestic rate poundage has existed in Scotland and has been set at the same level as the English Uniform Business Rate. Annual increases in the rate poundage are linked to the rate of inflation.

Revenue expenditure

Revenue grants support councils' recurring expenditure on the provision of local authority services. It also supports local authority costs in servicing debt from their capital investment funded from borrowing, leasing payments and approved PPP projects. The Scottish Executive grant support for revenue expenditure is termed Aggregate External Finance (AEF). The total level at AEF for the three forward years is determined by Scottish ministers and it is made up of three elements:

(a) Specific Grants
(b) Non-Domestic Rate Income (NDRI), and
(c) Revenue Support Grant (RSG).

Specific grants

Specific grants are set centrally and are linked to specific public policy initiatives and expectations. Specific grants constitute around 10 per cent of total AEF.

Non-domestic rates

Non-domestic rates are collected by local authorities, paid into a central pool and then redistributed to councils in proportion to their populations. The amount estimated to be available for distribution each year depends on forecasts of gross rate yield, losses from appeals and adjustments from previous years. Adjustments are made to the level of RSG (either up or down) to reflect variations between the estimated NDRI and the actual amount collected. As a consequence, the amount collected by an individual local authority has no direct impact on its AEF allocations.

Revenue support grant

Revenue Support Grant makes up the balance of AEF each year after estimates of specific grants and NDRI have been subtracted from the national AEF total.

Scottish Ministers, in reaching their decision on total revenue grant, must have regard to the impact on council tax levels. The proportion of local authority expenditure funded from the council tax is known as Local Authority Self Finance Expenditure (LASFE) and counts towards total public expenditure at national (UK) level.

Aggregate external finance: calculation and distribution

Aggregate External Finance (AEF) is distributed between Scotland's 32 local authorities using a "needs based" approach developed over a number of years in consultation between central and local government. The approach considers key factors which impact on councils' Relative Revenue Expenditure requirements. Grant distribution is calculated on the basis of councils' Total Estimated Expenditure (TEE) funded from both grant and local taxation. Councils' expenditure requirements are split between expenditure on services and debt servicing (loan and leasing charges). Once debt servicing charges and approved Public Private Partnerships project expenditure support have been calculated, their combined costs is top sliced from the TEE, the remaining provision is known as Grant Aided Expenditure (GAE) and is sub-divided between specific service and sub-service headings, knows as GAE allowances. The distribution system therefore requires the allocation of the aggregate level of GAE amongst services, this is known as "the GAE service split". The service split is a top-down process determined by the Scottish Ministers in consultation with COSLA. These consultations take into account a range of influencing factors including political priorities. Once the GAE service split has been made, there is a further distribution amongst sub-services. Each GAE allowance has its own distribution formula.

The next stage is to allocate to each authority a share of each sub-service GAE. The process for implementing this is known as the client group approach. This can be defined as an attempt to estimate the relative need of local authorities to incur expenditure on a particular service or sub-service. The approach takes into account variations in the demand for services and the costs of providing them to a similar standard and with a similar degree of efficiency. The approach is an attempt to objectify a subjective process as it requires consideration of demand and cost factors.

A primary indicator has to be determined for each service and sub-service and (if justified) one or more secondary indicators.

An example of a primary indicator in education would be the staff:pupil ratio in a school. A local authority's GAE is the sum of its share of each service or sub-service GAE. The details of the component elements of each local authority's GAE is contained in the "Green Book" which is produced each year.

The grant distribution formula is calculated on the basis of the council's total estimated expenditure. The gap between this level of expenditure and the total AEF is funded from the council tax. The distribution formula takes account of the resources that each council can raise from the council tax, by distributing the gap between local authorities on the basis of each council's tax base using the number of Band D equivalent properties within a local authority. A council's AEF allocation is calculated by deducting its estimated council tax income from its total estimated expenditure. Scottish Ministers have introduced a minimum grant "floor" within the settlement calculation to ensure that councils receive at least a minimum guaranteed increase in AEF for each year. Scottish Ministers have reserve powers to cap local authority expenditure where they consider an authority's expenditure to be excessive.

Capital expenditure

Capital expenditure is spending which creates long-term assets, whose benefits will last over a period of years. Local authorities' capital expenditure is determined by central government and is subject to statutory controls. Local authority capital expenditure is largely funded by borrowing. Control on spending on non-housing capital investment is exercised through the issuing of capital allocations.

Capital grants are funded direct from the Scottish Executive, whereas local authority capital expenditure is largely funded by borrowing for which councils receive loan charges support. In addition to grants and borrowing, councils can supplement their capital allocations by using current revenue for capital purposes, by spending capital receipts raised from the sale of council assets and by using European Union and other grants. Councils can also make use of Public Private Partnerships (PPP) projects as an alternative to direct funding.

Annual capital "allocations" issued by the Scottish Executive specify the level of expenditure on non-housing capital investment, these cover expenditure on education, social work, roads and transport, general services, flood prevention and non-council housing. This is normally issued in the form of a single allocation and councils can bid for additional resources for specific purposes. The allocations of capital consents were issued under section 94 of the Local Government (Scotland) Act 1973. These allocations are not grants but are "consents to borrow" up to a specified amount to fund capital projects. The single allocation allows councils to determine for themselves how the allocation is distributed amongst their service priorities. The single allocation for 2002–03 was approximately £325 million. Local authorities fund loan repayments from the revenue expenditure over the lifetime of the asset. The revenue grant support system takes into account the cost of repaying loan charges.

Council tax levels

Council tax in Scotland increased by an average of 4.4 per cent in 2004–05. The average Band D tax is £1,053, an increase of £43 on 2003–04. A feature of recent council tax settlements is the pattern of convergence in council tax rates across local authorities. There continues to be a reduction in the margin between the highest and lowest Band D charges. In 1996–97, the figure was £369 and it currently stands at £274.

Under the provisions of the Local Government (Scotland) Act 1973 local authorities require consent from Scottish Ministers to incur capital expenditure. These provisions were repealed by the Local Government in Scotland Act 2003 replacing them with a duty on the local authority to determine and keep under review the maximum amount which it can afford to allocate to capital expenditure. The 2003 Act also gives Ministers the power to set the maximum amount that a local authority may allocate to capital expenditure.

A code of practice known as "the Prudential Code" has been developed by the Chartered Institute of Public Finance and Accountancy (CIPFA) to provide a framework for local authority capital finance. The code sets out good practice in relation to the planning and management of capital expenditure. Regulations requiring local authorities to have regard to the code came into force on April 1, 2004.

Housing revenue

Income and expenditure in relation to a council's own housing stock is ring-fenced within the Housing Revenue Account (HRA). The main items of income and expenditure include income from rents, expenditure on managing, maintaining and repairing the housing stock and expenditure on loan charges.

Local authorities are expected to ensure that they collect sufficient income from rents to cover their HRA expenditure. Councils may transfer HRA surpluses to the general services account, however, they are not permitted to budget for a transfer of funds from general services into the HRA. The HRA is not allowed to be in deficit at the end of the financial year. If this happens, authorities must transfer funds from the general services account to cover the deficit.

Local authorities receive separate HRA capital "allocations" for expenditure on their own housing stock. These resources may not be used outwith the HRA. Councils can also supplement their capital allocations through the use of capital receipts and by using current revenue for capital purposes.

Councils raise substantial HRA capital receipts primarily from the sale of council house. Councils can also generate large surpluses from rental income in order to supplement their capital programmes. Gross HRA capital expenditure consists of capital allocations, capital expenditure funded from rental income and usable receipts (mainly from council house sales).

Direct Labour Organisations

Compulsory Competitive Tendering (CCT) was first established in the 1980s to introduce commercial pressures to certain activities undertaken by councils. As a consequence internal provider organisations known as Direct Labour Organisations (DLOs) were established. CCT was substantially suspended as a consequence of the 1996 local government reorganisation and this moratorium was extended as "best value" was developed. The Local Government in Scotland Act 2003 abolished CCT. Councils are now required to maintain and disclose trading accounts for their significant trading operations, and to achieve break-even on a rolling three-year basis.

PFI/PPP

In recent years, councils have entered into PFI/PPP contracts in a number of service areas, principally in education. Between 1998 and 2001, 12 councils signed contract under the first round of funding from the Scottish Executive for private sector delivery of school refurbishment or replacement.

Housing stock transfers

During 2002–03, Glasgow City Council and Scottish Borders Council transferred their council housing stock to local housing associations. Early in 2003–04, Dumfries and Galloway Council transferred its housing stock to community ownership. As part of these transfers, outstanding loans and costs associated with the early termination of loans were met by central government.

Financing the NHS in Scotland

The NHS in Scotland required some £7.7 billion in the financial year 2003–04 with £5.9 billion coming from the Scottish Parliament and £1.8 billion from National Insurance contributions, charges for prescriptions and dental treatment, and other sources of NHS income. The Scottish Parliament allocation is based on the Scottish Executive Health Department's Spending Plan. However, in the financial year 2003–04, the NHS in Scotland spent £7.8 billion with £6.6 billion being spent by the NHS Boards, £0.7 billion spent by Special NHS Health Boards and the remainder (£500 million) was spent by the Scottish Executive Health Department (SEHD) on centrally managed expenditure. The money is allocated principally in the form of the Revenue Resource Limit (RRL) and the Capital Resource Limit (CRL). There are other sources of finance including funding for family health services and financial resources for local health councils.

The RRL is the revenue budget allocated for the day-to-day operation of NHS services by the NHS Boards. If a NHS Board makes savings against its RRL budget, these savings can be carried forward to the next financial year, but over-expenditure must be repaid from future years' allocations. The CRL is the budgetary allocation for net capital investment. The Cash Requirement (CR) is the total funds required for the RRL plus the CRL. The RRLs are set by the SEHD and notified to the NHS Boards early in the financial year but can be changed in the course of a financial year as a consequence of supplementary allocations.

Recent financial performance

In 2003–04, four NHS Boards overspent against their RRLs to the tune of £61.7 million with the remaining 11 having a combined underspending of £47.5 million giving an overall deficit of £14.2 million. The Special Health Boards and other NHS bodies underspent by £12.7 million in total, resulting in a total deficit of £1.5 million for all NHS bodies in Scotland. In relation to the CRL and CR, 23 out of 24 NHS Boards, Special Health Boards and other NHS bodies achieved their targets for 2003–04. The SEHD expects all NHS bodies to achieve financial balance in 2004–05.

Scottish Executive Health Department funding for NHS Boards

There are three main elements to the funding of NHS Boards by SEHD.

Unified budget

The unified budget is allocated to cover expenditure on hospital and community health services, general medical services (GP support and team costs) and the costs of drugs dispensed. Allocations to individual NHS Boards are determined by reference to a formula developed in 1999, this is known as the Arbuthnott formula. This formula takes into account the share of the population living in each NHS Board area, the age structure of the population, levels of deprivation and the proportion of the population living in remote and rural areas. All NHS Boards receive a standard increase in funding to enable them to benefit from the growth in NHS expenditure. Capital funding is also determined with reference to the Arbuthnott formula, although adjustments are made to provide additional funds to NHS Boards with specialist teaching centres. The unified budget constitutes about 87 per cent of the total allocations the NHS Boards.

Family health services non-discretionary budget

Expenditure under this heading covers payments to family practitioners (GPs) based on the number of patients seen and prescriptions dispensed. This expenditure is therefore demand-led and thus it is not appropriate to make use of the Arbuthnott formula. Allocations are as a consequence only indicative and expenditure is met by an equal non-discretionary funding allocation. This budget constitutes approximately 10 per cent of the total allocations to NHS Boards.

Ring-fenced budgets

To ensure that NHS Boards spend appropriate amounts on particular public policy initiatives such as Drug Action Teams and HIV prevention measures, SEHD can ring-fence some of the total funds allocated to NHS Boards. Ring-fenced allocations comprised 3 per cent of the total allocations to NHS Boards.

Public sector audit

Public sector auditors give independent assurance on the financial statements of local authorities and report on:

- the local authority's arrangements for ensuring the proper conduct of public business;
- the management of performance;
- the use of public money; and
- the extent to which the local authority is achieving Best Value from public resources.

Contemporary audit practice goes beyond analysing and reporting to identifying areas for improvement and to encourage good practice. Audit Scotland helps the Auditor General and the Accounts Commission check that organisations spending public money use it properly, efficiently and effectively (Audit Scotland, 2005).

They do this by overseeing the audits of around 200 organisations including:

- 19 Scottish Executive departments and agencies
- 15 NHS Boards and 8 Special Health Boards
- 32 councils
- 35 police, fire and other boards
- 42 further education colleges
- 23 non-departmental public bodies (NDPBs), and
- Scottish Water.

Audits check whether public bodies manage their finances to the highest standards and achieve the best possible value for public money.

Three principles guide audit work:

- auditors are independent of the organisations they audit;
- reports are in the public domain; and
- auditors make sure organisations operate within the regulations that govern their work and deliver value for money.

The purpose of external audit is to support public scrutiny that is fair, equal and open, and that leads to more effective financial management and value for money.

The Auditor General is appointed by the Crown, is independent, reports to the Scottish Parliament and is held accountable for Audit Scotland's work. The Auditor General's role is to examine public bodies to see how they spend public money, to make sure they manage their finances to the highest standards and to make sure they achieve value for money.

The Accounts Commission was set up in 1975 and is independent of local councils and of government. The Accounts Commission can make reports and recommendations to Scottish Ministers. The Accounts Commission's role is to appoint auditors to Scotland's 32 councils and joint boards, to help these bodies manage their resources efficiently and effectively, to promote Best Value and to publish information every year about how councils perform. The Accounts Commission has powers to report and make recommendations to the organisations it scrutinises, to hold hearings and to report and make recommendations to Scottish Executive Ministers. The Commission can also take action against councillors and council officials if their negligence or misconduct leads to money being lost or breaks the law. There are between 6 and 12 members appointed by Scottish Executive Ministers.

The Accounts Commission is an independent body whose purpose is to hold local authorities to account. Issues arising from audits are reported to the Accounts Commission by the Controller of Audit. The Commission has the power to hold public hearings and to report and make recommendations to Scottish Ministers and local authorities.

Audit Scotland provides professional services to the Accounts Commission. This includes undertaking audits and the preparation of public reports as well as providing guidance and support on technical matters and monitoring auditor performance.

Financial threats

Local authorities participate in several pension schemes and each scheme has its own rules and funding arrangements. The management, funding and payment of pensions are long-term activities that require regular re-assessment of the health of the pension fund and the contribution rates necessary to sustain pension commitments. Employees' contributions to the scheme are fixed by statute. The employer's contribution rate is reviewed every three years by actuaries who certify a rate for employers' contributions to maintain the long-term solvency of the provision fund. Employers' contributions have increased in recent years partly as a consequence of the ageing of the local government workforce. In the NHS, future cost pressures include implementing UK-wide pay modernisation agreements, increasing pension costs and an increasing drugs bill.

Local government services

The services and functions of Scottish local authorities correspond in many respects to those administered by authorities in England and Wales. As local authorities are multi-purpose bodies, this range is extensive and covers all aspects of the life of the community. Water and sewerage services are now outwith local government administration but are not (as is the case in England and Wales) privatised.

Local government functions may be divided into three broad categories:

(a) Communal—These services are provided for the benefit of all, such as the provision of roads and paths, street lighting, planning and leisure services.
(b) Personal—These services are designed to assist individuals, and cover such areas as education and the welfare services. This is the most costly aspect of the local authority services.
(c) Protective—These services are designed to protect the individual from various dangers, through fire brigades, police forces, refuse collection, environmental health inspectors, trading standards inspectors and the licensing of public premises.

Communal services

Responsibilities for the communal services are dealt with as follows:

Planning

The Local Government Scotland Act 2002 provides a statutory basis for the community planning process. This Act requires local authorities to initiate, maintain and facilitate the community planning process in their area and to determine the means of consultation and co-operation.

Economic planning—contributing to national plans, advising on implications of national plans, formulating plans, controlling and directing capital investments, and using resources in accordance with plans.

Land-use planning—strategic plans to identify the broad pattern of physical development and transportation.

Other activities associated with planning include: control of buildings, responsibility for derelict land and industrial development strategy.

Building control includes comprehensive urban development policy, protection of listed buildings, establishment of conservation areas and the protection of ancient monuments.

With the decline of many of Scotland's traditional industries, increasing importance has been attached by central government and its agencies to attracting new industrial investment and to supporting and encouraging existing industries. Local authorities in Scotland have no specific statutory duties in the field of industrial development, but each tier can make use of general powers under various statutes to engage in the promotion and assistance of industry by, for example, providing land and buildings and by offering mortgages and other financial incentives.

Local authorities liaise with Scottish Enterprise, local development agencies and local enterprise companies on industrial and business development.

Roads and transportation

The responsibilites of local authorities include the provision, improvement and maintenance of public roads, the regulation of traffic and the implementation of road safety measures. They can also act as agents for the Scottish Executive for the maintenance and improvement of trunk roads and motorways.

The responsibilities, with regard to transportation, conferred on councils, cover the co-ordination of public transport services. Councils also have permissive powers to light roads and proposed roads for which they are, or will become, the highway authorities.

Leisure and recreation

Services in these areas are provided by local authorities for people to pursue leisure interests. With the growing emphasis on leisure and community pursuits, and with technological advances which will result in more leisure time, it is falling increasingly on local authorities to provide recreational facilities and services on an adequate scale, in the proper place and at the right time.

Leisure services include provision for the arts and entertainment, as well as sport and physical recreation. The main services provided are as follows:

(a) Libraries and cultural services: Local authority powers to operate public libraries were first introduced in the nineteenth century and the service has developed to its present form where local authorities are responsible for:

  (i) ensuring that facilities are available for the borrowing of, or the reference to, books and other printed matter, pictures, records, films and other material for both adults and children;
  (ii) encouraging the full use of the library service, through the provision of advice, bibliographical and any other information as may be necessary; and
  (iii) co-operation between library authorities and other authorities.

Councils may also provide and maintain museums and art galleries. No charges may be made for admission and the authority must take into account the need to secure that the museum or gallery plays its full part in the promotion of education within its area.

(b) Swimming pools and gymnasia: This is an expanding area of activity for the councils and is a good example of local authorities reacting to a changing need in the community for recreation by means of providing facilities for squash, badminton, table tennis, swimming, basketball and modern gymnasia.
(c) Parks: The powers conferred on local authorities by the Public Parks (Scotland) Act 1878 and the Local Government and Planning (Scotland) Act 1982 are to provide, among other things, parks, public walks and pleasure grounds.
(d) Tourism: Councils are responsible for tourism, its promotion and information regarding it and for the provision of facilities for recreation, conferences, trade fares and exhibitions.
(e) Countryside: Councils have powers to carry out works intended to preserve or to enhance the natural beauty of land in their areas, and provide a range of facilities to enable the public to enjoy the countryside or to engage in open air recreation. This can also include such things as

tree planting and the provision of picnic places, car parks and view points.

Personal services

The main personal services involve education, social work and housing.

Education

The education service is by far the most expensive of local government services and employs the highest numbers of people. Councils are required to secure an adequate and efficient system of pre-school and school education for their area. They are also responsible, among other things, for boarding schools, employing teachers and educational advisors, providing facilities for social, cultural and recreational activities and for physical education and training.

Local authorities provide education at three separate levels:

(a) Pre-school education: All three- and four-year old children in Scotland have access to free pre-school education. Most children receiving pre-school education attend education authority nursery schools or nursery departments, which consist of a nursery class or classes forming part of a primary school.
(b) Primary education: Compulsory primary education lasts from the age of 5 until about 12. Primary schools usually take both boys and girls and normally include infant classes for the first two years.
(c) Secondary education: The principle of comprehensive education has been traditional in many parts of Scotland. The majority of education authority secondary schools are six-year comprehensive schools. Because of local circumstances, however, there are some comprehensive schools whose courses may extend to four years only and from which pupils may transfer at the end of the fourth year to a six-year school.

New Community Schools

The New Community Schools (NCS) approach has the twin aims of promoting social inclusion and raising educational standards. The NCS pilot programme is supporting 62 projects with each project awarded funding of £200,000 a year for three years. The

Scottish Executive is supporting the roll-out of the NCS approach with the aim of having it introduced to all schools by 2007.

In addition to the above main areas of educational provision there is also an obligation on local education authorities to provide:

(a) Special education—This is provided for children needing it for any handicap, physical or mental.
(b) Adult education—This consists of non-vocational courses for people over 18. The subjects range from cookery to cultural subjects, including languages, drama and music.
(c) Community education—This is an area of educational provision which seeks to involve all age groups by providing facilities and organisers for youth clubs, recreation centres, outdoor centres and community centres.

The education service, therefore, includes many functions and requires vast resources, particularly a large labour force, to operate it. This makes it the costliest function of Scottish local government.

Social work

Social work services are provided by all authorities as they have a general duty to promote social welfare. The main components of this duty, at present, are the care and support of children, the elderly, the physically handicapped, the mentally disordered and other groups of persons in the community identified as being in need. Services are also provided within health service establishments and for offenders, both within and outside of penal institutions. There are services and facilities, too, provided directly by local authorities or in association with voluntary organisations acting on their behalf.

The main elements of social work are:

(a) The care of children—This involves the care of children deprived of normal home life, including the provision of assessment services; foster care; residential or other care; the giving or procuring of social, medical and other reports to the children's hearings and the care of children placed under supervision by these hearings, either in the community or in residential care; supervision of children privately placed in nurseries, day-care facilities or private foster homes or placed for adoption, and the inspection and registration of such places.
(b) The provision of social and other information to the courts—This is in respect of offenders and involves the

supervision of persons placed on probation or discharged from prison and other places of detention.

(c) The identification of, and the provision of assistance to, those in need—This group includes the chronically sick and disabled; those with impaired sight or hearing or other physical handicaps; mentally defective persons; and those in need, for any reason, of social work advice, support and guidance, including individuals or families in difficulty (which may include the elderly); arranging treatment in a hospital or under guardianship, voluntarily or by statutory provision, of the mentally ill and the care after discharge from hospital of such persons.

Housing

Housing is probably the public service which is most readily associated with local government in Scotland. In terms of expenditure, it is second only to education and, in terms of councils' time, it is certainly the most demanding of all. Compared to England and Wales, substantially more Scottish people live in council-provided accommodation. Added to this, housing has extensive and significant links with many other local government functions. The Housing (Scotland) Act 2001 contains provisions covering a number of areas including provisions in relation to homelessness, tenancy rights, regulation of the socially rented sector, and the roles and responsibilities of the Scottish Ministers, local authorities, Scottish Homes and other bodies.

Housing authorities have the following main functions:

(a) the comprehensive assessment of housing need, including need in the private sector;
(b) the provision of housing advice;
(c) the provision of new housing by themselves or by arrangements with other agencies, including the layout of housing schemes and the provision of necessary facilities and amenities such as shops, open spaces and playgrounds in the locality;
(d) the improvement of individual houses, either at their own hand or by making financial assistance available to private agencies or directly to individual occupiers, and the environmental improvement of housing areas in general;
(e) the acquisition and demolition of unsatisfactory housing and the re-housing of persons displaced from their accommodation by the operations of the local authority;
(f) the determination and collection of rents in respect of their own housing stock and the granting of rent rebates and allowances;

(g) the general management of housing stock, involving:
   (i) functions largely concerned with property (*e.g.* repairs and maintenance), and
   (ii) functions concerned primarily with tenants, including the allocation, transfer and termination of tenancies, together with housing welfare; and

(h) the administration of the Housing Act, 1985 and the "right to buy".

Protective services

The police

There are eight police forces in Scotland. Local authorities are no longer police authorities and, except for the Northern Constabulary (which covers the former Highland Region, the Western Isles, and Orkney and Shetland) and the Lothian and Borders Police, the territories of the Scottish police forces correspond with those of the former regions. For each force, there is a Joint Police Committee consisting or elected representatives of the local authorities within its jurisdiction area. The Joint Police Committee is the police authority and it is charged with the duty of maintaining an adequate and efficient force. The police authority provides the buildings and equipment needed and, subject to the Scottish Executive's approval, fixes the authorised establishment of both police and civilian personnel. The police authority, however, has no direct power to interfere in operational matters, nor in the deployment of members of the force within the police area.

The fire service and civil defence

There are eight fire brigades in Scotland and, as with the police, their territories correspond with former regional boundaries except for the Northern Fire Brigade and the Lothian and Borders Brigade (geographically as for the police). For each brigade there is a Joint Fire Committee which is the fire authority and it is required to prepare local contingency plans for civil defence and emergency planning.

Environmental health

Councils have wide-ranging powers in relation to environmental health, covering such matters as smoke, noise and pest control, standards for filling materials for upholstery, and the prevention of the spread of infectious disease.

Councils are responsible for food hygiene and safety under the Food and Drugs (Scotland) Act 1956, which deals with food standards, composition and labelling. Councils have powers under the same statute to supervise food hygiene and safety.

Local authorities also have certain functions under the Animal Health Act 1981 including the appointment of inspectors to enforce the relevant provisions of the Act and Orders made under it.

Legislation lays down conditions to ensure that animals (including poultry) which are intended for human consumption are slaughtered humanely in hygienic and sanitary conditions. Councils also have certain responsibilities in this area, which include the registration of private red-meat slaughterhouses and the licensing of slaughterhouse personnel.

The collection and disposal of refuse is another council responsibility and they also have powers under the Burgh Police Acts and local legislation to sweep and cleanse streets.

Consumer protection

The duties undertaken by councils in the field of consumer protection cover a broad spectrum of trade and business activities. They include checks for accuracy on weighing and measuring equipment, investigation of complaints about misleading or false descriptions of goods or services, enforcement of controls over credit and hire transactions designed to promote "truth in lending", enforcement of orders and regulations controlling trading methods and the provision of information to consumers.

Licensing

Local authorities have various licensing and related functions of which liquor licensing is the most important. Under the Licensing (Scotland) Act 1976, a local licensing board, composed of elected members, has complete responsibility for the granting or renewal of liquor licenses for its area.

Other licensing functions include the granting or renewal of licenses for cinemas and theatres, animal boarding and riding establishments, lotteries and taxis.

Miscellaneous services

Local authorities provide a comprehensive range of services not covered by the previous classification. These include:

Registrars services

The registration of births, deaths and marriages is essentially a central government function. The main responsibility for the service rests with the Registrar General for Scotland, who is required, under the Registration of Births, Deaths and Marriages (Scotland) Act 1965, to maintain a useful and efficient registration service. The Registrar General is the head of the General Register Office in Edinburgh.

The local registration authorities are the local authorities and they must appoint and pay Registrars and their staff and must provide and maintain office accommodation, including facilities for civil marriages.

District courts

Under the District Courts (Scotland) Act 1975, courts were established in the district council (as was) areas and the island areas. The councils there are basically responsible for the administration of the district court, including ensuring the provision of a legally qualified Clerk of the Court to advise the justices on matters of law, practice and procedure.

Many other minor functions and responsibilities are exercised by local authorities in Scotland including:

Aerodromes
Allotments
Burials and cremation
Caravan sites
Civic restaurants
Coast protection
Conservation areas
Employment of young persons
Ferries
Harbours
Health and safety at work
Public conveniences
Shops hours
War memorials

Table 4.1: Local Government Staffing

Estimated number and full-time equivalent number of staff employed by Scottish local authorities: June 2003

	Total number of staff						Full-time equivalent					
Service Group	Total	Male		Female			Total	Salary band (i)				
		Full-time	Part-time	Full-time	Part-time			A1	A2	B	C	Other
Corporate Services	4,574	1,502	89	2,241	742		4,166	121	232	1,071	2,643	100
Central Support Services	15,357	6,240	138	7,117	1,862		14,430	227	663	4,328	9,058	154
Planning and Economic Development	3,734	1,935	61	1,385	353		3,528	54	217	1,746	1,456	55
Education-Teachers	60,987	13,150	1,821	35,175	10,841	(ii)	54,607	n.a	n.a	n.a	n.a	n.a
Other Education Staff	45,951	4,406	1,774	10,873	28,898		30,677	124	334	2,183	24,529	3,508
Social Work	53,853	6,134	1,826	18,046	27,847		41,377	88	269	7,527	23,567	9,927
Housing	8,038	3,114	107	3,719	1,098		7,437	41	121	1,143	5,179	953
Roads and Transport	7,351	3,412	1,135	1,083	1,721		5,611	54	197	1,491	2,480	1,390
Arts, Sport and Leisure	6,730	1,852	1,226	1,354	2,298		4,738	27	62	568	2,109	1,972
Libraries, Museums and Art Galleries	5,515	1,062	329	2,010	2,114		4,130	13	43	546	3,274	255
Trading Standards	759	381	8	290	81		718	15	38	272	394	0
Environmental Services	3,263	1,930	85	917	332		3,062	29	79	868	1,166	921
DLO/DSO	62,560	26,970	2,625	4,403	28,562		44,907	58	163	1,476	4,719	38,492
Police and Related Services	21,672	14,581	92	5,762	1,237	(ii)	20,995	n.a	n.a	n.a	n.a	n.a
Fire Services	5,553	4,813	19	540	181	(ii) (iii)	5,460	n.a	n.a	n.a	n.a	n.a
Other staff	1,614	879	47	357	331		1,400	5	21	131	450	793
Total all staff	**307,511**	**92,360**	**11,382**	**95,272**	**108,497**		**247,243**					
			Full-time equivalent for all staff excluding teachers, police and fire service staff:				**166,181**	**854**	**2,435**	**23,350**	**81,023**	**58,519**

National Health Services

In this section contemporary NHS services are summarised before the chapter conclusion considers finance and services in the context of New Public Management.

The Scottish Executive Health Department (SEHD) is responsible for health policy and the administration of the National

Health Service in Scotland. The Chief Executive of the Scottish Executive Health Department leads the central management of the NHS, is accountable to ministers for the efficiency and performance of the service, and heads a Management Executive which oversees the work of 15 area health boards responsible for planning health services for people in their area. In addition to the 15 area NHS Boards there are seven Special Health Boards responsible for providing a range of NHS related services.

NHS Education Scotland

NHS Education Scotland is charged with developing the skills of doctors, nurses, therapists, dentists, scientists, psychologists and all other staff central to the aim of improving standards of patient care. NHSES combines three predecessor organisations that were individually involved with the education needs of doctors, dentists, psychologists, nurses, midwives, health visitors and pharmacists.

(a) The National Board for Nursing, Midwifery and Health Visiting for Scotland
(b) The Post-Qualification Education Board for Pharmacists
(c) The Scottish Council for Postgraduate Medical and Dental Education

The NHS Education Scotland plan focuses on five key issues that will build on the existing skills of NHS staff and contribute to improvements in patient care. The five areas are:

(a) Providing education that is fit for purpose;
(b) Adding value from all educational developments;
(c) Extending educational support to all NHS staff;
(d) Developing partnership working with stakeholders;
(e) Ensuring educational provision matches the needs of NHSScotland.

The NHS in Scotland has around 132,000 staff, including more than 63,000 nurses, midwives and health visitors, and over 8,500 doctors. There are also more than 7,000 family practitioners, including doctors, dentists, opticians and community pharmacists, who are independent contractors providing a range of services within the NHS in return for various fees and allowances.

NHS Health Scotland

NHS Health Scotland is the national resource for improving Scotland's health. It is a Special Health Board, formed in April 2003 through the bringing together of the Public Health Institute of Scotland (PHIS) and the Health Education Board for Scotland

(HEBS). NHS Health Scotland staff are drawn from an exceptionally broad range of professional backgrounds: from health promotion, public health and other health professionals such as doctors and nurses, to research specialists, training managers, health information specialists, librarians, information managers, publishing specialists, graphic designers, advertising and PR professionals, project managers, administrators, HR managers and finance managers. Together they provide professional leadership and support for specific aspects of the health improvement effort in Scotland.

Health Scotland plays a key role in improving the understanding of Scotland's health problems, the reasons behind them and the rationale for tackling them; working with partners throughout the NHS and in every other sector of the Scottish economy. Its key functions being to:

(a) collect, analyse and communicate information on health and health improvement;
(b) develop and use research evidence to inform health improvement policy-making and practice;
(c) develop health improvement programmes, and create advertising, publications, and training and development opportunities which deliver them;
(d) review international, national and local developments that lead to more effective approaches to health improvement in Scotland.

NHS 24

NHS 24 is a national 24–hour service which provides clinical assessment and referral, health advice and information by telephone throughout Scotland. NHS 24 works in partnership with local health systems, NHS organisations and local communities. The integrated service structure allows patients to treat their symptoms at home or, if they need to see a doctor, this can be arranged for them. NHS 24 works particularly closely with GP Out-of-Hours Services, the Ambulance Service and Accident and Emergency Departments. In addition NHS 24 provides a Health Information Service.

NHS Quality Improvement Scotland

The role of NHS Quality Improvement Scotland (NHS QIS) is to improve the quality of healthcare in Scotland by:

- setting standards;
- monitoring performance; and
- providing advice, guidance and support to NHSScotland on effective clinical practice and service improvements.

Quality improvement for NHS QIS means improving patients' outcomes and experiences. In order to promote this, it relies on understanding the scientific evidence, the needs and preferences of patients, and the experience of health professionals. NHS QIS achieves its aims by developing and implementing, in partnership with healthcare professionals and the public, a national framework to:

- determine, share and promote consistent high-quality care across Scotland through:
    - clinical audit
    - collecting and publishing clinical performance data
    - learning lessons from adverse events and near misses
    - assessing the clinical and cost effectiveness of health interventions
    - clinical guidelines
    - best practice statements
- set clinical and non-clinical standards;
- review and monitor performance through self-assessment and external peer review, and investigate serious service failures;
- support implementation of clinical governance.

Scottish Ambulance Service

The Scottish Ambulance Service serves all of Scotland and is a Special Health Board funded directly by the Health Department of the Scottish Executive. The Scottish Ambulance Service provides Accident & Emergency and Non-Emergency Services to the people of Scotland from a total of 152 locations. These locations are a mix of ambulance stations and home-based operating points. The Scottish Ambulance Service also operates a Helicopter Emergency Medical Service from two dedicated air bases; one in central Glasgow and one at Inverness Airport.

The Service has two main functions—the provision of an accident and emergency service to respond to 999 calls and a non-emergency service, which performs an essential role in taking patients to and from their hospital appointments. An Air Wing consisting of two helicopters and four fixed-wing aircraft provides emergency response and invaluable hospital transfer for remote areas.

The service is managed by a Board made up of a non-executive chairman, seven non-executive directors and a chief executive and four executive directors. Services are delivered locally across Scotland in six divisions.

The State Hospitals Board for Scotland

The State Hospitals Board for Scotland provides care and treatment in conditions of special security for around 240 patients from Scotland and Northern Ireland with mental disorders who, because of their dangerous, violent or criminal tendencies, cannot be cared for securely in any other setting. It is a public body accountable to the First Minister for Scotland through the Scottish Executive and is designated as a Special Health Board, the only hospital of its kind within Scotland.

The State Hospital is located at Carstairs and has state-of-the-art security systems managed by specialist staff, allowing care and treatment to be carried out safely; thus minimising the potential dangers to society posed by individual patients, whilst maximising the opportunity for care and treatment. The aim of the State Hospital is to provide the highest quality care and treatment for patients whilst respecting their dignity and individuality.

NHS Professions

At September 30, 2004, there were 149,896 staff in NHSScotland. The chart below gives a profile of the NHSScotland workforce by staff group. Almost half (43.3 per cent) of staff is in the Nursing & Midwifery staff group.

Figure 4.1

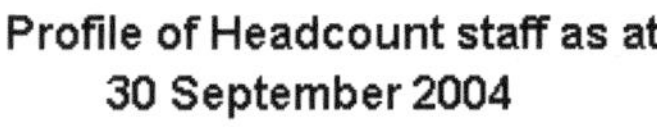

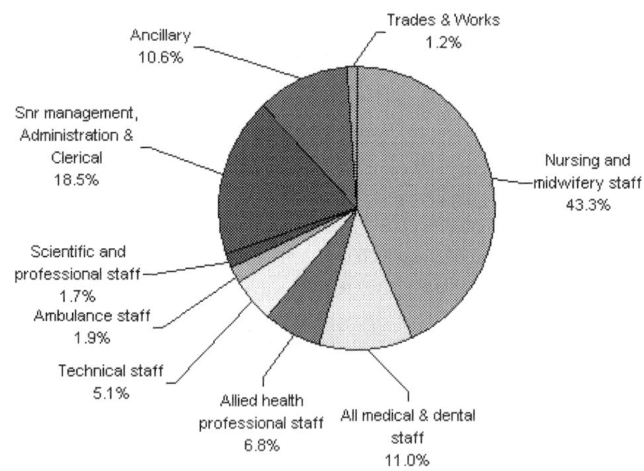

Source ©: ISD Scotland

Nursing

Nurses and midwives are the most visible and recognisable symbol of the health service, and embody the values people want to see in NHSScotland. They not only have the ability to assess and treat injury and illness, but also possess the skills to promote good health in individuals and communities, and the expertise to design, co-ordinate and deliver services.

The four main aspects of nursing are:

- Adult
- Mental health
- Children
- Learning disabilities

Midwifery is a separate career, but involves caring for women during their pregnancy and delivery.

Doctors

Doctors are responsible for the diagnosis, care and treatment of illnesses, diseases, infections and well-being of people. They may work in a variety of settings such as in a hospital or as a family doctor (GP). Hospital doctors can go onto specialise in particular areas such as surgery, psychiatry and paediatrics. There are opportunities in other areas such as public health, teaching and research.

Learning to be a doctor involves a long and expensive course of study. It can take a minimum of nine years to train as a general practitioner (GP) and 12 years before a doctor is suitably qualified to apply for a post as a hospital consultant.

Allied Health Professionals

Allied Health Professionals (AHPs) are critical to people's ongoing assessment, treatment and rehabilitation throughout their illness episodes. They support people of all ages in their recovery, helping them to return to work and to participate in sport or education. They enable children and adults to make the most of their skills and abilities and to develop and maintain healthy lifestyles. They also provide specialist diagnostic assessment and treatment services.

While advances in medical science are aimed at saving and prolonging life, the particular skills and expertise of AHPs are often critical to the well-being of individuals. Practical interventions from AHPs can often be the most significant factor in enabling people to recover movement or mobility, overcome visual problems, improve nutritional status, develop communication abilities and restore confidence in everyday living skills, consequently helping them to sustain and enjoy quality of life even when faced with life-limiting conditions. Professions include speech and language therapy, physiotherapy, dietetics, occupational therapy and radiography.

Planned Expenditure

Table 4.2: NHS in Scotland Spending Plans 2004–08

£m	**2004–05**	**2005–06**	**2006–07**	**2007–08**
National Health Service	7,903.89	8,623.81	9,348.45	10,093.61
Health improvement	65.90	78.37	81.27	84.17
Other health services	55.95	65.19	71.45	71.83
Community Care	21.94	21.63	21.83	21.89
Total	**8,047.68**	**8,789.00**	**9,523.00**	**10,271.50**

Table 4.3: Local Government Spending Plans 2004–08

£m	**2004–05**	**2005–06**	**2006–07**	**2007–08**
Local Government				
Revenue (AEF)	7,737.22	8,028.00	8,306.45	8,503.82
Capital (FPS)	385.46	395.46	407.97	413.70
Total FPS Local Government	**8,122.68**	**8,423.46**	**8,714.42**	**8,917.52**

Conclusion

Local government and the NHS in Scotland consume vast sums of public money, £16,169 million in 2004–05, and this will increase to £19,188 million by 2007–08. There is also a shift between the services. In 2004–05, local government spent £75 million more than the NHS in Scotland but by 2007–08 the NHS will have overtaken local government and will spend £1,354 million more than local government. These figures are based on the Scottish Executive's budget plans in the publication, *Build a Better Scotland* (2004) and assume efficency savings acrosss most public services funded by the Scottish Executive.

There is little doubt that Scottish local government and the NHS in Scotland have been greatly influenced by the changing nature of management in the public sector. This NPM has impacted on these services since the early 1980s and has now permeated through to all levels of management in local authorities and NHS organisations in Scotland. Changes to local government in Scotland cannot be considered separate from changes in other areas of public administration and management. The range of policies implemented by successive Conservative governments from 1979 impacted directly on the nature of local government in Scotland. The most significant change of the 1980s was the introduction of compulsory competitive tendering (CCT) to a range of local government services.

Local authorities in order to comply with the legislative provisions governing CCT had to create separate provider units, Direct Service Organisations (DSOs) and Direct Labour Organisations (DLOs), to compete with the private sector for the right to obtain a contract for local authority work.

The Private Finance Initiative (PFI) is a scheme designed to encourage the private sector to invest in public sector projects and improve the delivery of services through better value for money (VFM).

The PFI provides an alternative approach to funding public sector activity and this is achieved by transforming the risks related to the ownership of assets to the private sector. A development of this has been the growth in partnership working on major local authority projects. The partnerships, or Public Private Partnerships (PPPs), involve the local authority working with a private company on a project but Pyke (1998, p.217) notes that the only incentive for the private sector for such an arrangement is to make a profit.

Stewart and Walsh (1992, pp.504–508) identify a number of key themes in the "transformation of public service management" including:

- separation of the purchaser role from the provider;
- growth of quasi-contractual arrangements and quasi-markets;
- greater accountability for performance;
- emphasis on the public as customer.

This ties in closely with Christopher Hood's seven "doctrinal components" of New Public Management (see Ch.1). The overall effect of Conservative policy between 1979 and 1997 was to change the public sector and as a consequence local government and the NHS in 1997 were radically different from the local government and the NHS of the 1970s.

One of the key developments set out in the Scottish Health White Paper, *Partnership for Care*, is the evolution of LHCCs into strong Community Health Partnerships (CHPs), with new and enhanced roles at the heart of a decentralised but integrated healthcare system. These partnerships will be expected to play a pivotal role in improving the health of local communities.

Particular priorities are to ensure that CHPs can play a key role within community planning, and that they put local population health improvement at the heart of their new and enhanced role in health service planning and delivery. Important aspects of this will be the full involvement of patients, local communities and a broad range of healthcare professionals, working in substantive partnership with local authorities. Within the context of community planning each CHP will have an associated public partnership forum, and these forums should have important parts to play in local health improvement.

Therefore it is not the case that the services provided are different from the services provided 25 years ago, but there have been changes within services to respond to the changing demands of the Scottish population. Responding to these changes has been costly and the current Scottish Executive has identified the importance of identifying potential areas that can yield efficiency gains while at the same time maintaining service quality. This is the "doing more for less" approach which has been a central theme of the New Public Management.

CHAPTER 5

DEMOCRACY, PUBLIC INVOLVEMENT AND CONSTITUTIONAL STATUS

INTRODUCTION

The Wheatley Commission 1966–69 defined democracy as:

> "That form of government in which supreme power is vested in the people collectively and is administered by them or by representatives appointed by them." (Wheatley, 1969)

The effective power of decision-making must rest, and be seen to rest, with local elected representatives of the people, that is, councillors. The councillors must be directly accountable locally to the electorate. This chapter considers the ways in which local government and the NHS in Scotland promotes democracy and public involvement by discussing elections, councillors, party politics and public participation, and the constitutional status of local government.

LOCAL GOVERNMENT ELECTIONS

Widdicombe

The overall purpose of local government elections is to link the people (the electorate) to their community government.

The Widdicombe Committee Report (1986) identified three attributes of local government:

(a) pluralism;
(b) participation; and
(c) responsiveness.

All these features are enhanced by the democratic process. Elections contribute to the legitimacy of local government, helping to diffuse power from the centre—Westminster and Holyrood. Thus, local authorities may be regarded as power centres in competition with the national government. Competing centres of power are an essential element of pluralism.

Participation, which is important to the maintenance of a healthy democracy, can be achieved in many ways, but the most widely practised is through voting. Casting a vote also gives the ordinary citizen influence over public affairs and engenders responsiveness amongst representatives. Councillors have to face the electorate at regular intervals and so take notice of their views.

There are many criticisms of local democracy in practice. Electoral arrangements have been attacked because of:

(a) the low level of electoral turnout and general voter apathy;
(b) the under-representation of minorities;
(c) the concentration of power with the majority;
(d) the increasing influence of political parties;
(e) the increasing intervention of central government.

Despite these drawbacks, there is a continuing demand for participation of all kinds in local government and a concern for local democracy. The debate about whether the correct structure, enabling this to be achieved, has been created remains unresolved.

The McIntosh Commission

The Commission on Local Government and the Scottish Parliament (1999) (the McIntosh Commission) consulted on the type of electoral system which should be utilised for local authority elections as part of its consideration as to how "councils can best make themselves responsive and democratically accountable to the communities they serve" (p.4). The Commission found substantial and widespread support for the move to a system of proportional representation (PR) for local government elections and concluded as follows:

> "We believe that, as far as is practicable, every vote should count, and that Councils, in their composition, should reflect the range and balance of views within the communities which they service. It is critical that the democratic credentials of councils should be no less strong than those of the Parliament. Since the Parliament has been elected under a form of proportional representation we see this as a compelling reason for adopting PR for Scottish local government too." (p.22)

The Commission did not recommend a particular form of PR for local government elections, but did recommend that the Additional Member System (AMS), Single Transferable Vote (STV) and Alternative Vote (AV) Top-up were worth particular consideration. Instead, the Commission established five criteria which it considered should be utilised to assess the effectiveness of alternative forms of PR for Scottish local government elections. These were:

- proportionality—where the number of seats won by a party is proportionate to the total votes cast for it;
- maintenance of a link between councillor and ward;
- a fair chance for independents to be elected;
- allowance for the geographical diversity among local authorities, particularly between urban and rural areas; and
- a close fit between council wards and natural communities.

Report of the Renewing Local Democracy Working Group

The Renewing Local Democracy Working Group (2000) (the Kerley Working Group) applied the five criteria established by McIntosh against a range of PR systems (but not against First-Past-the-Post). The findings of the Working Group against each of the five criteria are summarised below as they relate to STV.

Proportionality

The Kerley Working Group considered that STV was a proportional electoral system whilst also noting that "the greater the number of seats per ward, the more proportionate the result is likely to be" (p.60).

Councillor-ward link

The Working Group recognised that ward size would be larger than is currently the case with First-Past-the-Post (FPTP) and that each elector would have an equal link to several councillors under STV. Kerley noted that the role of each representative would have to be clearly communicated to the electorate and recommended that a "programme of voter education will be an essential component of the successful introduction of a new electoral system for local government" (p.60). Kerley also recognised that multi-member wards existed in Scotland prior to 1975 and are currently in place in many English authorities and suggested that "concerns may be ill-founded" with regard to multi-member wards.

Independents

The Working Group considered that STV offered scope for independents to be elected.

Geographical diversity

The report of the Working Group highlighted that there currently exists considerable variation in the size of wards in Scotland, but noted that these would increase in size with a multi-member system albeit that there would be a number of councillors to represent constituents in those wards. It was also noted that larger wards would "impact disproportionately on independents".

Natural communities

As STV would result in larger ward sizes, the Working Group considered that this would reduce the "risk that communities would be split, or that areas which feel no common community will be put together" (p.62).

The Working Group considered that STV best met the criteria which had been established by McIntosh. However, three members from the 10 persons comprising the Kerley Working Group, were unable to support this recommendation. Two members considered that STV would undermine the councillor-ward link and one member preferred the Additional Member System (AMS) to STV. The majority of the Group went on to recommend a version of STV consisting of multi-member wards containing three to five members. In recognition of the larger ward sizes which would be present in sparsely populated parts of Scotland, the Group recommended that two members per ward would be appropriate in exceptional circumstances.

The Partnership Agreement and electoral reform

The 2003 Partnership Agreement between the Scottish Labour Party and the Scottish Liberal Democrats contains a commitment to:

> "Introduce for the next local government elections the proportional Single Transferable Vote system of election. The multi-member wards would have either 3 or 4 members, depending on local circumstances." (Scottish Labour Party and Scottish Liberal Democrats, 2003, p.46)

The Agreement also contained several additional commitments designed to enhance local democracy including:

- reforming voting arrangements;
- removing unnecessary political restrictions on standing for local authority election;
- lowering the age limit for local government candidates to 18; and
- establishing an independent remuneration committee for councillors and bringing forward severance and pension arrangement for local authority councillors.

The Local Governance (Scotland) Act 2004

The Local Governance (Scotland) Act 2004 contains provisions to introduce STV for local government elections, to widen access to council membership and to modify arrangements for councillors remuneration, pensions arrangements and severance payments.

Each local government ward will elect either three or four members per ward. The area of wards and the number of councillors per ward will be determined following a review of the electoral arrangements by the Local Government Boundary Commission for Scotland. The STV system will be used allowing voters to express preferences for as many candidates as are standing in a ward.

The Single Transferable Vote (STV) Working Group, chaired by David Green, former convener of Highland Council, was set up by the Executive in September 2003 to look at the practicalities of operating STV. It was asked to examine the procedures necessary to facilitate council elections being held using STV, and how multi-member wards would operate in practice.

The Local Governance (Scotland) Act 2004:

- introduces STV for the next local government elections;
- brings the age at which people can stand as a councillor down to 18;
- removes unnecessary political restrictions on council employees standing for local authority elections; and
- establishes an independent remuneration committee for councillors.

Access to council membership

The 2004 Act allows employees of a council to stand for elections but requires that person to resign from employment on the first working day after the individual is declared to be elected. The Act also amends s.29 of the Local Government (Scotland) Act 1973 reducing the age at which an individual can be nominated, elected and hold office as a councillor from 21 to 18.

The 2004 Act reclassifies "politically restricted posts" and abolishes the link between salary level and political restriction. The fact determining political restriction is the nature of the post not its level of remuneration.

The Local Government (Scotland) Act 1973 disqualified a person who is a councillor or has ceased to be a councillor, from being appointed to a paid position within the local authority (other than the posts of convener or depute convener). The Act amends that provision so that former councillors are disqualified for a period of three months from being appointed to a non-politically restricted post, and for a period of 12 months from being appointed to a politically restricted post. Current councillors are barred from obtaining any post with a local authority.

Councillors remuneration

The Act enables Scottish Ministers to make provision for the payment of local authorities of remuneration, pensions, allowances and expenses. The detailed provisions being determined by the Scottish Local Authorities Remuneration Committee.

It also enables Scottish Ministers to make regulations concerning severance payments for councillors who decide not to stand for re-election prior to the next local government elections. A councillor who has received a severance payment will not be eligible to stand for election at any future local government election.

The local government franchise

The law relating to the franchise was consolidated into the Representation of the People Act 1983, as amended by the RPA 1985.

The law is also to be found in various statutory instruments made under this legislation, *e.g.* the Representation of the People Regulations 1986.

Electoral areas

For the purpose of the election of councillors, every local government area is divided into electoral wards. Each ward at present returns one councillor and there is a separate election for each electoral division or ward.

Electoral areas must be reviewed periodically to take account of population movements. The Local Government (Scotland) Act 1973 established the Local Government Boundary Commission for Scotland, which reviews the local government areas and makes proposals for changes. The Commission considers changes that are desirable in the interests of effective and convenient local government. The changes can be carried out by any of the following means or by any combination of these means:

(a) The alteration of a local government area.
(b) The constitution of a new local government area.
(c) The abolition of a local government area.
(d) A change of electoral arrangements for any local government area, as a result of a change in the local government area.

By law the Boundary Commission must review all local government areas at periods of 10 to 15 years to ensure that the areas are conducive to effective and convenient local government. Individuals, or a local authority, can put a request to the Boundary Commission for changes in local government areas and the Boundary Commission is required to consider the request. If the Commission decides to carry out a review, it must do so through a procedure which involves full consultation with all interested parties.

The register of electors

The key to the exercise of the franchise, *i.e.* the right to vote, is inclusion on the Register of Electors. The Register is compiled by the Electoral Registration Officer once a year. It comes into force on February 16 each year, the "qualifying date" being the previous October 10.

Usually, the chief executive is the officer nominated by the council to be the Electoral Registration Officer, although often the day-to-day work is carried out by local government officers.

The returning officer

The date prescribed for ordinary local government elections is the first Thursday in May. The conduct of such elections is in the hands of the Returning Officer, appointed by the Council in which elections are to take place. The duties of a Returning Officer are to:

(a) announce the elections;
(b) accept the nominations of candidates;
(c) arrange for the poll in the event of a contested election;
(d) supervise the ballots and the counting of the votes;
(e) announce the result of the election; and
(f) scrutinise the expenditure by the candidates.

The frequency of elections

Councillors are elected for periods of four years under normal circumstances, *e.g.* other than where elected to fill a casual vacancy. Casual vacancies are those which occur outwith the normal pattern of elections. There are many reasons why such vacancies occur, *e.g.* the death or resignation of a councillor, disqualification by surcharge or conviction, or the election being declared void. In these cases, the position is filled through a by-election. There will be a Scottish local government election in 2007.

Nomination for election

The first step in holding an election is the publication by the Returning Officer of the Notice of Election. This indicates the place and time for the lodging of nominations, applying for postal votes, etc. To be capable of being legally nominated, a person must be duly qualified and not disqualified in any way. Each candidate must be duly nominated by two electors from the electoral area concerned—as proposers—and by eight other electors for that area, assenting to the nomination. The nomination includes the relevant information about the candidates, *e.g.* name, address and, where appropriate, the name of the political party.

The candidate

A candidate must name a person as an election agent, although a person may be his/her own agent. The object of this is to relieve the candidate from the technicalities of election law and procedure and to safeguard the public by ensuring that the election is properly conducted.

The sum a candidate may incur by way of election expenses is limited by law. Election expenses are sums incurred before, during and after an election on account, or in respect of, the conduct or management of an election. The sum that may be incurred is determined by the Scottish Executive and is expressed in terms of a lump sum plus a sum per entry on the Register of Electors for the ward in which the candidate is standing. All expenses (apart from the candidate's personal expenses) must be paid through the election agent. A candidate or agent who knowingly contravenes the rules is guilty of an illegal practice.

Turnout

There has been a consistently lower turnout at local authority elections compared to parliamentary elections. In 1974, the electoral turnout was over 50 per cent. In 1995, the turnout was 44.9 per cent, in 1999 it was 58 per cent. The overall turnout at the 2003 elections was 49.6 per cent. Table 5.1 illustrates the 2003 results.

Table 5.1

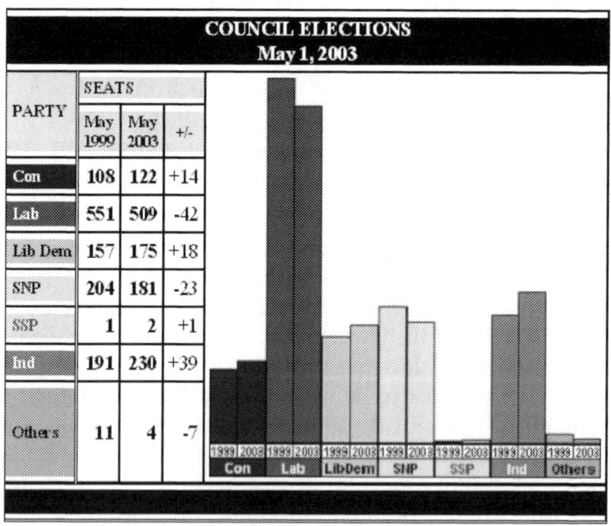

COUNCIL ELECTIONS
May 1, 2003

PARTY	SEATS		
	May 1999	May 2003	+/-
Con	108	122	+14
Lab	551	509	-42
Lib Dem	157	175	+18
SNP	204	181	-23
SSP	1	2	+1
Ind	191	230	+39
Others	11	4	-7

Source ©: Scottish Liberal Democrats Website *www.scot.libdems.org.uk*

COUNCILLORS

Characteristics

Scotland elects 1,222 local government councillors. The average Scottish councillor is a white, male, 55year-old with a degree or a professional qualification, and who owns a house and a car.

The latest Scottish councillors' survey, which was carried out immediately after the May 2003 council elections, shows that the profile of Scotland's councillors has not changed much since the last survey was carried out in 1999.

The 2003 councillors' survey carried out by COSLA with the support of the Scottish Executive has provided very valuable information about the profile, experience and interests of Scotland's 1,222 councillors. The data from the survey was used to inform the work of the Widening Access to Local Government and the Councillors' Remuneration Progress Groups established by the Executive to consider key aspects of the Local Governance (Scotland) Act 2004.

A total of 740 councillors responded to the 2003 COSLA survey. This represents a 60.5 per cent response rate which ensured that the sample of respondents is representative of all councillors and provides an accurate insight into the background experience, lives and interests of Scotland's councillors.

A copy of the full report, including over 40 tables is available on the COSLA website *ww.cosla.gov.uk/publications*. A summary is contained in *COSLA Connections*, issue 7, December 2003.

The Council, which is, in legal parlance, a "corporate body", consists of a number of elected councillors. Even with regard to size, the differences between councils are obvious, so it is difficult to make generalisations. The law is not a unifying factor, as, broadly, it only requires that there shall be an elected council for each local authority and that certain committees shall be established.

These restrictions are relatively minor and so the structure and operation of authorities varies. There is a trend towards greater uniformity, but this is by no means complete. Consequently, the role of a councillor is often what he or she makes of it.

The legal position of councillors

Councillors must be qualified to stand as candidates and then gain plural majority support in the election. Having gained a seat on the council, it is a basic legal requirement that a councillor ceases to be a member in failing, without due cause and without the permission of the council to attend any meeting of the authority for a period of six months.

Perhaps the most important restriction placed on councillors relates to the avoidance of corrupt practices. Members are directly involved with vast amounts of money and steps are necessary to prevent abuses. The Local Government (Scotland) Act 1973 restricts the freedom of councillors to participate in decision-making related to items in which they have a "pecuniary interest". A member must declare when he or she has a financial interest in the matter before the Council. (This, of course, also applies to committees and sub-committees). Declaring an interest precludes participation in the discussion or voting.

Examples of what constitutes a pecuniary interest are:

(a) Where a councillor is employed by, is a partner in, owns, or has a financial interest in a company with which the council is proposing to make a contract.
(b) Where a councillor lives in a council house and council rents or rates are being discussed.
(c) Where a councillor has a child who has dinners at a local school, and school meals charges are under discussion.

The 1973 Act empowers the Secretary of State to grant a "dispensation" to allow councillors to participate if disqualification would "impede the transaction of business". Such dispensations have been issued in respect of both (b) and (c) above.

The criminal law also imposes heavy penalties on councillors who abuse their office for corrupt purposes or make fraudulent claims for attendance allowances. Councillors are, however, expected to maintain even higher standards and a National Code of Local Government conduct has been produced covering:

(a) public duty and private interest;
(b) the disclosure of pecuniary and other interests;
(c) the chairs of council committees and sub-committees;
(d) councillors and officers;
(e) the use of confidential information;
(f) gifts and hospitality;
(g) the use of allowances;
(h) the use of council facilities.

All these are areas where abuses could occur.

To do their job, councillors need information and the law demands that they have access to such information. A councillor's rights in this respect were based on "the need to know", allowing access to information necessary in the course of normal duties. The situation was, however, never entirely clear.

The right of members to inspect documents was greatly extended by the Local Government (Access to Information) Act 1985. This gave councillors the right to see all documents in the possession of, or under the control of, the council which contain material relating to any business to be transacted at council, committee or sub-committee meetings.

Members also have the rights enjoyed by any member the public:

(a) The right of admission to meetings (also extended most recently by the 1985 Act);
(b) The right to inspect accounts at each audit.

The status, duties and powers of a councillor are subject to the law, but are not so closely defined as to prevent wide variations in practice.

The role and duties of councillors

Councillors are, basically, ordinary citizens who devote part of their time to community service through the local authority. They are not, in principle, professional politicians, but part-time lay people who receive allowances for the work that they do. As councillors should not benefit financially from the system of allowances, they must, therefore, be motivated by other factors. These include:

(a) a chance for self-expression;
(b) an opportunity to indulge in a hobby or an interest;
(c) a means of influencing local affairs;
(d) a wish to enter public life.

The traditional role of the councillor as a representative and servant of the local community is set out in the National Code of Local Government. This code is a guide for councillors, but does not override the law or the particular local authority's Standing Orders. In relation to public duty and private interest, the Code contains the following points:

(a) Your over-riding duty as a councillor is to the whole community.
(b) You have a special duty to your own constituents, including those who did not vote for you.
(c) Whenever you have a private or personal interest in any question which councillors have to decide, you must not do anything to let that interest influence the decision.
(d) Do nothing as a councillor which you could not justify to the public.
(e) The reputation of your council, and of your party if you belong to one, depends on your conduct and what the public believes about your conduct.
(f) It is not enough to avoid actual impropriety, you should at all times avoid any occasion for suspicion or the appearance of improper conduct.

Councils use a committee system to deal with the wide range of their work. The committee system is especially essential as councillors are part-timers. The work of committees is governed by Standing Orders, which are similar in each authority, but not completely standard. The Scottish Executive publishes "Model Standing Orders" as a guide. Standing Orders lay down the rules governing such things as:

(a) the order of business at meetings;
(b) the rules debate;
(c) the procedure for moving motions and amendments.

Councillors work together with officers in managing the affairs of the authority. The traditional view of their respective roles was that members were responsible for policy-making, while officers implemented this policy. It is doubtful whether local government ever operated on these simplistic lines and this view is certainly no longer widely accepted. The emphasis now is on the interlocking roles of members and officers.

Public Participation in Local Government

The present system of local government in Scotland provides many opportunities for the public to participate. Some methods permit a greater degree of participation than others and some methods are more direct than others.

Participation in elections takes two forms:

(a) Voting; and
(b) Standing for election

Voting is the most popular form of participation in local government, although the turnout at local elections is significantly lower than a parliamentary elections. The turnout at local elections varies from 30 to 50 per cent (see, *e.g.* Table 5.1 above).

Standing for election in practice, concerns only the minority of the public, but nevertheless there is ample scope for members of the public to stand for election as a councillor, provided that they are qualified, not disqualified and properly nominated under the terms of the relevant legislation.

It has, however, been argued that, in effect, many people are debarred from a political career at local government level for three main reasons:

(a) By reason of being employed by the local authorities in whose areas they reside.

(b) By reason of the present system of allowances which imposes a financial burden on councillors, in that they can lose quite substantial sums financially, which they cannot reclaim.
(c) By reason of the fact that the vast majority of councillors are elected through a political party and candidates who are not members of a political party have little chance of success.

There is in fact a shortage of candidates at local elections with the result that:

(a) some seats are uncontested, depriving the electorate of the right to vote; and
(b) elected members tend to be unrepresentative of the community they serve, in terms of age, occupation, etc.

Co-optation

Apart from the specific provisions governing individual committees, there is a general power to appoint to committees persons who are not elected members, provided at least two-thirds of the members of the committees are elected members. This general power to add members is called the power to co-opt.

In the case of some statutory committees, the composition of the committee is set out in specific legislation. For example, an education authority can appoint to their education committee persons who are not members of the authority, but at least half of the members appointed to the committee shall be members of the authority. In addition, the co-opted members on the education committee must include representatives of the church and at least two teachers employed in educational establishments under the management of the authority.

A co-opted member is a full member of the committee or subcommittee, which means he or she may speak and vote. Although co-option is designed to introduce technical expertise onto committees, it has increasingly been used as a political tool, favouring the supporters of the majority party.

Despite the opportunities for public participation in the electoral process, there appears a widespread reluctance to do so. Some reasons for this may be:

(a) A belief that local government is remote from the people.
(b) A belief that local government issues are less controversial than those dealt with by central government.
(c) A belief that central government control is so great that local government is irrelevant.

Party politics

Party politics is now commonplace in local government, although arguments about its effects continue. Whatever its overall impact, it can influence the level of participation in the following ways:

(a) selection of candidates for councillor;
(b) support for a candidate at an election;
(c) drafting the election manifesto;
(d) selecting the chairs of committees;
(e) influencing votes through pre-meetings;
(f) membership of community councils;
(g) membership of groups.

The Widdicombe Committee, which reported in 1986, regarded the continued presence of political organisation in local government as inevitable for the foreseeable future. Indeed, the Committee saw an intensification of the trend, even in authorities which, at present, were relatively apolitical.

The Committee found that, in most authorities, politics had not created a problem, although in some isolated cases power had been abused. The Report advocated the acceptance of the existing situation and the modification of the entire system of local government to accommodate formally the political dimension. As they found it, the system did not really recognise the political process and so politics was conducted on an informal basis. A framework better able to cope with the increased trend towards politicisation would strengthen democracy.

Attending meetings

All members of the public may attend local authority and health board meetings, in accordance with the rules laid down in:

(a) The Public Bodies (Admission to Meetings) Act 1960;
(b) The Local Government (Scotland) Act 1973;
(c) The Local Government (Access to Information) Act 1985; and
(d) The Freedom of Information Act 2002.

The Local Government (Access to Information) Act 1985 extended to all sub-committees the right of the public to attend council and committee meetings. This opened up local government considerably, although the public can still be excluded in certain instances. The public, including the press, may be excluded by a resolution of the meeting whenever publicity would be prejudicial to the public interest by reason of the confidential nature of its business, or where business is designated as "exempt". A reason has to be given for the exclusion. Exclusion should, however, be used with caution and there is evidence that it is used in some cases merely to enable controversial decisions to be taken with the minimum of fuss.

All meetings must be adequately advertised and copies of agenda and reports should be open to public inspection. The press must be afforded reasonable facilities for reporting meetings, are entitled to receive copies of all agendas and non-confidential reports, and may receive any other documents supplied to council members, if the proper officer approves.

The Access to Information Act also provided for greater public and press access to minutes, reports (including background papers) and other documents. Many documents must be preserved for six years after the relevant meeting. Local authorities are now obliged to publish certain information as well.

The public and the press have extensive rights to attend and investigate local authority meetings of all kinds. These rights are not, however, exercised to any great extent in the normal course of council business. The nature of the business transacted does not encourage public attendance and, usually, the press does not show any great interest.

The Freedom of Information Act 2002 considerably increases public access to information. An independent Scottish Information Commissioner has been appointed to promote and enforce the legislation, with powers to order disclosure of information.

Other forms of public participation in local government

Apart from membership of political parties, there are other means which an ordinary citizen can influence decisions of the council.

Community Councils

These are not local authorities in any real sense of the term, They were established by the Local Government (Scotland) Act 1973 for the general purpose of ascertaining, co-ordinating and expressing to the local authorities for their areas, and to other public authorities, the views of the communities which they represent. District councils may make contributions towards the expenses of community councils within their areas and may also make loans.

Community Councils have achieved varying degrees of success. In some areas they have improved the community spirit, but in others they function with less than the requisite number of councillors, because of apathy. They do, however, provide another means of public influence on local authority decision-making.

The Stodart Committee (1980) detected a good deal of frustration in Community Councils concerning their limited powers and the lack of attention paid to their views by local authority councillors.

Interest or pressure groups

A pressure group does not seek power, only to influence those in power, often on a specific issue. Some groups are of a more or less permanent nature, because the object of their concern is not likely to disappear, *e.g.* a council taxpayers' association. Other groups are short-lived, disbanding when their objective is achieved or lost, *e.g.* opponents of a school closure.

Such groups operate in various ways:

(a) by contacting individual members of the council and giving them advice and support;
(b) by presenting petitions or sending delegations;
(c) by putting up candidates for election to the council;
(d) by making representations at public inquiries, especially in the field of planning.

Groups are likely to have more impact on decision-making than individuals acting alone.

Pressure groups can illuminate neglected issues, bring expertise to debate and allow a wider range of public participation. They may, however, be regarded as divisive, secretive and a distorting factor in respect of public opinion generally.

Voluntary bodies

Public participation can also take the form of relieving the local authority of the task of providing a service, through a voluntary organisation. Such bodies often perform activities which supplement, replace or duplicate the work of the Council in a particular area.

This can achieve two objectives:

(a) The involvement of local people in the work, including decision-making.
(b) The saving of expenditure.

Local authorities usually liaise closely with such groups in order to co-ordinate activities. Many local authorities recognise the support that voluntary bodies provide and so give them grant-aid. The main importance of voluntary bodies is in the field of the social services.

The local authority and the individual

Various steps can be taken by an individual citizen who is dissatisfied by the action (or lack of it) by the local authority such as:

(a) Complaint to Audit Scotland.

(b) Appeal to an appropriate minister, where the law provides for this, *e.g.* a citizen who is aggrieved by a refusal of planning permission.
(c) Action in the courts, *e.g.* where a citizen considers that a local authority has exceeded its powers.
(d) Contacting the local Member of the Scottish Parliament (MSP). Many MSPs have been local councillors.
(e) Most councillors hold "surgeries" which their constituents can attend to discuss problems or refer to specific issues.
(f) Writing to the council. There is, however, a difficulty here, because many citizens do not know which department of a local authority is responsible for the matter with which they are concerned.
(g) Writing to the individual's own councillor, or to the chair of a committee.
(h) Contacting a pressure group or voluntary organisation.
(i) Contacting the media, *e.g.* writing to the local newspaper.

Public Involvement in the NHS

Unlike local government, there are no direct elections to NHS Health Boards, but Boards must comprise non-executive lay members, non-executive stakeholder members and executive members. The NHS Reform (Scotland) Act 2004 places a duty on Health Boards, Special Health Boards and the Common Services Agency to take action with a view to securing that patients and the public are involved in the planning and development of services as well as decisions that are to be made by those bodies which will significantly affect the operation of services.

The overall functions of Health Boards are the development of strategy, resource allocation, the implementation of the health plan and the performance management of the NHS system in their area of responsibility.

There are concerns that the NHS in Scotland has become must less democratic than local government. These concerns are not new but there is renewed interest in increasing democracy and accountability in all areas of the public sector. Health services are accountable to the public primarily through the Scottish Executive and MSPs but the NHS Reform (Scotland) Act 2004 seeks to require enhanced levels of public participation.

NHS Quality Improvement Scotland (NHS QIS) involves the public in its work, in order to improve the quality of health services in Scotland by ensuring that these are sensitive to the needs and preferences of patients. By involving people NHS QIS aims to:

- promote openness and transparency by enabling the public to review the quality of the NHS by being a vital part of our work;

- learn from the experiences of patients and carers to improve our understanding of their needs and preferences;
- focus our work on patients and encourage public accountability by providing an essential complement to the expertise from health professionals and information from scientific literature.

The UK-wide Patient's Charter was launched in 1991, and no longer reflects the current position within NHSScotland. The Patient's Charter is being replaced with a more comprehensive package that will incorporate:

- a guide to the NHS;
- standards focusing on patient entitlements, based on generic standards produced by the Clinical Standards Board for Scotland;
- the responsibilities of patients using the NHS;
- information about medical records, legal rights, and the complaints procedure.

NHS QIS is currently developing a framework for achieving an effective partnership with patients, carers and the public. Their involvement is viewed as an integral and essential part of all aspects of NHS QIS activities, which will significantly contribute to the continuous improvement of health services in Scotland. The four themes of this framework are:

- Involvement: ensuring public involvement is an integral part of all NHS QIS activities to improve healthcare in Scotland.
- Building capacity and communications: developing the ability to take effective action to improve services and to make sure that communications with people are clear, consistent and appropriate to promote public confidence.
- Responsiveness: ensuring a range of opportunities for involvement are offered which are flexible and sensitive to the needs of individuals and communities, making it as easy as possible for people to participate fully.
- Patient information: ensuring that people have the information that they require to be involved in decisions about their own care and to participate fully in the activities of NHS QIS.

Constitutional Status

There have been recent debates concerning the constitutional status of regional (local) government within the European Community (EC). In Scotland, the Convention of Scottish Local Authorities (COSLA) commissioned research to clarify the legal position of local government. The paper by Burrows *et al.* (2005) identifies a range of European governance issues likely to impact on Scottish local government. The paper highlights the fact that proposals from the McIntosh Committee on a covenant between the Scottish Parliament and local authorities setting out commitments on both sides have not been implemented. Neither, as recommended by McIntosh, has a power of general competence been conferred on local authorities who do, however, have the power to promote or improve the well-being within the area of a local authority under the terms of the Local Government (Scotland) Act 2003.

The research highlighted the issue of subsidiarity which is the right of local government to achieve "parity of esteem" with other levels of government under the terms of the European Constitution. COSLA in the first instance will seek to achieve parity of esteem through developing the existing Partnership Agreement with the Scottish Executive (this topic is further discussed in Ch.10).

Conclusion

This chapter has considered various ways in which people can influence local government and the NHS in Scotland. There is clearly a fundamental difference between local government and the NHS in Scotland in relation to the extent to which they are democratic. Local authorities are now subject to re-election every four years and in future will make use of the single transferable voting system which will promote a higher degree of correlation between the preferences of the electorate and the composition of councils. NHSScotland is not undemocratic but is less democratic than local government. Health Board members are appointed not elected but health is a matter devolved to Holyrood and therefore MSPs have a responsibility to the electorate for health services in Scotland.

There is doubtless a renewed interest in local democracy and community planning processes require the participation of individuals and communities in local decision-making. This trend is a move away from the more managerialist approaches that were popular in the early days of New Public Management particularly in the periods of Compulsory Competitive Tendering (CCT) and post-Griffiths general management in the NHS (see Ch.6).

Local government remains highly democratic because of elections and party politics, NHSScotland much less so. The NHS Reform (Scotland) Act 2004 places a duty on NHSScotland to developed its processes of public participation and NHS QIS has developed its Patient Focus and Public Involvement Framework and it will be interesting to see the extent to which participation is meaningful and sustained.

CHAPTER 6

MANAGEMENT AND DECISION MAKING

INTRODUCTION: MANAGEMENT

This chapter examines the ways in which Scottish local government and the NHS in Scotland have embraced managerialism. The chapter begins by explaining generic management before going on to consider the ways in which generic management has been adapted for application in the public sector. The chapter develops by discussing contemporary approaches to decision-making and policy advice.

Defining management

Henri Fayol (1949) wrote that to manage is to forecast and plan, to organise, to command, to co-ordinate and to control. This analysis still forms the basis of one of the most frequently adopted views of management. Fayol was one of the first theorists to stress the key position of the formal organisation chart and job descriptions. He also firmly advocated the belief that management could, and should, be taught.

Forecasting and planning

This involves assessing the future and making provision for it. The problems of forecasting and planning are many, but managers should ensure that within the organisation there is unity of direction, continuity, flexibility and precision. Planning is the process used by managers to identify and select appropriate goals and courses of action for an organisation. The planning function determines how effective and efficient the organisation is and determines the strategy of the organisation.

Organising

Organising ensures that the organisation has the necessary resources in terms of staff, money and materials and that they are brought together in the correct balance. In organising, managers create the structure of working relationships between organisational members that best allows them to work together and achieve goals. Managers will group people into departments according to the tasks performed. Managers will also lay out lines of authority and responsibility for members. An organisational structure is the outcome of organising. This structure co-ordinates and motivates employees so that they work together to achieve goals.

Commanding and leading

This involves the maintaining activity among the employees by making decisions and communicating them to subordinates. In leading, managers determine direction, state a clear vision for employees to follow, and help employees understand the role they play in attaining goals. Leadership involves a manager using power, influence, vision, persuasion, and communication skills. The outcome of the leading function is a high level of motivation and commitment from employees to the organisation.

Co-ordinating

Co-ordinating involves the manager in liaison with others in the organisation ensuring that activities occur at the right time and place and do not adversely affect other areas of organisational activity. This can only be attained by a two-way flow of information, and by meeting others.

Control

This activity checks on the extent to which the organisation is functioning according to plan. Controls must exist throughout the organisation and must be capable of reacting quickly to deviations from desired levels or standards of activity (Fayol, 1949). In controlling, managers evaluate how well the organisation is achieving its goals and takes corrective action to improve performance. Managers will monitor individuals, departments, and the organisation to determine if desired performance has been reached. Managers will also take action to increase performance as required. The outcome of the controlling function is the accurate measurement of performance and regulation of efficiency and effectiveness.

Management has been well defined by Henry Mintzberg (1989) as having the following basic purposes, to:

(a) ensure the efficient production of goods and services;
(b) design and maintain the stability of organisational operations;
(c) adapt the organisation, in a controlled way, to the changing environment;
(d) ensure that the organisation serves the ends of those persons who control it;

(e) serve as the key information link between the organisation and its environment;
(f) operate the organisation's status system.

Management roles, competences and standards

Managerial roles

Described by Mintzberg (1973), a role is a set of specific tasks a person performs because of the position they hold. Roles are directed inside as well as outside the organisation. There are three broad categories of roles:

1. Interpersonal
2. Informational
3. Decisional

Interpersonal roles

Managers assume different roles to co-ordinate and interact with employees and provide direction to the organisation:

(a) Figurehead role: symbolises the organisation and what it is trying to achieve.
(b) Leader role: train, counsel, mentor and encourage high employee performance.
(c) Liaison role: link and co-ordinate people inside and outside the organisation to help achieve goals.

Informational roles

These are associated with the tasks needed to obtain and transmit information for management of the organisation:

(a) Monitor role: analyse information from both the internal and external environment.
(b) Disseminator role: transmit information to influence attitudes and behaviour of employees.
(c) Spokesperson role: use of information to positively influence the way people in and out of the organisation respond to it.

Decisional roles

These are associated with the methods managers use to plan strategy and utilize resources to achieve goals:

(a) Entrepreneur role: decide upon new projects or programmes to initiate and invest.
(b) Disturbance handler role: assume responsibility for handling an unexpected event or crisis.

(c) Resource allocator role: assign resources between functions and divisions, set budgets of lower managers.
(d) Negotiator role: seek to negotiate solutions between other managers, unions, customers, or shareholders.

Managerial competences

Kanter (1984) elaborates on the need for organisations to change in order to be successful. They have to employ the four Fs: focused, fast, friendly and flexible. Focused means developing internal synergies in leaner, more integrated organisations. Fast means exploiting opportunities rapidly. Friendly means establishing positive internal and external relationships including partnerships. Flexible organisations have given up bureaucracy and reduced hierarchy to promote a high degree of capability for change. Kanter (1995) uses the term *post-entrepreneurial management* to describe new forms of management designed to promote effectiveness in the global economy based on three principles.

Figure 6.1

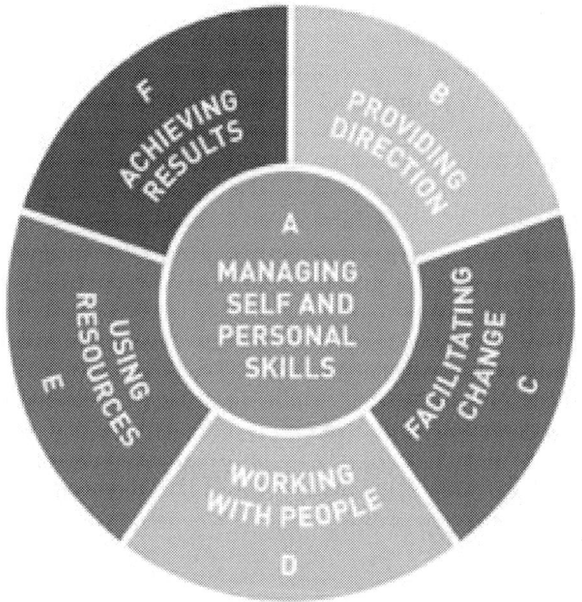

Source ©: Management Standards Centre

1. Minimise obligations and maximise options.
2. Derive power through influences and alliances.
3. Keep the organisation fluid by encouraging change and innovation

Management standards

The Management Standards Centre (MSC) is the government recognised standards setting body for the management and leadership areas. The MSC has been engaged in a publicly funded project to develop a new set of National Occupational Standards (NOS) for management and leadership. The new standards, which were approved in May 2004, describe the level of performance expected in employment for a range of management and leadership functions/activities.

In the 1980s, the UK Government launched a skills challenge initiative which led to the introduction of sector specific "Lead Bodies" to set standards for effective performance. The Management Charter Initiative (MCI) is an independent body set up in 1988 by employers and backed by the Government. Its mission is to shape and promote management development—particularly competence-based management development—for the benefit of organisations and individuals. MCI introduced Management Standards in 1989 and these were updated in 1997 and 2004. The Management Standards are arranged in a logical sequence to cover every aspect of management at every level in an organisation. There are six key roles each divided up into units, these key roles are:

(a) Managing self and personal skills;
(b) Providing direction;
(c) Facilitating change;
(d) Working with people;
(e) Using resources;
(f) Achieving results.

Scottish Public Management

In November 1998, a study by the Eglinton Centre Consultancy (Eglinton, 1998) on the potential impact of the Scottish Parliament on the role and function of public sector managers concluded that public managers faced challenges and changes as a consequence of devolved government in Scotland. The study also identified a range of public management competences and particular "gaps" in management development provision. Certain knowledge, skills and behaviours were identified as being important to public managers, these are:

(a) Leadership;
(b) Strategic behaviour;
(c) Political awareness;
(d) Breadth of sector knowledge;
(e) Entrepreneurship and risk-taking;

(f) Focus on results;
(g) Delegation;
(h) Influence;
(i) Policy management;
(j) Partnership working;
(k) Financial management;
(l) Self management;
(m) Communications;
(n) Respect for the political process;
(o) People management;
(p) Openness;
(q) Behaviour aligned to values.

This represents a move away from the competence approach but recognises the generic nature of managerial work in particular employment sectors.

Managers in the public domain are increasingly expected to fulfil their managerial responsibilities by carrying out their roles to support performance governance, performance management and increasingly to promote enhanced consumerism, quality and responsiveness. In so doing, managers are required to demonstrate a range of management competences and their underpinning knowledge and understanding.

The Eglinton Centre Study stimulated a renewed interest in public management development in Scotland. There was a general consensus amongst the contributors to the study that any particular solution to the public management development problem did not require new or additional investment, but that a proportion of the current spend could be invested differently. The study concluded that a "Foundation" could be a middle way between the fixed overhead of a physical centre and the need to have strategic direction in commissioning management development options. As a consequence of this report a Task Force was set up, led by the Scottish Executive, to consider the hypothesis that the creation of the Scottish Parliament would have an impact on the work of a wide range of public sector managers.

Senior managers from across the public sector agreed that the key challenges for them, in working with the new Parliament, would be:

(a) Policy analysis and development;
(b) Common vision and values;
(c) Strategic behaviour;
(d) Collaborative working;
(e) Removal of hierarchies; and
(f) Public accountability.

Faced with these challenges, the development of key skills and attributes were essential for the public sector to deliver. The Task

Force also agreed that a Scottish Leadership Foundation should be established with the following characteristics:

(a) to be employer led;
(b) to be funded in a number of ways;
(c) to have a small commissioning team;
(d) to provide a focal point to commission research, design and delivery of novel approaches; and
(e) to broker secondments across different parts of the public sector.

The Scottish Leadership Foundation became operational in 2001 (Scottish Leadership Foundation website, 2002).

Public Policy Models

Public policy analysis has a contribution to make both to academic study and to the development of better policy making. Public policy by definition has to be generated or at least process within the frameworks of governmental procedures, influences and organisations (Hogwood and Gunn, 1983). Public policy models have influenced policy makers in the Scottish Executive, local government and the NHS, and it is therefore of paramount importance to students and practitioners to understand the contribution of policy models to public decision-making.

A satisfactory model of the policy-making process must be realistic, aid in the development of a policy science, and attempt to improve the quality of current policy-making systems. There are many models of policy, but they can be grouped for analysis into three broad classifications:

(a) rational models;
(b) non-rational models;
(c) combined models.

Models provide a focus for policy analysis, and as such help us to understand and explain real phenomena.

Rational models

Pure rationality

Rational models are widely held conceptions about how decisions are and ought to be made. The rational model (Dror, 1968) attempts to approach the study of policy scientifically and with as wide a scope as possible. Under this model the policy-making process is seen as being broken down into several stages.

(a) The first step is to posit the general goal that the political system wishes to achieve.
(b) Once this has been done, the general goal must be broken down into its component operational goals, on the basis of their value position in society.
(c) The third stage requires the analyst to attempt to determine what other values will be affected by the new policy. This forces the politician (*i.e.* the person deciding policies) to reconsider priorities and to decide whether or not the new programme is more important than the programme that will be affected.
(d) If the politician agrees that the new policy must go forward the analyst (*i.e.* the politician's "technical advisor") must then produce the entire range of alternative means of achieving the goals within the range of possibility given the available resources. Accompanying each of these alternatives should be an extensive cost-benefit analysis, clearly spelling out the effects of each alternative on other valued policies.
(e) Finally, the analyst must present the decision-maker with a clear indication of the probability that each alternative is realistic and will produce the desired results.
(f) On the basis of this information the decision-maker will then choose the best policy. Normally this will not entail much effort, because the analysis will clearly indicate that one approach is far superior to the others in achieving the goals.

Objections to the pure rationality model

There are several serious problems with this approach to policy-making and policy analysis.

(a) It assumes that vague general goals like "achieving a better educational system" can be used in determining alternatives.
(b) It requires political leaders who are prepared to state, *e.g.* that creating a better educational system is more important than solving problems of urban deprivation and inner-city decay. Few politicians would be willing to make such a decision, as the supporters of urban renewal may have a greater (or equal) degree of popular support as the educationalists.
(c) It assumes that all alternatives can be known by rational means. Since no individual or group of people, no matter how intelligent, is completely rational, the accomplishment of this task is impossible.
(d) It clearly postulates that the political leaders really have such a wide range of feasible alternatives. Some alternatives may be rational but are not politically acceptable, as they would result in serious objections from a section of the community.

(For example, one option for licensing policy might be to prohibit all consumption of alcohol; but this would create a backlash led by the majority of the population and the licensing trade.)

(e) Finally, it is a fallacy to assume that somehow a perfectly rational policy-making process would exist in a political system, which cannot be completely rational.

These limitations seriously restrict the utility of the pure rationality model.

Economic rationality

One development based on the pure rationality model is the economic rationality model put forward by Charles Hitch. Hitch (1965) argues that this approach has been applied usefully in the United States for the purpose of developing weapons systems. This model proposes an approach that is similar to that of the pure rationality model, but which requires that the cost of the policy analysis process must be less than the increased benefit such a process will bring for existing or new programmes.

Because of the similarity of this model to the rational model, it has several of the same limitations.

It assumes that goals can be operationalised in such a way as to be capable of quantitative analysis, and that the analysis will produce an alternative that obviously contains the best mix of cost/output.

There are political limitations as well which can be most clearly seen by looking at the period to which Hitch refers. The major weakness of this model lies in the assumption that the political system can behave rationally when economics is an important factor. In the real world of politics, however, political, moral, social and other considerations often preclude accepting the most economically rational proposal. Economic rationality does not appear to be very useful tool for understanding and analysing public policy.

Non-rational models

Incrementalism

Charles Lindblom (1959) provides a model which he claims illustrates the real process of policy-making as practised in the United States. He argues that rational models are inapplicable to the American experience and that rational policy analysis is beyond the capabilities of the political system. Existing forms of policy analysis, he states, often become part of the bargaining process in which advocates of different policies produce their own analyses to convince others that their solution is the best. Instead Lindblom presents his concept of "incrementalism" as being both the reality and the best possible way of making policy.

In each functional area of responsibility the decision-makers proceed by making slight changes. If the reaction to the changes is favourable, they will respond with another slight step in the same direction. If not, they can retreat without losing much political support. This system is inexpensive, and allows for the usual bargaining and compromise approach to political decision-making.

Professor Lindblom is supported in his analysis of the policy-making process by Aaron Wildavsky (1966), who argues that recent attempts at rational policy analysis will only lower the quality of analysis.

Critics of the incremental approach agree that it does realistically represent the existing process, but they argue, this is not sufficient to make it useful. Societies are faced with several crises and the solutions to them appear to be increasingly complex. Incrementalism is far too simplistic a process to provide meaningful solutions.

Incrementalism encourages a conservative approach to decision-making, at a time when social and political conditions require increased creativity and innovation. In essence, the critics claim, the processes of the nineteenth century will not provide the answers to the problems of the twenty-first century. Even though incrementalism provides a realistic approach to the policy-making process, its utility is severely restricted by its failure to suggest ways by which the system could be improved.

Sequential Decision-Making

This approach is a non-rational model. It involves the search for alternative means of achieving the desired objective using appropriate quantitative techniques where possible. Of these perhaps two or three might seem feasible. The political leader is unsure of the best one and responds by attempting all of them simultaneously. After a short period the approach which functions best will become obvious and the others can be safely ended.

The political repercussions of such an approach are obvious. The political leader who announces a three-pronged attack on poverty and then attempts to drop two of the "prongs" will be faced with severe criticism. Critics will make accusations of indecision and will attempt to show that the leader has no real commitment to solving the problem, because he or she has just cancelled two valuable programmes.

Sequential decision-making can be an important guide on how to time experimental policies and delay the final policy selection, so as to reduce both uncertainty and wasted time as much as possible.

This would be especially important where different paths were being considered. Rate-payers and taxpayers may become incensed at the political leader who seems to be squandering funds by introducing policies in packages of two or three programmes. This system may not be efficient economically if the political leader were to accept the proper alternative then the costs of the other one or two courses of action would not be incurred.

This approach is limited to certain kinds of policy issues.

Satisficing

Another model which can be included in the non-rational category is the approach suggested by Professor March (1958). He argues that people do not search for the best solution to their problems, but rather that they attempt to find a satisfactory solution. This latter process, which he calls "satisficing", can take place if two necessary conditions are met:

(a) There must be a set of criteria which describes minimally satisfactory alternatives;
(b) The alternatives in question must meet or exceed these criteria.

If none of the alternatives meets these criteria, the decision-makers simply lower their concept of what is satisfactory until they discover a suitable answer.

There are two major weaknesses with this approach. First, who defines what is a "satisfactory" solution to a political problem? There will be as many solutions as there are political groupings in the policy-making organisation. Secondly, satisficing is essentially a conservative way of making policy decisions, at a time when radical solutions might well be required to provide "satisfaction". Satisficing does not provide the necessary guidelines required to improve the policy-making system, and thus lacks this vital requirement of normative instrumental models.

Perception in policy making

Sir Geoffrey Vickers (1964) points out that not all decision-making is rational. Most decisions do not involve achievement of goals (at least in the manner suggested by the rational models), but rather regulation of current affairs in accordance with accepted social norms. Intuition, hunches and sudden insight on the part of the decision-maker play an important role in this process.

For Vickers, the critical factor is perception of the situation which must be dealt with.

If the information available results in a new "appreciation" of the problem, rather different solutions from those considered previously will become obvious. The key to improving the policy-making process is to improve the perception stimuli, in such a way as to produce a broader and more realistic view of the situation.

There is no doubt that Vickers is correct in emphasising the non-rational elements in policy making. His emphasis on perception, however, does little to improve the process of governmental decision-making, because it concentrates on individual behaviour. The varying skills and capacities of individuals involved in this policy-making situation envisaged will produce policies of uneven quality, and the process will proceed spasmodically. It is important that the process be as rational as possible, so that human deficiencies can be overcome.

Vickers provides insight into existing systems but his emphasis on individual processes prevents the practical political leader from gleaning suggestions for improving the decision-making system.

Combined models

Mixed scanning

Professor Etzioni (1967) advocates a truncated approach to policy analysis. He argues that there is not sufficient time to carry out rational analysis of all policies, even if this were operationally possible. Policy-makers should proceed on their usual course for most decisions, but should submit the remainder to the vigorous form of analysis suggested by the pure rationality model. By following such a process, Professor Etzioni feels that the normal brokerage features of politics would continue, but its output would be at least slightly improved by those better quality decisions taken after the extensive study of alternatives.

There are several practical and methodological shortcomings to this model. First, it is impossible to even approximate purely rational analysis for most policy areas. The most important social problems must be exempt from this kind of study. Secondly,even if it were possible to apply these sophisticated techniques to all policy proposals, who would decide which policies undergo extensive analysis? It seems highly unlikely that political leaders would be able to remove the highly sensitive issues from the normal process of politics.

The obvious arguments suggest that only minor problems will be dealt with rationally, and thus the improvement in output quality is likely to be marginal. There is also the danger, in an approach such as this, of using pseudo-analysis as part of the bargaining process to convince others of the validity of one's proposed solution. Finally, it is possible that the economic and political costs involved in the truncated approach will be greater than the improvements in output. The result of such an approach to policy making might well be a net loss in terms of the efficiency and perhaps effectiveness of the policy-making system.

Optimality

Dror (1968) presents one of the more elaborate models of the policy-making process. He divides it into four stages:

(a) Metapolicy making: at this stage the political system attempts to develop knowledge about policy making, to create new resources for use by political leaders in developing and executing policy, and to set general goals for the political community.
(b) Policy making: at this stage the policy analyst prepares the organisation's goals for action, develops and evaluates alternatives, and relates them to other government programmes and policies. The outcome of this stage is a decision to adopt a particular policy.
(c) Post-policy making: this stage involves the mobilisation of public support for the policy, the execution of the policy and evaluation of the effectiveness of the policy.
(d) Feedback: this stage provides information for and coordination between all phases of the process.

This optimal model is basically a combination of the economic rationality model, supplemented by extra-rational elements.

Not all alternatives can be compared in the same way and there is a serious possibility of error being built into the system. The optimal model can be viewed as a model representing existing policy-making systems.

Rationality and incrementalism

In discussions of policy analysis the two models most often used are the rationalist model and the incrementalist model. The main proponent of the rationalist approach is Professor Herbert A. Simon who is a Nobel Prize winner. The main proponent of the incrementalist approach is Professor Charles E. Lindblom. Both positions are worthy of more detailed examination.

Simon's rationality model (1947)

The main activities involved in rational policy making are set out below:

(a) Intelligence Gathering: Intelligence is here used as in the sense of "military intelligence", namely the gathering of information prior to taking action. In a completely rational world, any policy-making agency would continually and systematically scan the horizon, seeking to identify all present and potential problems and opportunities relevant to its mission or interests.
(b) Identifying All Options: Several policy responses (or "behaviour alternatives") are usually possible when a problem or opportunity is perceived. The completely rational policy maker would identify all such options and consider them in detail.

(c) Assessing Consequences of Options: In considering each policy option, it would be necessary to know what would happen if it were to be adopted. This perfect knowledge is unattainable in real life, but would be essential for complete rationality (in Simon's terms, "objective" rationality, where the reasoning is not only rational in intention but correct in the event, unlike "subjective" rationality, where reasoning is intendedly rational but proves, with hind-sight, to have been incorrect). Thus the fully rational policy maker would identify all the costs and benefits ("consequences") of all his or her policy options.

(d) Relating Consequences to Values: From the preceding gathering of data about problems, options and consequences, the rational policy maker would now have a large amount of information; a great many facts. But facts alone are useless if they cannot be related to a set of criteria or some sort of preference-ordering procedure. Thus for Simon, "rationality is concerned with the selection of preferred behaviour alternatives in terms of some system of values, whereby the consequences of behaviour can be evaluated."

(e) Choosing Preferred Option: Given full understanding of, and information about, all problems and opportunities, all the possible policy responses, all the consequences of each and every policy option, and the criteria to be employed in valuing these consequences and thus assessing policy options—then, and only then, would the policy maker be able to arrive at a fully rational policy.

Simon indicates the extent to which policy makers fall short of rationality but, nevertheless, (he believes) there is a need for decision-makers to become more rational.

Lindblom's incrementalist model

Charles Lindblom (1959) recognises limits to rationality in real-life policy making. He emphasises the "costliness of analysis", and is particularly strong on the political environment of policy making and the constraints of the given situation in which policy is made. Lindblom's model has the following characteristics.

(a) Attempts at understanding are limited to policies that differ only incrementally from existing policy.

(b) Instead of simply adjusting means to ends, ends are chosen that are appropriate to available means.

(c) A relatively small number of means (alternative possible policies) is considered, as follows from (a).

(d) Instead of comparing alternative means or policies in the light of postulated ends or objectives, alternative ends or objectives are also compared in the light of postulated means or policies and their consequences.

(e) While these actors are self-interested they are not blindly partisan, and are capable of adjusting to one another, through bargaining, negotiating and compromise ("partisan mutual adjustment").

(f) A value is placed in most pluralist liberal democracies upon "consensus seeking", so that what emerges is not necessarily the one best policy but rather that compromise policy upon which most groups can agree.

Decisions by consent, however, will ultimately reflect the interests of the most powerful. This could lead to a situation where the demands of the underprivileged and politically unorganised would be underrepresented.

Incrementalism also neglects innovation and change as it focuses on the short run and tries to achieve no more than limited variations from past policies. The result can be action without direction.

Policy models help to promote a better understanding of the nature of policy. We have examined a number of policy models, and compared the rational and the incremental approaches. If policy makers pursued and were capable of complete rationality they would produce "perfect" policies. However, most policy makers are not capable of complete rationality, and many have developed more incremental approaches to policy making. A useful approach to policy models is to divide them into three types:

(a) *Ideal type*: This does not exist in real life, but can help understanding and explanation by exploring underlying ideas or concepts (such as "rationality").

(b) *Descriptive model*: This relates to a real-life situation, and its purposes are those of description, exploration and understanding.

(c) *Prescriptive model*: This relates to what is desirable. It is concerned with what ought to be rather than with what is.

Most policy theorists employ models which emphasise the process of policy making and the cyclical nature of that process over time. Some models are prescriptive, some are descriptive. Certain theorists use a "mixed model" which combines both descriptive and prescriptive elements. Simon's approach is to consider rationality as a prescriptive idea but then to argue that more policy makers should move towards the rational policy model. Lindblom believes that incrementalism is the way policy is formulated, and argues that it should remain so.

The value of public policy models is that they are based on studies of decision-making in a public services context unlike many of the contemporary "business-like" management decision-making techniques. Decision-takers in Scottish local government and NHSScotland must learn to combine the best of public policy analysis with business-like approaches contextualised for the public sector.

Local Government Management

England and Wales

The development of local government management has been closely linked to a series of reports by Royal Commissions and other committees. These reports increased the status of management in English and Welsh local authorities, but none was concerned with Scottish local government, although all had a degree of persuasiveness.

The main reports covering England and Wales are as follows:

The Third Report of the Royal Commission on Local Government (1925–29) (The Onslow Report)

The Onslow Report commented on internal management and control and recommended that the Clerk should be responsible for co-ordinating the activities of the authority, but should not interfere with technical staff on technical matters.

The Haddow Report (1934)

This report also mentioned the co-ordinating role of the Clerk who, it was stressed, should exercise general supervision over the authority, although, again, without interfering with heads of departments on technical matters.

The Maud Committee (1967)

This Committee was concerned specifically with management in local government and it identified a number of weaknesses, notably, the fragmented nature of local government activities. It recommended that the Clerk should be the undisputed head of the whole paid service, with the other principals, or chief officers, forming a team under him or her. This team would report to the council through the Clerk. This was the initial idea leading to the conception of the post of the Chief Executive Officer.

The Bains Committee (1972)

The Bains Committee was concerned with the managerial implications of the reorganised structure of local government in England and Wales. The report highlighted the absence of unity in the internal organisation of most local authorities and, to combat this, recommended that there should be a chief executive in every authority, to head the council's paid service. In addition, it was suggested that committees should be related to policy areas or programmes, and departments should be related to functions or services.

In order to understand management in Scottish local government it is necessary to consider in detail the changes that have taken place in recent years in public management.

Scotland

The significance of the Hughes and Paterson Reports

In Scotland, comparatively little has been done by local authorities to organise recruitment and training. One attempt in this direction was the *Report on the Staffing of Local Government in Scotland*, which was published in 1968, after investigations under the chairmanship of A.A. Hughes. Its terms of reference were:

> "to consider the future recruitment, training and employment of local government officers in Scotland, having regard to the recommendations of the Committee on the Staffing of Local Government in England and Wales (the Mallaby Committee)."

A major recommendation of the Hughes Report was that local authorities in Scotland should establish a central organisation to provide comprehensive services fitted to the needs of local government in Scotland. This central organisation was to have the following principal objectives:

- (a) to perform the functions of the Local Government Training Board (England and Wales) insofar as these were required and considered necessary in Scotland;
- (b) to undertake the duties of a central staffing organisation;
- (c) to provide such central or regional management services as may be considered necessary;
- (d) to establish appropriate links with English or other organisations operating in the field of staff development and management services.

Although these recommendations were accepted in principle, the local authority associations were not persuaded that there was any urgency in acting on them and, in fact, they were largely ignored.

The Paterson Report is the title given to the *Report of the Working Group on Scottish Local Government Management Structures*. The chair of the Advisory Group was Ian Paterson who was, at the time, County Clerk of Lanark County Council. The report, published in

1973 was, in effect, the Scottish equivalent of the Bains Report. The Paterson Report followed closely the structure and recommendations of the Bains Report for England and Wales (1972). Paterson advocated a strategic approach to overcome the traditional departmentalism of local government. Chief Executives, policy planners, management teams, policy-led resources committees and the rationalisation of departmental and committee structures would all contribute to a corporate management approach (Midwinter and McGarvey, 1995, p.7).

Paterson began with a diagnosis of failings of the existing managerial structures, caused by excessive specialisation and fragmentation and inadequate arrangements for co-ordination. The Paterson Report envisaged a new structure which would provide a means of achieving a unified approach to the formulation and implementation of policies to meet the real needs of the community. The report regarded the need for a corporate approach to the business of local government as established beyond doubt and recommended the adoption of what is broadly termed "corporate management" in the new local authorities.

It was suggested that the following be established in every authority.

(a) *A chief executive*

Paterson followed the suggestion of Bains and recommended that a chief executive should be appointed as head of the council's paid service. This officer should have direct authority over, and responsibility for, all other officers.

The chief executive would be the council's principal adviser on matters of general policy, be responsible for co-ordinating advice on financial planning and would lead the management team in securing a corporate approach to the affairs of the authority.

Paterson, however, deviated from the Bains concept of a chief executive in two ways. First, Paterson suggested that, whilst in the larger authorities, the chief executive should not have responsibility for a conventional service department, in the smaller authorities, the duties of departmental head and chief executive could be combined. Secondly, the report stressed that the chief executive should be supported by an executive office in large authorities and by a department of policy planning in the large regions. The executive office would consist of two or three chief officers (administration, finance and policy planning). The policy planning department was to be responsible, in addition to that function, for research and intelligence and programme area team negotiation.

(b) *A management team*

A team or officers should act together as the focal point for the preparation and presentation, to the council, of co-ordinated advice on policies and major programmes or work. This would be done via the policy and resources committee and the service committees.

(c) *A policy and resources committee*

Reiterating Bains, Paterson argued that, at elected member level, there was a need for a policy and resources committee with a remit to "guide the council in the formulation of its policy objectives and priorities."

(d) *A "programme-based" organisational structure*

Paterson echoed Bains in its proposal that departments and committees should be organised, where possible, on a programme area basis.

All Scottish authorities appointed a chief executive for the 1975 reorganisation, but more than half or the districts and one region made this officer responsible for a department. The Paterson proposals have been followed least in respect of the support for the chief executive.

The vast majority of authorities made only minimal organisational changes which would assist the development of corporate management. Most have relied on the chief executive and the management team themselves to develop corporate management.

Management Development in Scottish Local Government

The "modernisation" agenda has led to a fundamental re-examination of the traditional public sector managerial roles. The establishment of the Scottish Parliament in 1999 resulted in a range of public policy initiatives promoted through the Scottish Executive and impacting on local government managers in several ways. There is a greater than ever demand for transparency and ethical management. There is closer scrutiny of local government than ever before. The influences and demands of community leadership, partnerships, intervention, and political management coupled with policy initiatives on social inclusion, sustainable development, Best Value, quality and equality, benchmarking, performance management and performance indicators all necessitate changes in the knowledge skills and competences of local government managers.

For over 35 years, management development in Scottish local government has featured on the political agenda yet, despite greater environmental turbulence than ever before, the policy to promote centrally co-ordinated management development has suffered from piecemeal implementation. Management development in local government can be defined as learning opportunities, by a variety of modes, to enhance the knowledge, skills and competences required both now and in the future by local government managers to promote their personal effectiveness and the effectiveness of their employing local authority.

In local government in England and Wales, two reports in 1967 impacted on management in local government. The Maud Committee looked at *Management in Local Government* and the Mallaby Committee examined *Staffing in Local Government*. The Mallaby Report in particular provided a useful definition of management in local government in the late 1960s:

> "Management involves the setting of objectives and planning how these objectives are to be achieved, the organization and harmonization of the work of various individuals and groups of people, the controlling of costs and the appraisal of results." (Mallaby, 1967)

During the period 1966–67, discussions were taking place on the establishment of a Local Government Training Board (LGTB) covering England and Wales and the first meeting of the LGTB took place in September 1967.

It is against this background that the "issue search" stage of the public policy process on management development in Scottish local government begins. In late 1966, Professor W.J.M. Mackenzie of the University of Glasgow wrote to the Secretary of the Royal Commission on Local Government in Scotland (The Wheatley Commission, 1966–69) to ascertain whether or not the Royal Commission would consider training and development in Scottish local government as part of their review. The reply was negative, but in April 1967, in a letter from the Scottish Development Department to the local authority associations, the Government intimated that training and development was on the policy agenda:

> "It seems to the Secretary of State that it would be desirable to consider in relation to Scottish local government the same range of problems and in doing so to take into account the recommendations of the Mallaby Report." (Association of County Councils in Scotland, Minutes, 1967, pp.190–192)

A Working Party was appointed in June 1967 with A.A. Hughes, Assistant Secretary at the Scottish Development Department, as Chair and it reported in 1968. The report highlighted that:

> "Training to meet the needs of local government was a matter, which was not accorded much priority."

and

> "There would be a need for systematic performance appraisal linked to comprehensive management development."

The Working Party made 55 recommendations including the establishment of a Central Training Organisation for Scottish local government. Most of the recommendations lacked detail and a further Working Party was set up to develop the policy so that it could be implemented. The progression of the issue from the Secretary of State to the Hughes Committee clearly confirms that the policy was on the political agenda.

In 1970, a draft constitution was agreed and financial support was offered by the Scottish Office to the local authority associations to help the creation of a Central Training Organisation with a broad remit including management development for local government managers. The Working Party was reporting to a Steering Committee of elected members, but following the 1970 local government elections, a number of elected members were no longer in office and had to resign from the Steering Committee. This led to delays, a loss of expertise, and a loss of continuity. Further discussions took place in the early 1970s with the Employers Secretariat of the local government Joint Negotiating Bodies playing a key role in the policy network. There had been six drafts of the constitution by April 1971 and no agreement reached. There was a "failure to agree" between the Working Party (officers), the Steering Group (elected members) and the local authority associations. Subsequent to this, the policy lost its impetus and the issue failed to appear on the agendas of the local government associations largely due to the run-up to the 1975 local government reorganisation.

The Report of the Advisory Group on *The New Scottish Local Authorities: Organisation and Management Structures* (the Paterson Report) in 1973 had little to say of direct relevance to training and development. Indirectly, however, many of its recommendations had implications for management development. The Paterson Report followed closely the structure and recommendations of the Bains Report for England and Wales (1972). Paterson advocated a strategic approach to overcome the traditional departmentalism of local government. Chief executives, policy planners, management teams, policy-led resources committees and the rationalisation of departmental and committee structures would all contribute to a corporate management approach (Midwinter, 1995, p.7).

Therefore the policy failed to progress to implementation by 1975. At the time of the 1975 reorganisation of Scottish local government there had been no forecasting of demand for management development provision, no setting of objectives and priorities, no consideration of options and as a consequence, no preferred option. The management development policy had not therefore reached the implementation stage of the public policy process after eight years of sporadic deliberations.

In August 1975, the newly established Convention of Scottish Local Authorities (COSLA) conducted a survey on the training requirements of member councils. The data from the survey confirmed that the position had not changed since the late 1960s in that training for professional qualifications received a great deal of attention, but training for management was largely neglected. The policy process was beginning all over again. In early 1977, COSLA's Manpower Committee requested a report on the steps which might be taken to establish a training organisation for Scottish local authorities. This is clearly a return to "deciding how to decide". The report recommended a joint committee of employers' representatives and trade unions separate from COSLA and the Scottish Joint Negotiating Bodies. The report was accepted with reservations concerning the accountability and control of this joint committee subject to further consideration of its implications.

At this stage, an agency of the UK Manpower Services Commission, the Training Services Agency (TSA), was invited into the policy network. The Scottish Office expressed concerns about the funding of the joint committee but the TSA were willing to "pump-prime" the organisation for three to four years. Deliberations continued on the constitution of the joint committee and COSLA decided to review the entire proposal and to conduct a further survey of councils in 1977.

The 1977 survey confirmed the 1975 survey and the findings of the Hughes Committee 1968. This was clearly "paralysis by analysis" and there had been no initiatives forthcoming, yet COSLA continued to seek reassurance that there was still a demand for a central training organisation. In 1978, COSLA decided to restrict trade union participation to advisory and consultative input and COSLA would be the sole decision-taker. A further draft constitution followed and this was approved in 1979. This resulted in the creation of the Advisory Committee on the Education and Training of Scottish Local Government Employees in 1980. The Advisory Committee had a Management Development Sub-Committee and it requested a management development proposal from the University of Edinburgh. The proposal was received and submitted to the COSLA Policy Committee for funding but no action was taken on the proposal.

The policy was largely shelved during the 1980s with larger authorities beginning to initiate their own management development programmes in-house and through external providers. In the late 1980s, COSLA approached the University of Strathclyde to be the home of the Scottish Local Authorities Management (SLAM) Centre and agreed to fund the centre for a three-year period. Funding from COSLA was eventually withdrawn and the SLAM Centre became an integral part of the Human Resources Management Department of the University of Strathclyde. From its inception the SLAM Centre provided a range of management development and consultancy services to Scottish local authorities on a commercial consultancy basis, but found its level of activity declining in the run up to the 1996 reorganisation.

Progress was slow during this period and the end result (the Advisory Committee and the SLAM Centre) were options that had never been fully considered as entirely appropriate to meet the requirements of the Scottish local authorities. Indeed the smaller authorities had little better management development provision in 1996 than they had in 1975. Larger authorities fared better but even then progress was patchy. Strathclyde Regional Council initiated their management development programme in 1990, 15 years after the 1975 reorganisation. Of the 2,000 middle and senior mangers in Strathclyde Regional Council, less than 5 per cent had been afforded management development opportunities prior to the launch of their bespoke management development programme. This is clearly a period of policy procrastination with no sense of the way in which the policy should respond to the changing management development requirements of Scottish local government managers. The policy formulators seem to become stuck on the need for surveys, constitutions and finance with little systematic policy development. COSLA was also considering its future under a changed local government structure (COSLA, 1995).

(The information contained in this and the previous section was obtained from the Minutes of the local authority associations 1967–75, the minutes of Convention of Scottish Local Authorities and from interviews with local government officers).

COSLA in the period from 1996, first expanded its training and development activities, but in 2000 reduced its role in the promotion of management development in Scottish local government. The policy at last seems to have progressed beyond the debate phase. Implementation is only now beginning in earnest and lies in the hands of COSLA, the Scottish Leadership Foundation, local authorities and providers such as the SLAM Centre and the Scottish Universities.

In a survey conducted by the author for COSLA in 1999 (Mackie, 1999), the data revealed that management development in Scottish local government remains piecemeal at best. The larger local authorities benefit from in-house provision and the capacity to subcontract to private providers with the SLAM Centre being the most active provider of development opportunities to officers and elected members. However, the smaller authorities remain disadvantaged because of their lack of resources (finance and time) to commission in-house provision and to access more generic provision provided externally.

This review provides an insight into management development in Scottish local government over a 35-year period. In many respects, there are no surprises with the larger authorities making progress, while the smaller authorities are left behind due, in part, to the failure of the policy network to provide a central organisation promoting management development in Scottish local government. In consequence, management development practices are fairly standard, with little evidence of innovative approaches which look strategically at the importance of effective management practices at all managerial levels in an authority, in a rapidly changing public management environment. There is widespread use of "standard" menu-driven approaches using traditional modes of delivery. There is little evidence of partnership and consortia arrangements to share costs and provide opportunities for development outwith the individual's own employing authority. This may constrain the likelihood of improving decision-making in Scottish local government and will impact on the effectiveness of Community Planning initiatives.

Health Service Management

The growth in managerialism in the NHS can trace its roots from the early 1970s. The NHS reorganisation of 1974 clearly established a key role for managers in the provision of a positive and supportive climate to health professionals in pursuit of efficient and effective health services. The UK Government has been able to exercise close control over NHS expenditure since 1948 and this was strengthened in the 1970s through the introduction of the "cash limit" system of public finance, in place of the volume-based approach employed prior to this period. NHS managers were effectively charged with ensuring that cash limits were not overspent.

Decisions taken within budgetary constraints were made by clinicians substantially free from Government policy directives and managerial objectives. In the period prior to the Griffiths Report (before 1983), health service managers were not strategically influential, tended to be re-active, inward looking and complacent (Harrison, 1988, Ch.3).

By 1983 this had changed, largely due to the finding of the Committee of Inquiry into the Management of the NHS chaired by Roy Griffiths (subsequently Sir Roy Griffiths), Deputy Chairman and Managing Director of Sainsbury's. The Griffiths Report identified consensus management as a serious problem whereby decision-making was slow. There was no strategy, no prioritisation, no plans, no implementation and no performance evaluation and review. The health service as a consequence lacked strategic direction and a capacity for change. The NHS took little account of its consumers or clients. All of these deficiencies were addressed in the Report's recommendations and the means by which change was to be achieved was through general managers at all levels of the NHS with responsibility for strategic management and its operationalisation as well as resource management throughout the NHS system. This led to a major shift away from clinicians to managers and a consequent movement from producer values to consumer values (Klein, 2001, p.129).

Further developments took place in the early 1990s with the creation of health trusts and the purchaser-provider split. All of this impacted on the knowledge, skills and competencies required of NHS managers. In Scotland, the Common Services Agency Management Education and Training Division (CSA-METD) co-ordinated management development events across the country. Many NHS managers undertook training and development in generic business management rather than public administration and management.

STRATEGIC DECISION-MAKERS

Councillors

In local government, the key decision-makers are the elected councillors. Decisions are substantially made by Council Committees which operate under a scheme of delegation as laid down in the local authority's standing orders. Typically, the full council devolves authority to service and other committees to take decisions on its behalf, with the meetings of the full council formally approving any recommendations made to it. Committees, comprising cross-party membership and responsible for major service or policy areas such as education and social work, hold local authority departments to account for their performance.

In recent years, partly in response to national and local initiatives on joined-up government, some councils have moved away from the traditional committee-based structures. Others developed committees covering, for example, social and community development and lifelong learning, which covered the professional responsibilities of a number of departments and services so that councillors could consider the full range of issues relating to a particular policy area.

Councillors in Scottish local authorities are key policy makers and decision takers in sophisticated business-like organisations that have developed in response to environmental influences, changing legislation and government policy, reports and recommendations. They are organised through a system of committees designed to integrate policy formulation and decision taking across the whole of the authority's activities—a corporate approach. It was not always thus, for prior to the 1970s, the usual practice was to have a series of committees, each dealing with its specific responsibilities and making its own policies. Although the full council was paramount, there was little central co-ordination or management control. The Maud Report (1967), the Bains Report (1972) and the Paterson Report (1973) focused on these deficiencies, recommending fewer committees, but with one of special power to achieve a corporate approach. Parallel with this, co-ordination of the officer component was urged, which led to the widespread appointment of chief executives when reorganisation was under way.

It must be understood that while there is a general pattern to the way local authorities organise their committee structure—especially as so many of their activities are prescribed by law—there are nevertheless significant variations to be found among them. Each one, however, will have a council comprised of all the councillors, and a system of committees and sub-committees to which a wide range of detailed decisions and issues are delegated. It is not feasible for the full council to deal with a mass of detail since councillors, being mostly part-timers, could not possibly meet frequently enough. Nor would they, for the most part, have a sufficiently wide grasp of detail to reach meaningful decisions on all matters. It is therefore the very essence of local authority committee work that members seek appointment to those committees dealing with matters of which they have some experience or particular interest. In this way, they can build up a reputation for special knowledge, as a result of which their contribution in discussion and debate will be accorded special significance by their fellow members.

The full council must by law hold an annual meeting, but otherwise may only meet four or five times a year, when committee chairs will submit the minutes of their committees for ratification. These will include details of decisions taken under the delegated powers given to the committee by the council. Also included will be reports and perhaps recommendations on major policy issues that require council approval, such as the closing of a school or the building of a children's community home. These will either be approved as they stand, accepted with amendments, rejected, or referred back to the committee for further consideration. Officers do not make any contribution to the discussion in council, unless it be the chief executive on a legal or procedural matter, though chief officers are available in the chamber to give advice to their chairs, if requested.

At its first meeting the council must appoint a chair to take charge of proceedings. This will not normally be the leader of the council, because it is desirable that the chair of the full council be seen as a relatively independent person without strong political ties. It takes a very special person to hold the respect of all parties and at the same time to be the representative of the council in a range of public activities. The council must also allocate members to the various committees it establishes, though this will usually mean little more than confirming recommendations already made by a special committee. However, since the Local Government and Housing Act 1989, which gave effect to certain recommendations of the Widdicombe Committee, the council must in allocating members to committees have regard to maintaining the same political balance as exists on the full council. This marks a major step forward in democratising the work of councils, since prior to this politically-led councils would sometimes try to weaken the representation of political opponents on important committees and exclude them altogether from the policy and resources committee.

The council must decide what powers it wishes to delegate to committees and also what functions to allocate officers. But there are two matters the council cannot delegate—determining the amount of the council tax and the decision to borrow money.

Health board members

The overall purpose of the unified NHS Board is to ensure the efficient, effective and accountable governance of the local NHS system and to provide strategic leadership and direction for the system as a whole, focusing on agreed outcomes.

The role of the unified NHS Board is:

- to improve and protect the health of local people;
- to improve health services for local people;
- to focus clearly on health outcomes and people's experience of their local NHS system;
- to promote integrated health and community planning by working closely with other local organisations; and
- to provide a single focus of accountability for the performance of the local NHS system.

The functions of the unified NHS Board comprises:

- strategy development—to develop a single Local Health Plan for each NHS Board area which addresses the health priorities and healthcare needs of the resident population, and within which all aspects of NHS activity in relation to health improvement, acute services and primary care will be specified;
- resource allocation to address local priorities—funds will flow to the NHS Board, which will be responsible for deciding how these resources are deployed locally to meet its strategic objectives;
- implementation of the Local Health Plan; and
- performance management of the local NHS system, including risk management.

Membership of the unified NHS Board carries with it collective responsibility for the discharge of these functions. All members of the NHS Board will be expected to bring an impartial judgment to bear on issues of strategy, performance management, key appointments and accountability, upwards to Scottish Ministers and outwards to the local community. Members will provide independence of thought and action in reflecting the public interest. The creation of unified NHS Boards is not intended to result in more centralised decision-making. On the contrary, the goal is Boards which empower those in the front line to plan and deliver services, but in the context of clear strategic direction and rigorous performance management.

The diagram below illustrates the relationship between the component parts of the local NHS system and the role and functions of the unified NHS Board.

Figure 6.2

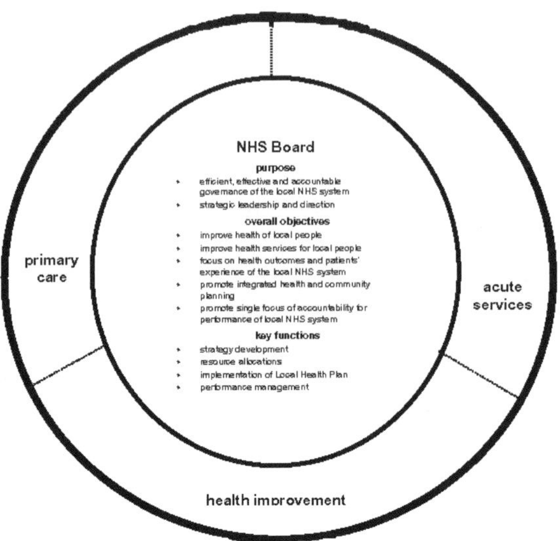

Source ©: ISD Scotland

Local government representation on health boards

Health improvement cannot be delivered by NHSScotland in isolation. NHS Boards and local authorities must work closely together across a range of health and community planning issues. The Scottish Executive intend to reinforce this partnership by further promoting greater integration of planning and decision-making between local government and the NHS and other partners.

Some health board already have members who are also elected local authority members. In future, this will be the norm across NHSScotland. The presence of elected representatives on NHS Boards is intended to:

- improve communications between the NHS and local authorities; and
- support closer partnership working, consistent with the principles of community planning.

More specifically, local authority members of NHS Boards will play a vital role in helping to strengthen collaboration between NHSScotland and local authorities—not just in planning but across a range of activities, including service delivery and community care. The presence of local authority members on NHS Boards should help ensure that the Local Health Plan for each NHS Board area is consistent with the components of the community planning process in each local authority area. It will not, however, be the local authority member's function to provide the primary link to the community planning process. Senior representatives of the NHS Board will be members of community planning partnerships in their own right.

Local authority members will have a key role in facilitating interaction and co-operation between the local authority and local NHS systems and with wider communities. This interaction and co-operation is crucial to the shared objective of improving health. As full members of NHS Boards, local authority members will be bound by the need for collective responsibility. In this context, they will also be expected to participate fully in the committee structures of the local NHS system. It is vital that local authority members of NHS Boards enjoy the full confidence of their authorities, and are able to commit to decisions on health and health service matters which could affect their local communities. The Scottish Executive will invite local authorities to nominate either:

- their Leader; or
- their Deputy Leader; or
- the senior member of the local authority with designated responsibility for public health-related issues

to be appointed, by the Minister, as members of their principal NHS Board.

University Medical School members of the NHS Board

At present, those health boards which have a University Medical School within their area have an additional seat for a member from the University. This is felt to have proved valuable. The participation of the University member facilitates strategic planning for both the NHS Board and the Medical School and reflects the degree of influence which medical education has on service delivery—and vice versa. This practice will continue in those new NHS Board areas which include University Medical Schools. Nominations will be sought from the Universities in line with the guidelines issued by the Commissioner for Public Appointments.

Clinical and other professional input to the NHS Board

It is essential that NHS Boards are able to draw on professional skills and expertise from across the local NHS system as a whole for advice on clinical and other professional matters. Trusts, and where appropriate NHS Boards, will retain their own Medical and Nursing Director posts. These directors will have an important contribution to make to the work of the NHS Board. This will undoubtedly include attendance at meetings of the NHS Board, as necessary. The establishment of NHS Boards has provided an opportunity to examine and refocus local clinical advisory mechanisms. NHS Boards will also be expected to harness and access the range of expertise which exists in Area Professional Committees. There is substantial scope to strengthen the role of these committees in underpinning the design and delivery of quality services. These committees already have a duty to advise existing health board on clinical and other professional matters and may be consulted by the Board at its discretion.

Currently, provision exists for six Professional Advisory Committees at Health Board level covering:

- medical;
- dental;
- nursing and midwifery;
- pharmacy;
- ophthalmology; and
- the professions allied to medicine.

Additional members of the NHS Board

It is important that the total number of members of NHS Boards is sufficient to ensure that Boards can carry out the functions required of them. These functions will include providing an adequate degree of scrutiny over all the component parts of their local NHS system, including membership of committees. In addition to the membership discussed above, NHS Boards will therefore have the discretion to seek the appointment of up to two additional members. The exact number is to be decided locally. The number of members of the NHS Board needs to reflect a balance between the desire for inclusiveness and the need to ensure that the NHS Board is of a manageable size, consistent with the effective discharge of business. This balance may vary in different areas.

Directors of existing health boards

At present, not all directors of health boards are appointed to the governing board of the health board. The only directors who are appointed to the governing board on the basis of their position are chief executives. Other directors, including the Directors of Public Health and Finance, are appointed to the board as members following recommendation from the chair. A small number of directors, who are currently appointed members of the board, may not be appointed to the NHS Board. However, this will not materially affect the level and importance of their contribution to the work of the new NHS Board. Their status and areas of operational expertise and responsibility will be undiminished.

Based on the proposals discussed above, the following table illustrates the likely composition of a typical NHS Board.

Table 6.1: The size of the NHS Board

Typical unified NHS Board (covering 2 Local Authority areas): up to *15 Members*
Board Chair
2 Local Authority Members
Staff Side Chair of the Area Partnership Forum
Chair of the Area Clinical Forum
University Medical School Member (*where appropriate*)
(*up to*) 2 additional members
Board Chief Executive
Director of Public Health
Finance Director

Committees

For the most part, a council can set up whatever committees and sub-committees is necessary to discharge its functions, except that where it has responsibility for these services it must have separate committees for the police, education, and social work—known as statutory committees. Since the advent of corporate management, the most important committee will be that of policy and resources. This committee is usually responsible for co-ordinating and directing the overall strategy of the authority.

It makes recommendations to the council on the budget and the policies and standards to be applied by all committees. It is also responsible for overseeing the management of the council's financial, personnel and property resources.

It is in the number and function of the remaining committees that local authority practice shows wide variations. The system has always been to divide the operational work between a number of departments, each headed by a chief officer responsible to a committee. Thus there may be a planning officer, a planning department, and a planning committee, and similarly with housing, finance, highways, environmental health, architecture, and so on.

But local authorities vary in the degree to which they have amalgamated departments under one officer and one committee.

For example, housing may be combined with environmental health, or planning and architecture may be grouped under technical services. Finance may be made a responsibility of a sub-committee of policy and resources. Each authority will have its own preferred system, the significant point being the general tendency to reduce the number of committees, departments and chief officers, thus moving in the direction of a model of corporate management.

Committees having a specific output to the community, such as education, social service, or housing, are called service committees and are sometimes described as vertical committees. In contrast, the term horizontal is used to distinguish those committees, such as policy and resources, finance, and personnel whose decisions reach across and affect all committees and departments of the local authority but have no direct impact on the public.

This is developed into a corporate system by amalgamating departments where appropriate, appointing a chief executive to head a chief officers management team and creating a high-powered policy and resources committee to set guidelines for all the other committees.

As with the council, the first task of a committee is to appoint someone to the chair. This is a post of vital importance, for the whole tone of the committee, and the quality of its decisions and recommendations will depend on the ability of the chair to absorb a great deal of information, to keep discussion balanced and directed to the matter in hand, and to defuse tensions with good humour. Committees are usually less formal than council meetings and the chief officer and his assistants play a larger part, clarifying reports and explaining action taken under delegated powers. The extent to which officers may make a contribution to any discussion depends very much on the ethos of the particular committee and the style adopted by the chair. Their contributions will in any case be strictly non-political and limited to legal, technical or professional aspects of the subject under discussion.

The appointment of the chair is followed by deciding what recommendations to make to the council regarding co-opted members.

Any committee, other than the finance committee, may co-opt persons from outside the council, the purpose being to allow representation of important community interests—such as voluntary organisations—and to utilise the contribution of persons with particular skills or experience. Standing Orders of the council will indicate the number of co-options that can be made. Again, the education committee must include persons with experience in the subject, so that if no councillor members meet this requirement, suitable persons must be co-opted. Widdicombe noted that co-options could upset the political balance of committees, and was no aid to democracy. Consequently, legislation now prevents co-opted members from having voting rights on all but non-executive committees.

Committees can set up sub-committees, working parties, panels, review groups and liaison committees to deal with any particular aspect of their responsibility. This is especially necessary where committees have a wide span of operations, as with education and social work. These sub-committees may have delegated powers and be executive in nature, such as a tenancy sub-committee of housing. Others will be deliberative only, dealing with reviews, liaison or forward planning, and reporting back comments and proposals to the full committee. Sub-committees are less formal than full committees and member/officer discussion will be fuller and freer. The chief officer will generally be represented by an assistant or a principal officer, having specialist knowledge of the particular area of responsibility.

The agenda for a full committee will be prepared by the chief officer and the chair, in consultation with the chief executive. Since the chair will usually be a member of the policy and resources committee, and the chief executive heads the chief officer team, this ensures that the business of the committee is underpinned by a corporate approach. Before the committee meeting, the chief officer and chair, usually together with the vice-chair will meet and go through all the papers to ensure that the chair is fully briefed.

It is common practice for a committee to authorise the chair to make certain decisions on its behalf between meetings. The need for this arises where a chief officer is faced with a problem that is judged to require a committee decision, but where it is imperative to act quickly. The chair must, however, act with caution, as it has been shown in law that no general authority can be given to the chair to act in this way. Committees are minuted by committee clerks from a central services department under the chief executive. A solicitor from the same department will often be present also, since legal and procedural questions frequently arise.

The committee system is a long-standing and well-tried feature of local government. Although sometimes criticised as being cumbersome and inefficient, it is in fact a very effective method of providing detailed and concurrent coverage of all the business activities of the council. It facilitates contact between members and officers and between councillors of different political persuasions. It is difficult to see how better to demonstrate local democracy working in the community. Nevertheless, the Government began in 1998 a comprehensive review of certain aspects of local government and the Scottish Parliament, suggesting there may be good reasons for change.

The McIntosh Commission

Audit Scotland is increasingly promoting improvements in management practice in local government.

In June, 1999, the Commission on Local Government (the McIntosh Commission) reported on a number of aspects of local government, including decision-making structures (see Ch.5). The McIntosh Commission proposed, *inter alia,* that:

- Local authorities should carry out a review of business and working practices under the guiding principles of accountability and accessibility.
- The aim of the review should be set on a formal, open and accountable footing, the political leadership in the form appropriate to the circumstances of the local authority.
- Local authorities should consider formalising the political leadership in an executive "cabinet" but should also consider other options.

In response to the McIntosh Commission, the Scottish Ministers formed the Leadership Advisory Panel to advise councils on the review of their decision-making and policy development processes, and working practices which support those processes and to advise Ministers accordingly. In April 2001, the Leadership Advisory Panel identified that local authorities had adopted three main strategies in response to McIntosh:

(a) streamlined committee structures;
(b) the formation of an executive structure; and
(c) devolved and semi-devolved structures.

Ultimately, it is for councils to determine their decision-making and policy development arrangements. The majority of councils in Scotland have retained the traditional approach to committee structures. A minority, however, have developed approaches to "cabinet" style government which demonstrate many similar principles although they may differ in detail. Using one council for illustrative purposes, "cabinet" style government involves the following:

- The full council is responsible for setting an annual budget and council tax level, determines the council's strategic objectives and corporate policies, and delegates functions to officers. It appoints on an annual basis 13 members of the full council to act as an executive.
- The executive exercises strategic leadership of the council. It takes executive decisions within the budget and policy framework approved by the full council, develops new policies consistent with the overall strategic approach of the council, sets targets for service delivery and provides political accountability for the council's performance. Members of the executive are each allocated a special area of responsibility such as transport, education, social work, housing, environment and leisure and culture.

- Seven subject scrutiny panels, appointed by the full council from councillors who are not members of the executive, scrutinise the activities of the executive and hold it to account for its performance. The scrutiny panels are responsible for monitoring the performance of the executive and departments against service delivery and financial targets, for commissioning reviews of particular issues and policies and for submitting recommendations to the executive and the full council. They may request executive members or senior officials to answer questions or submit and report on any matter that is relevant to their responsibilities. Scrutiny panels make reports to the council on their activities every six months.
- Six local development committees comprising councillors advise the executive or security panels on matters of interest in their local areas and allow local issues to be discussed at a local level. They are intended to improve consultation with voters by acting as sounding boards for council proposals, to develop community strategies and to monitor local performance against targets. Local development committees are accountable to the full council and make an annual report to the council on their activities and plans.

Regardless of whether the local authority adopts a traditional or "cabinet" style of government, the elected members of the council are ultimately accountable to the electorate for its performance. Officers are responsible for delivering the policies of the local authority. Chief officers, as heads of departments, report to the chief executive as head of paid service and the most senior of the chief officers. The chief executive and the chief officers are accountable to the elected members. In addition, the chief executive as head of paid service has a particular role established in statute to report to the council where he considers it appropriate to do so as a range of matters. These include the manner in which the discharge of the local authority's functions is co-ordinated and the organisation and management of staff (Audit Scotland, 2002).

Policy advice

The Scottish Academy for Health Policy and Management (SAHPM)

The National Health Service Scotland is facing an unprecedented era of reform and investment, and politicians and the communities they serve have increased expectations that this will result in improvements in the management and delivery of services. Since devolution, major health policies have sought to address the barriers to improving Scotland's health. These service strategies have been underpinned by a sound clinical evidence base, however, less evidence is available to support clinicians and managers in the delivery of services through a series of different management and organisational structures which require new ways of working across professional and geographic boundaries. In addition, all service improvement in NHSScotland is underpinned by a commitment to joint working with local communities and partner organisations, particularly local authorities and the voluntary sector, and there is a need for a sound understanding of how this can best be achieved.

The concept of evidence-based policy and decision is now a standard of best practice in government. Increased public scrutiny and accountability has created a heightened awareness of the need for politicians and decision-makers to have a range of evidence to support policy development and decision-making in the public sector. A major programme of civil service reform (*Change to Deliver*) is underway in the Scottish Executive and the Permanent Secretary has made a commitment to improvement at all levels in the policy making process. Improving access to evidence and engaging with stakeholders is at the heart of this programme.

In Scotland, whilst there is a highly acclaimed clinical research community, less attention and funding is focused on research and evidence-gathering to support service delivery, management and organisation improvement. Policy makers and NHS managers are therefore vulnerable to criticism from clinicians and practitioners when asked to identify the evidence that underpins policy and management decisions especially when this results in structural change. The reform of the NHS in England is supported by a national R&D programme dedicated to improving service delivery and organisation (SDO). Additional resources are allocated to the Department of Health Policy Research Programme to inform ministerial policy and priorities. As health policy diverges north and south of the border, it is evident that there is an immediate need for similar dedicated resources in Scotland. The Academy represents the Scottish response to this identified need.

SAHPM: Aims

The Academy aims to provide:

- a collaborative network to identify and co-ordinate clearly defined research and evidence to support policy, strategy and service development in SEHD, NHSS and other partner organisations;
- dedicated resources to support policy implementation, service development and management practice;
- management education and skills development to support implementation and improved service delivery, in particular

the NHS Leadership Strategy currently being developed by SEHD;
- a "knowledge exchange" facility to store and disseminate knowledge and learning.

The following diagram illustrates how the activity of the Academy will be defined and driven by stakeholders and partners.

Figure 6.3

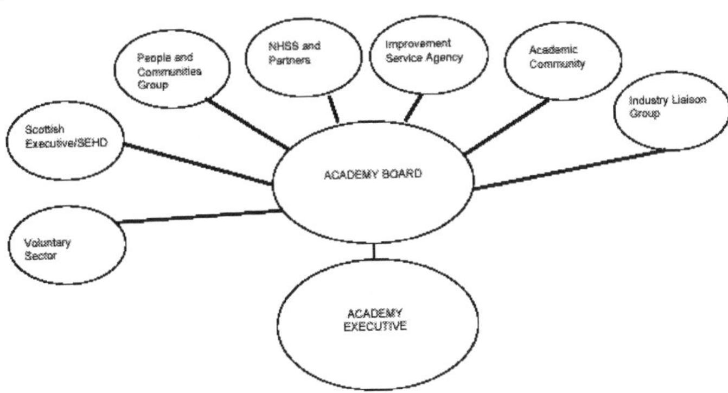

Source: Scottish Academy for Health Policy and Management, Position Paper, March 2004, Crown copyright.

The Academy will provide dedicated resources to support Ministers and SEHD officials in the policy development process. It is of vital importance that there is a formal relationship between the SEHD and the Academy. To ensure a seamless connection between the Department and the Academy, the possibility of a joint SEHD/ Academy liaison team is being considered to provide the interface between dedicated policy resources in the Health Department and the Academy networks. At a wider Scottish Executive level, it may also prove appropriate to formally link the Academy to the Strategy and Delivery Group of the Office of the Permanent Secretary. In addition to formal links to SEHD at a general level, the Academy will have strong relationships with Departments and Directorates on designated activities.

Local Government Policy Advice: COSLA and the Improvement Service

The Convention of Scottish Local Authorities (COSLA)

COSLA is a key stakeholder in Scottish local government. Every local authority is a separate organisation, but a co-ordinating body is necessary to represent the interests of all Scottish local authorities together. Prior to 1975 there were four national local authority associations:

(a) The Counties of Cities Associations
(b) The Convention of Royal Burghs
(c) The Association of County Councils
(d) The District Councils Association

In addition to those natural associations, there were a number of associations of a local nature, such as the Borders Burghs Convention. However, the Wheatley Commission stated that there was a need for one strong central association to represent local government as a whole in order to balance the power and influence of central government. In July 1974, the Scottish Development Department of the Scottish Office convened a meeting of representatives of all the new authorities in Scotland to discuss the arrangements for a local authority association. In October 1974, representatives were asked to vote in principle for a single association. All region and islands representatives voted in favour and only 12 of the 53 district representatives voted against. The inaugural meeting of COSLA was held in Glasgow in April, 1975.

The McIntosh Commission (1999) made three specific recommendations aimed at establishing a permanent constructive relationship between local government, the Scottish Parliament and the Scottish Executive. The recommendations were:

(a) A joint agreement (covenant) between the Scottish Parliament and the 32 councils setting out the basis of their working relationships;
(b) A formal working agreement between local government and Scottish Ministers;
(c) A standing Joint Conference where the Scottish Executive, MSPs and local government representatives may discuss issues on the basis of equality.

Greater constitutional standing has to be supported by greater financial autonomy. Adequate, sustainable and flexible funding is essential, according to COSLA (1993), to deliver effectively jointly agreed national priorities and also to recognise the importance of individual councils being given capacity to address local priorities (see Ch.10).

In 2003, COSLA committed itself to a manifesto which states that if Scottish local government is to flourish, free of the constraints and centrally imposed policies that characterised the last two decades of the twentieth century, there has to be a new relationship between local and central government. This new relationship needs to be founded on a parity of esteem and on greater financial freedoms for local authorities. COSLA's organisational structure has recently been reviewed and a new internal structure is being put in place. The old structure of four teams—Chief Executive's, Finance, Organisational Development and Policy & Legislation—is being replaced with seven themed teams working across the disciplines. The aim is to increase COSLA's capacity and effectiveness to approach issues in a coherent and holistic way.

The themed teams will cover the following areas:

(a) Children & Young People;
(b) Community Resourcing;
(c) Environment & Regeneration;
(d) Health & Social Care;
(e) Governance & Democracy;
(f) Image, Media & Communication ; and
(g) Resourcing & Capacity

The mission of the Convention of Scottish Local Authorities (COSLA), is to act as the representative voice of Scottish local government. COSLA promotes this mission by developing external relationships with bodies such as the Scottish Executive and the Scottish Parliament, and by addressing and influencing key constitutional issues for local government, including modernisation, democratic renewal, structural change and the status of local government. COSLA also seeks to influence the development of the public policy framework in line with the political direction set by its political leadership and to protect and influence the resourcing of local government.

COSLA also acts as the employers' association on behalf of its member councils, negotiating salaries, wages and conditions of service for local government employees in Scotland with the relevant trade unions.

Local Government Improvement Service

The Improvement Service has been established to support, promote and assist in the delivery of excellent public services—through learning, sharing and delivering improvement solutions. The Service is a company limited by guarantee with a budget of £4 million over three years provided by the Scottish Executive. It has three partners—COSLA, the Scottish Executive and the Society of Local Authority Chief Executives (SOLACE).

According to COSLA (2004, p.1), the Service aims to support the delivery of continuous improvement by building on the expertise in local authorities and through working in partnership with local government stakeholders across the public, voluntary and private sectors. The purpose of this improvement service is to provide local authorities with positive assistance to support continuous improvement in service delivery in a manner that responds to the needs of customers, the delivery of excellent services and the promotion of Best Value.

Core objectives are to:

- Promote a learning culture across local government and to support the opportunities for collaborative working within the local government and wider public sector communities to support change management and business redesign;
- Build capacity within local government to improve and increase the skills of both officers and elected members;
- Gather, identify, understand and offer methods to promote good practice across local authorities and partnerships in Scotland, as appropriate;
- Promote the use of knowledge management within local authorities, using human resources alongside IT to support sharing and learning; embrace the e-governance agenda; and support business re-design to deliver continuous improvement; and
- Access the opportunities that exist beyond Scotland and share the learning from further afield.

Supporting objectives are to:

- Support councils in responding to the outcomes of the new Best Value audit;
- Promote opportunities for new ways of working that can deliver improvement in services;
- Promote success in local authorities and recognise the skills and innovation of staff at every level, that are making a real difference to communities across Scotland;
- Support benchmarking and learning groups for local authorities and partners; and
- Communicate the work of the service and seek feedback from members.

The Scottish Executive has committed £4.5 million over the three years 2003–06.

The expectation on local authorities to seek continuous improvement in their performance is now enshrined as a statutory obligation through the Local Government in Scotland Act 2003. This reflects the commitment of the Scottish Executive to working with councils to build better services for citizens.

Strategic Public Management

Explaining strategic public management

A strategy is a decision or series of decisions made within an organisation which determines its medium to long-term objectives, priorities and overall direction. It re-positions the organisation in relation to its external environment including the availability of key resources. Strategic management refers to a set of processes comprising strategy formulation, strategy implementation, monitoring and control.

Strategic management has the following characteristics:

- an active (or pro-active) rather than reactive approach;
- a deliberate, self-awareness process in which managers "plan to plan";
- a top-down approach;
- fundamental questions about purposes, priorities and options;
- a review of existing policies in the light of changing circumstances;
- major acts of choice, often leading to significant changes in direction;
- new frameworks for subsequent decision-making;
- a longer-term perspective than is typical of "normal" decisions;
- a wider or more strategic perspective than usual;
- a deeper, more analytical or "rational" approach.

Strategic management is a process comprising strategic analysis, strategic choice and strategy implementation. It is a systematic, comprehensive and continuous process which takes account of the resources and capability of the organisation and the environment within which it has to operate. Strategic management attempts to achieve a situation where the needs of the client/customer are viewed as a whole. The activities of the organisation should be planned, directed and controlled in a unified manner to make the best use of available resources.

A strategic management model

According to Bryson (1988), strategy helps public organisations and communities respond effectively to changing situations. A model of strategic management based on the work of Bryson consists of 10 activities:

1. Development of an initial agreement (plan to plan)
2. Identification and clarification of mandates
3. Development and clarification of vision, mission and values
4. External environment assessment
5. Internal environment assessment
6. Strategic issues identification
7. Strategy options appraisal
8. Strategy selection and formalisation

9. Strategy implementation
10. Strategy evaluation

Each activity requires elaboration.

The initial agreement (1) should identify the rationale for strategy, the organisational arrangements for the development of a strategic plan (composition of planning committee) and the milestones and timescales for the strategy formulation stages of the process.

Activity 2 involves clarification of internal and external mandates; these are those functions and services which the organisation must provide.

Activity 3 involves a clarification of future aspirations linked to organisational values and purposes and Activity 4 comprises environmental scanning to determine current and future external influences on the organisation.

Activity 5 is an assessment of the organisations strengths and weaknesses taking into account organisational resources (inputs), present activities and strategy (process) and current performance (output and outcomes). Activity 6 is the result of stages 1–5 where those issues fundamental to the future success of the organisation are clarified. This requires a succinct statement of what the issues are, why are they significant, and what the consequences would be of failure to address the issue.

Bryson (ibid.) identifies three approaches to issues identification: the direct approach; the goals approach; and the scenario approach. The direct approach is a product of the consideration of mandates, mission and vision linked to SWOT (strengths, weaknesses, opportunities and threats) analysis. From this strategic issues are identified. The goals approach is where the organisation formulates goals and objectives and then develops strategies to achieve them while the scenario approach involves the formulation of a "vision of success". The strategic issues then concern how the organisation can move towards this strategic vision and the scenarios are alternative paths to success.

Activity 7 involves subjecting strategic options to a range of appraisal techniques to determine their suitability (does the option address identified strategic issues?), acceptability (will the option meet the demands of resource cost, risk and stakeholder reactions?) and feasibility (does the organisation have the resources and competences to implement successfully?). (Johnson and Scholes, 2002 pp.384–398).

Activity 8 involves the selection of the preferred strategy and communicating this to all stakeholders. In a Scottish public sector context, this may require the approval of councillors, Health Board members, government agencies and the Scottish Executive.

Activity 9 (implementation) translates the selected strategy (plan) into action (see Ch. 9).

Activity 10 concerns the assessment of the success or otherwise of the strategy to inform further strategic development. The strategic management process is cyclical and ongoing. It is not uncommon for strategic plans to be submitted to government (or its agencies) on an annual basis.

Conclusion

The New Public Management (NPM) has shifted the onus of effective implementation from the public policy formulators to those organisations and individuals charged with responsibility for implementation. Such implementors have in the past had limited control over policy content and policy planning but community planning provides an opportunity to extend involvement in the policy process to multiple stakeholders. Community planning implies delegation and such delegation of responsibility is part and parcel of the NPM and requires more people to possess policy implementation competences. Community planning cannot succeed in the absence of policy implementation competences in decision-takers. This necessary competency enhancement cannot be achieved without comprehensive training and development programmes for all stakeholders involved in the community planning process. There has been a tendency in recent years to replace public administration training and development with generic management training and development, but this does not address the special nature of management in the public sector.

Public policy implementation literature tends to reflect the public administration context of its heyday in the 1970s and early 1980s. The focus then was on improving policy formulation to take account of potential implementation problems and thus to counter the failures due to bad policy identified in the multiplicity of real case studies. However, there has clearly been insufficient attention given to policy failures due to bad execution and bad luck. This, coupled with the changing context of public policy and the advent of New Public Management, has shifted practitioners' requirements. Public managers need theory from the academic literature to guide practice (implementation is discussed more fully in Ch.9).

Under community planning, public policy is formulated by multiple stakeholders. Policy implementors in Scottish local government are local government officers, and both formulators and implementors need (and want) training in strategic and operational management to develop competences, including: public policy implementation; project management; operational planning, monitoring, review and evaluation; leadership and motivation; communication; performance management; and the management of change. There will always be policy implementation failures due to unforeseen circumstances in the real world but public policy implementation literature has tried to make all stakeholders more aware of those factors likely to contribute to such failures believing that being forewarned allows for forearming. Community planning is at the beginning of its implementation, time will tell whether it becomes a public policy success or a failure.

This chapter has considered the range of influences on local government decision-making in Scotland. Traditional approaches to decision-making focused on the local government committee system but in contemporary practice decision takers have become much more managerial, taking into account environmental constraints and the concern to promote effective public policy implementation. Scottish local government elected members and managers have to work in partnership to promote the strategic objectives of the authority. In order to promote compliance and effectiveness local authorities and NHS Boards have to manage performance and this subject is discussed in Ch.9.

CHAPTER 7

ACCOUNTABILITY, REDRESS AND RESPONSIVENESS

INTRODUCTION

In this chapter we explore the linkages between local authorities, health boards and their stakeholders. Some stakeholders provide resources and others are clients and consumers of public services. Public accountability requires many means of accounting. In recent years, lines of accountability in the public domain have become less clearly defined as new forms of organisation develop but nevertheless, public sector organisations must be accountable for their actions and expenditures. Stakeholders must also have access to redress processes to facilitate the resolution of disagreements between citizens and public service organisations. Responsiveness means public sector organisations responding to citizens by taking into account diverse needs and wants and the various pressures that stakeholders can bring to bear on the public sector organisation.

ACCOUNTABILITY

Gray (1983, pp.29–31) suggests that it is helpful to consider accountability in the context of a principal/agent relationship, using the senses of the term found in the common law of contract. Agents will normally be found by two distinguishable responsibilities, one for the action they take, and the other for accounting for those actions to their principals. It is the second responsibility that we know as accountability.

According to Greenwood, Pyper and Wilson (2002, pp.232–233), accountability has several components, the first and weakest of which is answerability, or explanatory accountability. The stronger and more complete version of accountability adds to answerability the components of sanctions, amendatory accountability and redress of grievances.

The Scottish Ministers are responsible, with Parliament's approval, for determining the amount of funding to be made available to local authorities, but they are not accountable for the way in which the funding provided is utilised. It is for local authorities to determine their expenditure priorities from the different resources available to them, following consultation with their local electors. The 32 local authorities in Scotland are independent legal entities accountable to their local electorate. Responsibility for the determination of local authorities' strategy lies with local elected councillors. The conduct of councillors in relation to openness, accountability and transparency is governed by a code of conduct issued by the Scottish Ministers and approved by the Scottish Parliament in March 2002 under the Ethical Standards in Public Life etc. (Scotland) Act 2002 (Audit Scotland, 2002).

There are many ways in which Health Boards and local authorities are held accountable and this chapter will first examine accountability and redress in its traditional forms including public accountability, legislative accountability and accountability to Government, before considering the additional, contemporary, regimes of accountability.

A key principle in public administration is public accountability. Public bodies have to account for their activities to their stakeholders. Stakeholders include government and other funding bodies as well as clients and communities. In carrying out their functions local authorities are expected to act equitably in their dealings with others and to comply with legislative constraints on their activities. There are many sub-elements of public accountability.

Political accountability

This includes the accountability of politicians to the electorate, the accountability of officials to politicians and the accountability of nominated persons to their sponsoring organisations. There is also "ministerial responsibility" on the part of government ministers for actions carried out by or under the auspices of the minister's government department and the accountability of the minister to Parliament.

Managerial accountability

This is concerned with making those managers with delegated authority answerable to their hierarchical superiors for carrying out agreed tasks to pre-determined standards of performance. Dimensions of this, according to Day and Klein (1987, p.27), include:

> "fiscal or regularity accountability to spend according to rules and regulations; process or efficiency accountability to demonstrate value for money; and programme or effectiveness

accountability to ensure that a given course of action achieves its intended result."

The term "accountable management" is one version of managerial accountability and involves more systematic use of management accounting, the creation of cost or responsibility centres to clarify managerial tasks by establishing links between resources and objectives, and sub-dividing departmental activities into separate accountable units (Fulton, 1968, para.150).

Financial accountability

This concerns the responsibility of the agent for the financial resources made available by the principal. Financial accountability is through annual accounts and internal and external audit. Improvements in accounting practices in the public sector are seen as being able to assist in locating the inefficiencies of the past and ensuring that better performance is achieved in the future, not least by making public sector management and employees accountable for their actions and decisions.

Professional accountability

This can be identified in situations where professional bodies have documented codes of conduct for their members. This normally results in the very limited need for supervision or control among professionals. Accountability is through compliance with standards generated within the professional peer group and monitored by representatives of the profession.

Market accountability

This is a key element in the changes that have taken place in public management has been the introduction of markets and quasi-markets in different parts of the public sector. Developments such as compulsory competitive tendering (CCT) and charges for public services to external and internal "customers" created "market-place surrogates" in the public sector (Pyper, 1996). Failure to meet the demands of the "market" could result in loss of the contract for the delivery of services. Failure to generate sufficient "business" can lead to budget shortfalls.

Legislative accountability

Local authorities and health boards in Scotland are statutory bodies, created and given powers and duties by Acts of the Scottish Parliament. The structure and functions of local government and the NHS, however, can be, and frequently are, modified by legislation. Indeed, both systems ocould be lawfully abolished by an Act of the Scottish Parliament.

Local authorities and health boards must act, at all times, in accordance with the powers and duties conferred upon them by Parliament through the relevant legislation. To act outwith the law is to act "ultra vires" (beyond one's powers). The place of local governments in the political system is not, however, derived solely from its former constitutional relationship with a sovereign parliament. Sovereignty of the Scottish Parliament is underpinned by a body of custom and convention as to the manner in which that sovereignty should be exercised. The position of local government in the political system is, therefore, governed by constitutional convention as well as by the simple fact that it derives its existence and its powers from the Scottish Parliament.

There is, in fact, no validity in the assertion that local authorities have a "local mandate" by which they derive authority from their own electorate, thus seeking to place themselves above the law. The electoral basis of local government merely lends added authority to actions that are taken within the law and to any proposals made for changes to the law, but does not provide the right to act outside or above the law.

Through the legislative process, Scottish local authorities have, over the years, been given responsibility for administering a wide range of public services. Many of these services are diverse and seemingly have little in common; nevertheless local government ensures that the wide range of interests and needs, both current and future, of the community are considered and evaluated and that the services and functions are shaped and organised to meet these particular interests and needs.

Local Authority Functions

The Widdicombe Committee (1986) stated that the character of local government in Great Britain is determined by:

> "the fact that it is the creation of Parliament; and the particular legislative form that Parliament has given to it."

Local authorities are empowered to carry out certain functions and these fall into two major groups:

Mandatory or compulsory functions

These are services which the local authority must provide, *i.e.* they have a duty under statute to perform them. Most services come into this category, *e.g.* education authorities must provide schools and teachers.

Permissive functions

These are services which the local authorities may perform, at their discretion. The power to establish a local art gallery or theatre is given to the appropriate authority and they may be created if the council consider that such institutions are needed.

Statutory powers

Local authorities need statutory powers to carry out functions which they are required to perform by Parliament. The following are ways in which these powers are given to local authorities.

Public (or General) Acts of Parliament

These Acts relate to matters of public policy and are introduced directly by the Government or, individually, by Members of Parliament. These Acts may require a local authority to carry out a specific function.

Private Acts of Parliament

These Acts are used when local authorities wish to carry out some task for which they have no powers under existing legislation. Since local authorities may do only what the law permits, they must, in such circumstances, apply for the necessary powers through a Private Act.

These Acts are not very common in Scotland.

Adoptive or Permissive Acts of Parliament

These Acts are general, public Acts, which confer powers on those local authorities who choose to "adopt" them by taking the prescribed steps to make the Acts apply to themselves. The procedure allows a local authority to provide particular services, but does not make it obligatory.

Provisional Orders

These Orders enable local authorities to acquire powers more simply than by private bill legislation. Under the Private Legislation Procedure (Scotland) Act 1936, a local authority can apply to the Scottish Office for an order which will enable the authority to acquire the power. The provisional order is in effect a parliamentary bill, and it becomes legislation by the process of a Provisional Order Confirmation Act in Parliament which incorporates the provisional order as a schedule.

Secondary legislation

Increasingly, Acts of Parliament provide powers to Government Ministers to make regulations (statutory instruments) which direct or regulate local authority activity or describe the manner in which a power is to be exercised.

Subordinate legislation

Local authorities themselves have the power to make subordinate local legislation. The power to do so has to be granted in an Act of Parliament, however, the making of bye-laws is an important source of local authority power and they enable local authorities to regulate a wide range of activities carried out in their areas. A local authority can make bye-laws for the good rule and government of the whole or any part.

Other examples include local orders such as road closure orders, traffic regulation orders, compulsory purchase orders and other directions under various statutes.

Remedies in Scots law as identified by O'Donnell (1996) include:

- *Reduction*, whereby decisions of local authorities may be set aside as a consequence of the courts deciding that the local authority acted in excess of jurisdiction, in breach of natural justice or otherwise contrary to law;
- *Declarator* is an action where an interested party seeks to have a legal right declared without any claim on the defender to do anything;
- *Interdict* is a judicial prohibition preventing an action. An *interim interdict* is a temporary prevention order usually issued pending a fuller consideration of the claim;
- *Action for damages* is a claim for monetary compensation for loss suffered; and
- *Specific implement* is a remedy to enforce performance of statutory duties.

Central-Local Relations

Local authorities are separate, in law, from central government. They are not "the regional offices of the central government departments" nor agents of the Government or the Crown, although they may undertake to act on behalf of a government department. However, all governments are concerned with the ways in which public money is used by local authorities and the extent to which local authorities are accountable for their actions. As a consequence a complex relationship has developed between local government and central government which is partly about the use of public funds and partly about accountability.

Local government is not sovereign, and central government has an undoubted right and duty, ultimately, to control the executive actions of local government. On the other hand, local government, as an institution of government with an elective basis and with the power to raise some finance, enjoys a constitutional status which ought to be matched by genuine local answerability. Both levels of government, therefore, have powers and responsibilities and, to an extent, there is likely to be some conflict about local autonomy.

In theory, the Scottish Executive and the Scottish Parliament retain overall control over the shape and direction of new services provided in the locality while the actual running of those services, and the assessment of local priorities among those services, are recognised as the clear responsibility of local government.

Both groups of functions are indispensable and so, although the Scottish Executive is obviously much more powerful, in a real sense the relationship between central and local governments can be regarded as a partnership. At least, both sides must appreciate that their actions have a consequential effect on the other.

The relationships between central government and local authorities has developed and changed over the years. There was virtually no contact between the two before 1830 and, even after the creation of an embryonic local government structure on a national scale and the related legislation of the second half of the nineteenth century (*e.g.* concerning education, housing and environmental health), local authorities still enjoyed a high level of autonomy. The twentieth century saw a steady erosion of that independence, as central government came to recognise that many local functions are national in importance.

Nevertheless, local authorities still retain discretion in certain areas with regard to the day-to-day running of services, provided that specified minimum standards are met. Local authorities are thus relatively free to develop and to vary the scope of the services they provide to meet local needs. Indeed, the very fact that central government needs the co-operation of local authorities in the administration of various services gives the latter some opportunities for influence in the determination of relevant policies.

Central-local relations take many forms, each operating in a particular way, but the two institutions are bound together by the overall purpose of promoting a more effective local government service. On the part of central government, the emphasis in these relationships tends to be on control of local authority activities, whereas local councils want more freedom to make local democracy more meaningful. Inevitably, therefore, this relationship is complicated and contentious.

The role of the Scottish Executive

The Scottish Executive must concern itself with total local government expenditure and taxation. It also has responsibility for the development of policy for particular services. The Scottish Executive's role is, therefore:

(a) to ensure that local services reflect national priorities and national policies and are provided at broadly comparable standards;

(b) to ensure that, in aggregate, local government spending plans are compatible with the government's economic objectives;

(c) to ensure that activities of one authority do not have adverse effects on the area of another;
(d) to promote co-operation between local authorities and between local government and other complementary services;
(e) to ensure that the financial arrangements promote efficiency;
(f) to safeguard the interests of vulnerable minority groups in society, whose interests may gain a proper hearing only at national level; and
(g) to encourage and maintain local democracy.

This view of central government's role was set out clearly by the government in its response to the Layfield Committee (on local government finance (1976)) and can be summarised thus:

(i) to ensure that money is well spent;
(ii) to manage the economy; and
(iii) to ensure equality in the provision of local government services.

Local authorities have been subject to much closer scrutiny in recent years, as central government has exercised increasing control over the detail of their activities, especially in the most important sphere—local expenditure. Scottish local authorities are subject mainly to the control of the Scottish Executive, but also to Westminster; and the institutions of the European Community.

There are many justifications for this central government control of local councils. Local authorities secure most of their money, for both capital and revenue purposes, from central government. Therefore, it seems reasonable that, in such circumstances, central government has a right to impose controls. Also, central government represents the taxpayers, who are in effect funding local government and it is, therefore, its duty to ensure that this money is properly spent.

Thus, some degree of control may be justified, but the extent of central intervention is consistently criticised. Critics point out that in other systems, *e.g.* Sweden, local authorities receive even more money from the national government, but are freer to spend it as they wish.

Government is responsible for the economy as a whole and so must be concerned with the implications of local government expenditure. The Conservative Administrations tried to limit public expenditure, including that of local councils, as a means of reducing inflation, in pursuit of "monetarist" policies. This led to stringent limits on local spending, through such devices as imposing cash limits and rate-capping, and in reducing Rate Support

Grant, etc. As a result, the proportion of public spending attributable to local government has fallen over the last few years. Although spending has been limited, the demands on local authorities, however, have not been correspondingly reduced. Indeed, largely because of central government policies and direction, local councils have found themselves with greater tasks to perform, with less resources at their disposal. This trend has been maintained by the Labour Government and local authorities still feel that they are having to do "more with less".

Central government has assumed that economies could be made while maintaining the level of services, but this has proved very difficult to achieve. Although minor variations in standards of service are inevitable, in the interests of justice, levels of provision should be reasonably uniform nationally. This implies a certain element of central control, to ensure quality and equality.

Local autonomy

If local government is to be true to its name, then local authorities should really govern their communities, rather than merely acting as the agents of central departments. Ideally, local government implies democratic accountability and responsiveness to the wishes of the community. Other justifications for local autonomy are:

(a) *Legislative*

Statutes allocate the provision of services to local authorities within certain limits. Accordingly, if the local authority continues to operate within these legislative limits, it should, it is argued, be relatively free from central government intervention.

(b) *Democratic*

Local authorities have their own political power base. They comprise elected representatives of the community and so should be accountable to them, rather than to central government. On the other hand, central government can claim to be acting in the "superior" national interest.

(c) *Financial*

Local authorities have powers to raise a certain amount of revenue through council tax and business rates, as well as through revenue from charging service users.

(d) *Geographic*

Local authorities are responsible for the provision of services to a defined geographic area and, as such, the provision of these services will vary between local government areas. The totality of needs of the population in each area is unique and, therefore, central government should permit local authorities to decide how best to meet the particular needs of their specific population.

The various traditional central controls may be categorised, to illustrate the similarities of the controls as exercised over the different services and to demonstrate the wide range of restrictions employed. A four-fold classification is both the most obvious and the most useful, as follows:

(i) performance governance as legislative controls such as Acts of Parliament, provisional orders, statutory orders, delegated legislation and circulars;
(ii) performance governance as financial controls such as grants, borrowing, restrictions on general expenditure, audit and performance information published by audit scotland;
(iii) performance governance as administrative controls such as powers of direction, the approval of bye-laws, inspections, inquiries, powers to act in default, control over officers, the settlement of disputes and control over grants; and
(iv) performance governance as judicial controls such as *ultra vires* and actions as a consequence of a local authority's failure to perform its statutory duties.

Contemporary accountability

The traditional forms of accountability remain but they have been supplemented by a range of contemporary regimes which clearly impact on the ways in which local authorities are held accountable for their actions. Contemporary regimes tend to enhance the quantity and quality of information which must be made available to all stakeholders and generally promote clear, user-friendly complaints systems. As a consequence, contemporary regimes of accountability in Scottish local government promote answerability or explanatory accountability. In addition, many local authority commit themselves to responsiveness to stakeholder grievances and have developed systems for allowing stakeholders to lodge complaints and to have them considered within a set period of time.

Financial accountability

The extension of the powers of the Comptroller and Auditor General and the National Audit Office by statute has enabled these bodies to examine the use of public monies by public sector organisations. In evidence to the Treasury and Civil Service Sub-Committee on the role of the Civil Service, former civil servant Sir Kenneth Stowe argued that "the machinery of public audit in the UK is the most vital component of good practice." (HM Treasury and Civil Service Sub-Committee, 1994, para.28)

Public sector organisations are primarily publicly funded and there is therefore a concern in performance governance to ensure that public funds are used well. To this end government agencies try to monitor the extent to which public sector organisations deliver Value For Money (VFM), *i.e.* make good use of public funds. VFM is commonly sub-divided into three headings for the purpose of evaluation, these are, economy, efficiency and effectiveness. The first E is economy and is defined by the Treasury as, "a situation where the actual inputs are equal to or less than the planned inputs".

The Accounts Commission (1986, p.28) defines economy as involving:

> "The consideration of the way in which the public authority acquires resources (input). An economical operation acquires these resources in the appropriate quality and quantity at the lowest cost."

The second E is efficiency and is, according to the Accounts Commission (*ibid.*), the relationship between goods or services produced (outputs) and the resources (inputs) used to produce them. An efficient operation produces the maximum output for any given set of resource inputs, or uses minimum inputs for any given quality and quantity of goods produced or services provided.

The third E is effectiveness and, according to the Comptroller and Auditor General (1985), it is: "the achievement of established goals or other intended effects". Cost-effectiveness is therefore the achievement of goals or other intended effects at a reasonable cost, which normally means within the constraints of the available level of resourcing.

VFM uses the three Es despite conflicts between them and within them. The most efficiently delivered service may not be effective if its output fails to meet objectives or produce intended outcomes. VFM is arguably efficiency-led rather than customer-driven. It is concerned with supply not demand or user specification (Wilson and Hinton, 1993, p.65).

In order to meet the need of performance governance, government requires that public sector organisations have their accounts audited annually. Additionally, Audit Scotland and other auditing bodies have responsibilities for additional areas of scrutiny of performance through powers related to the publication of performance related in formation. For example, Audit Scotland sees these powers as part of an evolutionary process aimed at improving local authority performance.

Audit

Fiduciary care

Scottish public bodies are responsible for establishing proper arrangements to ensure that public business is conducted in accordance with the law and proper standards, and that public money is safeguarded and properly accounted for, and used well. The term "fiduciary care" informs the rationale of public audit. The basic concept is that a body charged with the administration, for definite purposes, of funds contributed, in whole or in part, by persons other than the members of that body, owes a duty to those persons to conduct the administration in a fairly businesslike manner, with reasonable care, skill and caution, and with a due and alert regard to the interests of those contributors who are not members of the body. In other words, council tax payers and government fund local authorities yet are not part of that organisation, therefore the local authority has a duty of fiduciary care to government and to council tax payers.

Audit forms

Audit plays an important part in promoting fiduciary care through comprehensive financial monitoring systems at all organisational levels. There are two main forms of financial audit in local government: internal audit, or external audit.

In relation to internal audit, local authorities employ their own auditors to conduct independent appraisals of financial management within the local authority. Internal audit has four main functions:

(a) verifying for management that there is an adequate system of internal control within the local authority;
(b) drawing to the attention of management any deficiencies in the organisation or the system of control;
(c) developing the control system; and
(d) carrying out special reviews or assignments on subjects worthy of further investigation or where management request such a review.

Therefore, internal audit is a management control which measures, evaluates and reports upon the effectiveness of the internal financial control system and the extent to which there is efficient use of resources within the local authority. There is now an extended remit in many local authorities to monitor performance and "Best Value".

External audit is carried out by Audit Scotland. Audit Scotland was established under the Public Finance and Scotland Act 2000 to provide audit services on behalf of the Auditor General for Scotland and the Accounts Commission. Audit Scotland levies charges on local government bodies for audits undertaken on behalf of the Accounts Commission (see Ch.4).

Under the code of audit practice the auditor's objectives are to:

- provide an opinion on the audited body's financial statements and the regularity of transactions;

- review and report on the audited body's corporate governance arrangements and aspects of its arrangements to manage its performance, as they relate to economy, efficiency and effectiveness in the use of resources;
- review and report on relevant local government bodies' arrangements for preparing and publishing specified performance information and compliance with requirements in relation to Best Value.

The financial statements of public bodies are an essential means by which they account for the stewardship of the resources made available and their performance in the use of these resources. Under the Public Finance and Accountability (Scotland) Act 2000, auditors appointed by the Auditor General are specifically required to give an opinion on the regularity of audited bodies' expenditure and receipts (see Ch.4).

Corporate governance

Corporate governance is concerned with structures and processes for decision-making, accountability, control and behaviour at the senior levels of the organisation. Each audited body has a responsibility to put in place arrangements for the conduct of its affairs, to ensure the legality of activities and transactions and to monitor the adequacy and effectiveness of these arrangements in practice.

The code of audit practice gives auditors a responsibility to review and, where appropriate, report findings on the audited body's corporate governance arrangements as they relate to:

- The audited body's review of its systems of internal control and reporting arrangement.
- The prevention and detection of fraud and irregularity.
- Standards of conduct, and arrangements in relation to the prevention and detection of corruption.
- The financial position of the audited body.

The Role of the Accounts Commission

The Scottish Ministers appoint the members of the Accounts Commission but they act independently both of central and local government. The Accounts Commission contributes to how local government bodes are held to account in a number of ways.

First, under the Local Government Scotland Act 1973, the Controller of Audit (a member of staff of Audit Scotland appointed by the Accounts Commission with the consent of Scottish Ministers) may prepare a report either at his discretion or at the request of the Accounts Commission with respect to the accounts of local government bodies. The Accounts Commission can hold a hearing into the report and/or make recommendations to the Scottish Ministers or to any local government body as appears to the Commission to be appropriate.

The Controller may also make a special report on a local government body to the Accounts Commission where in his opinion there has been illegal expenditure or a failure to account for money; where there has been a loss because of negligence, misconduct or because of the body's failure to carry out a duty; or where there has been a mistake in the accounts which the body is not putting right. The Accounts Commission may decide to hold a hearing, normally heard in public, so that it can have any matter raised in the Controller's report clarified or amplified. The Commission must make available a copy of its findings arising from the hearing available to the public. The sanctions available to the Commission include the censure of an officer or member, the suspension of a member for up to one year or the disqualification of a member for up to five years.

The Account Commission also undertakes, via Audit Scotland and appointed auditors, comparative studies designed to enable it to make recommendations for improving economy, efficiency and effectiveness in the provision of services by local authorities and for improving the financial or other management of such authorities. The results of such studies are published and auditors are subsequently expected, as part of their audits, to review how the Accounts Commission's recommendations have been implemented.

Finally, under the Local Government (Scotland) Act 1992, the Accounts Commission is required to give directions to local authorities requiring them to publish performance information. Audit Scotland assists in this process by annually consulting with local authorities and other bodies on the most relevant performance information to be collated. Auditors appointed by the Accounts Commission audit the performance information compiled by the local authorities, against common performance indicators prescribed for selected service areas. The resultant performance indicators, which are published by the Accounts Commission, enable service comparisons to be made between local authorities.

Local authorities have traditionally adopted a committee structure to support their decision-making processes, operated under a scheme of delegation as laid down in the local authority's standing orders. Typically, the full council devolves authority to service and other committees to take decisions on its behalf, with the meetings of the full council formally approving any recommendations made to it. Committees, comprising cross-party membership and responsible for major service or policy areas such as education and social work, hold local authority departments to account for their performance.

In recent years, partly in response to national and local initiatives on joined-up government, some councils have moved away from the traditional committee based structures. Others developed committees covering, for example, social and community development and lifelong learning, which covered the professional responsibilities of a number of departments and services so that councillors could consider the full range of issues relating to a particular policy area.

Accountability in local authorities is also further reinforced in stature by the requirement for councils to appoint two further members of staff with particular responsibilities. First, local authorities are required to make proper arrangements for the proper administration of their financial affairs and must appoint an officer, normally the director of finance or equivalent, with responsibility to administer these affairs. Secondly, local authorities must appoint a monitoring officer. The monitoring officer is responsible for reporting to the council if it, or one of its committees, has taken or is considering action which would result in a contravention to any statutory provision or maladministration or injustice (Audit Scotland, 2002).

Redress

The current NHS complaints procedure

The current UK-wide NHS complaints procedure was introduced in April 1996. It has three stages:

(a) *Local Resolution:* involves situations where the service provider attempts to resolve a complaint as directly and as quickly as possible, with the primary aim of being fair to both the person making the complaint and to its staff. Local resolution may involve an immediate informal response from frontline staff or it may require an internal investigation, use of conciliation or direct action by a Chief Executive.

(b) *Independent review:* where a complaint cannot be resolved locally, the person making the complaint may apply for an independent review. The right to have a complaint reviewed is not automatic. A request for a review is considered by the Convener, in consultation with an independent layperson who has received training in chairing review panels.

(c) *Ombudsman review*: where the person making the complaint is refused an independent review or is dissatisfied with the outcome of such a review, they may ask the Scottish Public Services Ombudsman to consider the matter. The person complained against can also seek an Ombudsman review in certain circumstances.

A complaints procedure should be credible, easy to use, demonstrably independent, effective and sensitively applied. Making a formal complaint can be stressful for people involved, both for those making the complaint and for the staff involved. The procedure must be seen to be fair to both sides. It must support the person making the complaint and be fair to the staff complained against. It must also ensure that the NHS can learn and grow positively from the experience.

Drawing on comments made on the evaluation report and the Cabinet Office's *Service First Principles* an effective complaints procedure would:

- be well publicised, accessible and subject to independent monitoring;
- contribute to achieving a patient-focused health service where comments and suggestions are welcomed as a learning opportunity;
- have clear lines of accountability for complaints handling;
- be integrated into the clinical governance/quality framework of the NHS organisation;
- provide support to those making and handling complaints;
- be demonstrably fair to both the person making the complaint and the staff complained against;
- resolve complaints within a "reasonable" time frame.

While the chief executive of each NHS organisation is ultimately responsible for the quality of care delivered by their organisation, they should appoint a named senior member of their executive team to take responsibility for delivering the organisation's patient feedback and complaints process. This individual should hold a position allowing them to remain abreast of major potential problem areas.

Each NHS organisation, including GP practices, should assign the task of dealing with complaints to a person of sufficient seniority to be able to deal with the issues raised quickly and effectively without needing to refer, in all but the most exceptional circumstances, to more senior staff.

Accountability within local NHS systems

NHS Boards will be strategic bodies, accountable to the Scottish Executive Health Department and to Ministers for:

- the designated functions of the NHS Board; and
- the performance of the local NHS system.

NHS Boards should not concern themselves with day-to-day operational matters, except where they have a material impact on the overall performance of their local NHS system. All members of NHS Boards will share collective responsibility for the overall performance of their local NHS system, including the performance of its separate component parts.

The Scottish Public Services Ombudsman

The Scottish Public Services Ombudsman Act 2002 established, from October 2002, a one-stop shop ombudsman service, headed by the Scottish Public Services Ombudsman. The new service incorporates the range of services previously provided by the Scottish Parliamentary Ombudsman, the Scottish Health Services Ombudsman, the Scottish Local Government Ombudsman and the Housing Association Ombudsman for Scotland. The new service will also take over the Mental Welfare Commission's function of investigating complaints relating to mental health and complaints against Scottish Enterprise and Highlands and Islands Enterprise whose External Complaints Adjudicators will be abolished.

The new arrangements are intended to be more open, accountable and accessible to the public by providing simpler and more effective means for members of the public to make complaints. In addition, the new service reinforces the Ombudsman's independence from the authorities within his or her jurisdiction and improves publicity and transparency of the Ombudsman's functions. The Ombudsman can investigate complaints from members of the public and requests from a listed authority. The latter allows a listed authority to request an investigation as a means of addressing cases where there has been public criticism of an authority but no resultant formal complaint by an individual. The intention is that this option should be used as a last resort.

Complaints may be made by the person aggrieved or their authorised representative and must be submitted within 12 months of the day on which the person aggrieved first had notice of the matter complained of. The process of investigation is at the discretion of the Ombudsman who has the same powers as the Court of Session in respect of the attendance and examination of witnesses and the production of documents. Complaints have to be in writing or by electronic communications, but the Ombudsman has discretion to accept oral complaints in special circumstances.

The new provisions remove any inconsistencies in the previous arrangements for consultation and co-operation between existing Scottish public sector ombudsmen and their counterparts in England and Wales. They also introduce new provision for the Ombudsman to share information with auditors, examiners and the UK and Scottish Information Commissioners. The overall aim is to provide a clear and consistent framework for co-operation, consultation and information sharing between office-holders within the public sector, and thereby promote joined-up working. The sharing of experience, expertise and knowledge should also be improved.

The main exclusions affecting local government are:

(a) matters affecting all, or most, of the inhabitants of an area, *e.g.* the general level of council tax;
(b) contractual and commercial transactions, except the sale or purchase of land;
(c) matters concerning professional judgement in education;
(d) personnel matters.

Investigation reports must be laid before the Scottish Parliament and sent to the listed authority investigated. The Ombudsman can make a Special Report on any case where it is considered that the complainant has suffered an injustice or hardship which has not been, or will not be, remedied. The Ombudsman must lay any special report before the Parliament and copy it to those who were sent the relevant investigation report. These provisions are more detailed than those of the former Scottish Parliamentary and Health Service Ombudsmen but are less prescriptive than those for the former Local Government Ombudsman. They enable the Ombudsman to publicise cases of unremedied injustice or hardship and to draw them to the attention of the Parliament. These arrangements allow a reasonable degree of flexibility, while being sufficiently rigorous to encourage compliance with the Ombudsman's recommendations.

The Ombudsman must lay before the Scottish Parliament each year a general report on the performance achieved in relation to functions. The annual report may also include any general recommendations which the Ombudsman may have, arising from the consideration of complaints and requests during the year covered by the report. The Ombudsman may also lay before the Scottish Parliament such other reports considered appropriate for the Parliament to consider.

The Ombudsman and deputy Ombudsmen are appointed by Her Majesty on the nomination of Parliament. The Ombudsman and deputies are prevented from holding certain public appointments or paid offices during their period of appointment. They are also disqualified from certain public appointments or paid office for three years after appointment. These disqualifications provisions are designed to avoid conflicts of interest or allegations of corruption. The Ombudsman is not subject to the direction or control of any MSP, any member of the Scottish Executive or the Scottish Parliamentary Corporate Body (except with regard to the form and content of annual reports or the maintenance of accounts) (*www.scottishombudsman.org.uk*).

Maladministration

The term "maladministration" is not defined in the Scottish Public Services Ombudsman Act 2002. Nor was it defined in previous Ombudsman legislation. However in 1967, Mr Crossman, Leader of the House of Commons, gave the following examples of maladministration: "bias, neglect, inattention, incompetence, ineptitude, perversity, turpitude and arbitrariness and so on". This is known as the "Crossman catalogue".

Matters which may be investigated include maladministration in connection with any action taken by or on behalf of: the Scottish Parliament and the Scottish Administration; Scottish Health Service Organisations; Scottish local authorities; registered social landlords (housing); Scottish Public Authorities; and cross-border public authorities. The Ombudsman may investigate these matters only where there is a claim that a member of the public has sustained injustice or hardship in consequence of the maladministration, service failure or other action as appropriate. This does not entitle the Ombudsman to question discretionary decisions taken without maladministration. The 2002 Act identifies a range of restrictions and exclusions including a restriction relating to matters for which the complainant has, or had, a right of appeal to a Minister or a statutory tribunal, or a remedy by way of proceedings in a court of law. The Ombudsman does, however, have discretion to conduct an investigation where it is not reasonable to expect the person to use, or to have used, those courses of action.

Additional examples of maladministration were quoted in the UK Parliamentary Ombudsman's annual report for 1993:

- rudeness (although that is a matter of degree);
- unwillingness to treat the complainant as a person with rights;
- refusal to answer reasonable questions;
- neglecting to inform a complainant on request of his or her rights or entitlements;
- knowingly giving advice which is misleading or inadequate;
- ignoring valid advice or overruling considerations which would produce an uncomfortable result for the "overruler";
- offering no redress or manifestly disproportionate redress;
- showing bias because of colour, sex, or any other grounds;
- omission to notify those who thereby lost a right of appeal;
- refusal to inform adequately of the right of appeal;
- faulty procedures;
- failure by management to monitor compliance with adequate procedures;

- cavalier disregard of guidance which is intended to be followed in the interest of equitable treatment of those who use a service;
- partiality; and
- failure to mitigate the effects of rigid adherence to the letter of the law where this produces manifestly inequitable treatment.

The Standards Commission

The Ethical Standards in Public Life etc. (Scotland) Act 2000 requires Scottish Ministers to issue a code of conduct for councillors which sets out principles and rules for councillors conduct and also sets out rules on the treatment of councillors interests. The Act provides for the establishment of the Standards Commission for Scotland.

The Standards Commission for Scotland has a minimum of three members appointed by Scottish Ministers and a chief investigating officer who is charged with investigating and reporting to the Commission on cases where it is alleged that a councillor or a member of a public body has contravened a relevant code. The chief investigating officer has powers to require any person who is able to give relevant information or produce relevant documents, to do so. The chief investigating officer has the same powers as the Court of Session when dealing with civil proceedings to enforce the attendance and examination of witnesses and the production of documents.

The chief investigating officer reports to the Standards Commission and where a report of the chief investigating officer concludes that a councillor or a member of a devolved public body has contravened the councillors' code or the members' code respectively, that report is not submitted to the Standards Commission unless the councillor or member of a devolved public body has been given a copy of the proposed report and has had the opportunity to make representations on the alleged contravention and the proposed report. At the same time that a copy of the proposed report is given to the councillor or member of a devolved public body, the chief investigating officer is required to give a further copy to the appropriate local authority or public body. The Standards Commission may publish a report submitted to it by the chief investigating officer in whatever form it thinks fit and send it to whomsoever it thinks fit. The Standards Commission may direct the chief investigating officer to carry out further investigations, may hold a hearing or may take no action.

The sanctions available to the Standards Commission on concluding that there has been a breach of the relevant code are as follows:

- censure;

- partial suspension from attending some meetings for up to one year;
- suspension from attending all meetings for up to one year;
- disqualification for up to five years from membership of the council or public body.

Appeals against a finding by the Standards Commission are heard, in the first instance, by the Sheriff Principal and thereafter there is a further appeal to the Court of Session.

Responsiveness and Excellence

An influential study of 62 companies in the United States with outstandingly successful performance, conducted by Peters and Waterman (1982), identified eight attributes which are characteristic of excellent, effective and innovative companies. These are:

(a) a bias for action;
(b) autonomy and entrepreneurship;
(c) close to the customer;
(d) productivity through people;
(e) hand-on, values-driven management;
(f) "stick to the knitting"; and
(g) simultaneous, loose-tight properties.

Some of these characteristics are transferable to public sector organisations in the United Kingdom. However, it is far from certain that "excellence" in public management means the same as it does in business. Nevertheless, the measuring of excellence, *i.e.* reaching for and achieving high standards of performance, is very important regardless of the environment in which you manage.

The originators of the interest in Reinventing Government Movement (REGO) in the United States, Osborne and Gaebler (1992), used a methodology similar to Peters and Waterman in that they looked at successful managerial and administrative innovations drawn from US State and local governments. Osborne (1988) states that the reinvention perspective is compatible both with a commitment to business values and the modern political interest in less government. It has been supported by legislative provisions, promoted by former Vice-President Al Gore and requires, among other things, changes in public performance measurement and its reporting to clients and funders. The REGO movement resembles the new public administration of the 1970s but identifies dichotomous couplets that, according to Frederickson (1996), define its focus. The REGO movement sees a changing role for government in public service provision based on the changes implied in the dichotomies such as: steering rather than rowing; replacing bureaucratic processes with market processes; meeting the needs of customers not bureaucracy; earning rather than spending; preventing rather than curing; and moving from hierarchy to participating and teamwork.

Public managers are substantially constrained by legislative provisions and organisational mandates, but they can identify and respond to opportunities which enhance service delivery. Tension exists between accountability and responsiveness in public management. Potter (1988) suggests five dimensions of responsiveness:

(a) Access and accessibility—deciding who has the right of access to services and communicating the criteria by which access decisions are taken.
(b) Choice
(c) Information
(d) Redress
(e) Representation

Public managers must be responsive to a range of stakeholders including clients/patients, funding bodies and government at various levels. Clients and patients can seek to influence responsiveness through "voice" and "exit". "Voice" is where clients express dissatisfaction, "exit" is where they seek other service providers. There is a different balance between "voice" and "exit" in the private sector. According to Hirschman (1970), the balance in the private sector favours "voice". Voice is about expressing judgments and preferences, and participating in decision-making processes in an effective way. Exit is not an option for most people in relation to public services such as health, education and housing. Many people have to take the service provided by their council or health board because choice requires personal financial resources to go "private".

Conclusion

This chapter has considered the various ways in which local authorities and health boards are held accountable for their actions. Local authorities and health boards cannot act in an autonomous manner free from the demands of Scottish Executive policy direction. Nor can they ignore the wishes and influences of their clients and stakeholders. Local authorities and health board must be responsive to individuals and groups with a legitimate right to express their views on these public services.

Failure on the part of a local authority or a health board to be compliant with the demands of accountability may result in punitive measures being taken against them by the Scottish Executive.

New Public Management has created much greater client/consumer awareness and public service providers have an obligation to continue to inform these groups and to continue to respond as appropriate.

Chapter 8

BEST VALUE, COMMUNITY PLANNING AND PARTNERSHIPS

Introduction

This chapter considers three key themes of contemporary public management in Scotland. The starting point is a consideration of the implications of "Best Value" for public managers. Following this there is a review of community planning before considering the trend for partnership working.

Compulsory Competitive Tendering

Compulsory Competitive Tendering (CCT) was introduced in 1980 and initially applied to those services provided by local authorities in relation to building construction and maintenance, and highways construction and maintenance. The legislation required local authorities to put the specified services out to competitive tender. The process required a comparison of the costs of in-house provision with those of any interested private contractors and the award of the contract to the most competitive bidder. The legislation was extended to cover additional services such as cleaning, catering, refuse collection, ground maintenance and leisure management. The legislative basis for CCT in Scotland was abolished by the Local Government in Scotland Act 2003.

The underpinning rationale for CCT is based on public choice theory which uses the methods of neo-classical market economics to analyse politics and this approach, according to Carter (1998, p.184), has encouraged the use of marketplace surrogates to improve public service provision.

Under CCT, contracts which were won by the in-house bid submitted by the council service were subsequently operated by Direct Labour Organisations (DLOs) or Direct Service Organisations (DSOs). Under Best Value, councils are no longer required to have separate DLOs or DSOs, but if they choose to operate trading or commercial activities they must keep separate accounts for these activities.

According to Wilson and Game (1998, p.349), CCT had a major impact on the management of local authorities including the creation of divisions within an authority and the establishment of client and contractor relationship between service commissioners and service providers (DLO/DSO). This fragmentation often leading to the organisational sub-divisions perceiving themselves to be organisations in their own right with unclear systems of accountability (sub-optimisation).

The Local Government in Scotland Act 2003 abolished the legislative basis of CCT but does allow local authority trading. The Act identifies three different forms of local authority trading:

- With another local authority, in this case the income generated is not subject to restriction;
- With other public authorities or bodies, in this case the local authority must trade from its own surplus capacity in staff services, property and facilities, although the income it makes is not subject to restriction; and
- With other trading partners, in this case the local authority must trade from its own surplus capacity in staff services, property and facilities, and the income it makes will be subject to financial limits set by Ministers.

Best Value

"Best Value" was introduced on a voluntary basis in 1998 following the Programme for Government and it became a statutory duty following the Local Government in Scotland Act 2003. The objective of Best Value is to ensure that management and business practices in local government deliver better and more responsive public services.

Best Value in local government is about local authorities:

- Balancing quality service provision against costs;
- Achieving sustainable development;
- Being accountable and transparent, by engaging with the local community;
- Ensuring equal opportunities;
- Continuously improving the outcomes of the services they provide.

Best Value policy objectives

The Scottish Executive and Scottish local government share a commitment to deliver better quality public services. There was a broad consensus that in a number of critical areas, statutory frameworks and business practices needed updating to allow local government to deliver better quality services. The Scottish Executive and local government have been working in partnership to develop new statutory and management frameworks which better suit the needs of both central and local government. These frameworks have become known collectively as Best Value.

The reforms in local government will accommodate new approaches to service delivery. The introduction of the power to advance well-being and the duty of community planning encourages local authorities to look increasingly at partnerships and joint ventures to help deliver their services. While innovation and initiative are welcome in the public sector, increases in risk, and the pace of change need to be managed carefully. Best Value is a flexible system that puts quality and effective management to the fore.

Best Value background

In 1997, the incoming Labour Government introduced a "Best Value" approach in local government. Councils, as a consequence, have to produce meaningful and robust information to allow those who benefit from and pay for council services to judge performance. Councils are required to take stock of their present ways of working and to map out a path of change.

The key principles of Best Value are:

(a) accountability;
(b) transparency;
(c) continuous improvement;
(d) a planning framework; and
(e) ownership.

In relation to performance indicators, auditors should confirm the integrity and comparability of performance information including performance indicators. The role of performance indicators is one of significant importance within a framework that is principally one of self-assessment by managers. Performance indicators will be required by the auditor to confirm progress (or otherwise) and it is already clear that performance indicators will also be used to report on how a council compares with other similar councils (Robert Black, Controller of Audit, Accounts Commission). Audit Scotland expects that VFM studies will identify key performance indicators that can be developed and will also support the development of benchmarking groups.

All local government services have been applying a Best Value approach since 1997, following the guidance of the Best Value Task Force. This approach has included a commitment to continuous improvement and providing user-focused cost-effective services.

Performance Management and Planning (PMP) is a process whereby council managers and auditors assess the extent to which the authority is achieving Best Value. The PMP follow up audit assesses progress in relation to identified improvement actions and whether those actions are achieving their desired improvement objectives. There are four main stages to the PMP follow-up audit:

(a) The council manager provides the auditor with two completed self-assessment reports covering progress in implementing improvement actions and progress in improving key aspects of performance.
(b) The auditor then reviews the self assessments, checks samples of evidence and provides feedback.
(c) Any revisions agreed between the auditor and the council should be incorporated into the self-assessments.
(d) The auditor submits individual reports to council managers and produces a summary report for the Chief Executive.

An important step in achieving performance improvement is identifying shortfalls in desired performance and taking steps to meet the shortfalls. The Improvement Action Progress Report (IAPR) records the extent to which identified action has been implemented and the extent to which improvements in performance have been achieved. The IAPR does not identify overall improvements in service and therefore a Best Value Achievement Report (BVAR) is also required. The BVAR is a concise, evidence based, summary of what the service has achieved. Improvements may relate to providing a better service for customers, achieving a better policy impact for citizens more generally, reduced costs or greater efficiency. The improvements may have come through a variety of means including Best Value reviews, government policy, use of quality models, responding to feedback from users and benchmarking studies.

The Local Government in Scotland Act 2003 specifies a duty on Scottish local authorities to secure Best Value. In the Local Government in Scotland Act 2003, Best Value is defined in loose terms to mean councils achieving continuous improvement in the performance of all of their functions. Best Value emphasises the need to ensure improvement in the actual outcomes as well as improvement in the process of delivering services. The Act states that in securing continuous improvement in a particular service, councils are expected to maintain an acceptable balance between the quality of the service delivered and the cost of service delivery. Local authorities are expected to consider economy, efficiency, effectiveness and compliance with the requirements of equal opportunities legislation (the 4 Es).

The Act additionally requires that action taken by a local authority in meeting the duty of Best Value should contribute to the achievement of sustainable development and the promotion of an integrated approach to improving the economic, social and environmental well-being of a community.

A local authority which fully embraces Best Value will reflect the principles of Best Value in its:

(a) political management structure;
(b) corporate planning;
(c) derived service plans;
(d) consultation with some stakeholders;
(e) communications with staff and others;
(f) codes of governance;
(g) allocation of resources; and
(h) review practices.

A Best Value organisation will demonstrate commitment, leadership, responsiveness, consultation with sound governance and the management of resources. In its management processes, it will make use of review and options appraisal and will take account of competitiveness in trading and in the discharge of local authority functions. A Best Value organisation promotes sustainable development, equality and accountability.

Community planning

The Local Government in Scotland Act 2003 provides a framework for the development of Community Planning in Scotland. Community planning seeks to promote the integration of service delivery for a local government area by encouraging all organisations involved in service delivery to that area to participate in the planning process. It is fundamentally about recognising the range of stakeholder organisations and the desirability of improving coordination to enhance the quality of service delivery. Community planning is a product of the political desire to promote "joined up government" recognising that fragmented decision-taking by a range of separate service providing organisations leads to inefficiency, lack of responsiveness and poor quality public services.

An additional purpose of community planning is to enhance delegated decision-making and, as a consequence, empower local communities, neighbourhoods and individuals by making service delivery more transparent and understandable. Such empowerment promotes a sense of ownership and fully supports those key elements of local government identified by the Wheatley Commission 1966–69, *i.e.* power, effectiveness, local democracy and local involvement.

Community planning aims to ensure that people and communities are genuinely engaged in the decisions made on public services which affect them and, allied to this, there is a commitment from organisations to work together to provide better public services. Community planning is an evolving process in that it is recognised as the key over-arching partnership framework helping to co-ordinate other initiatives and partnerships and where necessary acting to rationalise and simplify multi-agency service provision. Community planning therefore has a capability to improve the connection between national priorities and those at regional and neighbourhood levels. Community planning should not be an additional or parallel process to the various strategies or partnership structures already in place.

Community planning partnerships bring together key participants and as a consequence facilitate improved linkages between national and local priorities. This should be a three-way process whereby local community planning partnerships can influence national direction, but also can help to co-ordinate the delivery of national priorities in a manner which clearly enables local sensitivities and perspectives to be taken into account. This process also allows for local or neighbourhood priorities to be identified and considered.

The "top-down" perspective, according to Barrett and Fudge (1981, pp.3–32), falsely assumes that all initiative is from the top or centre along with the ability to control the periphery or subordinate actors. The "bottom-up" perspective considers policy makers and implementors as more equal and the interaction between them is crucial to the study of policy implementation. Individuals' and organisations' actions and reactions may determine policy as much as policy itself determines actions and responses. Successful implementation depends on achieving consensus in the policy process. This perception of effective policy management undoubtedly informs community planning.

Marsh and Rhodes (1992) suggest that there is a choice between ways of looking at the policy process between the "top-down" and "bottom-up" approach. Hill (1997, p.377) acknowledges that in British public administration there has been substantial change, clearly initiated from the top (government). Dramatic value shifts through institutional changes have been promoted through public policies in areas such as further and higher education. According to Hill (1997, p.383), government in the period from 1979 has not demonstrated any great concern for consensus in the policy process. Hoggett (1996, pp.9–32) comments on the ways in which government has tried to combine "rowing" and "steering", intervening inconsistently, using controls—particularly output controls—that are susceptible to manipulation and undermine trust. Hill (1997, p.383) concludes that the analysis of policies does not require the prescription of a correct starting point at the top or the bottom.

Community planning is a process intended to result in a local authority and other local agencies, including community, voluntary and private sector interests, coming together to develop and implement a shared vision for promoting the well-being of their area. This is expressed in a jointly-agreed strategy called a community plan. The planning process incorporates community leadership provided by the local authority; a strategic vision for the whole area; community involvement; and partnership working.

Decision-making in Scottish local government in the future will have to follow the community planning model, but it is not an entirely new concept. For several years, Westminster government, Holyrood government and local authorities have been trying to improve the effectiveness of decision-making and public policy implementation. There has been concern for many years about the tendency to blame administrators for policy failure. The first major study of the implementation process was by Pressman and Wildavsky (1973) and since then many academics both in the United States and the United Kingdom have made interesting contributions to the body of literature on public policy implementation.

Many writers advocate more rational and systematic policy planning where the potential implementation problems are addressed before they arise. There is less literature on the ways in which the policy is operationalised through implementation and on the stages addressing review and evaluation. The public policy implementation literature is therefore targeted at policy formulation and policy planning. The question faced by public managers of "what to do with a policy?" remains largely unanswered by theorists. It appears to be based on the assumption that those responsible for implementation are (using Hood's terminology) "perfectly competent". In the transition from public administration to New Public Management (NPM), there is less concern amongst policy makers with "how" the policy is implemented as long as it is implemented. Implementation theory is examined in more detail in Ch.9.

Partnerships

Joint working

Over the next 20 years the number of people aged over 65 and over in Scotland will rise from 800,000 to 1.2 million (an increase of 50 per cent), and those over aged 85 will double to 174,000. Planning healthcare services for older people cannot be done by NHSScotland alone. NHS bodies, local authorities and the independent sector need to work together to support people in their own homes; help prevent people being admitted to hospital; and provide support on discharge. The Joint Future agenda promotes better joint working between health and local government. These bodies are now expected to jointly resource and manage community care services for older people. The new Community Health Partnerships must build on the existing work of local partnerships. Audit Scotland will develop measures that provide information on the performance of community services and their outcomes.

Joint management covers the elements needed to ensure a more co-ordinated and effective approach to community care services including planning, commissioning and operational management. It can have a number of elements:

- a high level joint board or committee
- a joint senior management group
- a new partnership body
- a joint manager at either high-level or locality level, or both.

The critical factor is that the relevant range of services is under joint management.

A Local Partnership Agreement ("LPA") is central to the development of joint management. Full LPAs have been received from all 32 local partnerships. These LPAs have been evaluated by a team from Audit Scotland, the Social Work Services Inspectorate and Joint Future Unit.

Joint governance and accountability

The LPAs outline the arrangements that local partnerships have put in place to ensure the proper joint governance and accountability of partnership arrangements, which are open to public scrutiny. These arrangements must ensure clear statements about decision-making processes, operational and management arrangements, delegation of responsibilities, reporting lines to parent agencies and monitoring for joint services, are available to staff and managers.

Joint performance management

Local partnerships will wish to choose measures that demonstrate their improved performance and how they are meeting their objectives. They draw on measures from existing national frameworks, including the NHS Scotland Performance Assessment Framework (PAF) and supplement this with the commitment to local targets for joint working. The Joint Performance Information and Assessment Framework (JPIAF) has been used to evaluate each of the LPAs to ensure that there are nationally consistent performance measures in place. The performance measures in the existing JPIAF are process indicators. A group has been established to develop outcome indicators.

Joint Future

In 1998, the Joint Future agenda in Scotland was established to improve joint collaborative working in community care through "agencies working in partnership in localities through better operational and strategic planning, joint budgets, joint services and joint systems" (Scottish Office, 1998). There was a strong consensus that previous attempts at joint working had been unsuccessful. After the establishment of the Scottish Executive, the Joint Future Group was set up by the Scottish Health Minister (Susan Deacon) and chaired by the Deputy Minister for Community Care (Iain Gray) in 1999. In January 2001, the Group made a very clear recommendation, which was accepted by the Scottish Executive:

> "Local authorities (that is, social work and housing), health boards, NHS Trusts and Scottish Homes should draw up local partnership agreements, including a clear programme for local joint resourcing and joint management of community care services collectively or for each user group individually." (Scottish Executive, 2001)

The focus on users/clients has a direct line of descent from the 1980s and 1990s new managerial and new public management discourse, having a policy rhetoric and perspective of clients as consumers or customers of services (Hood, 1995; Hoggett, 1996; Pollitt, 1990, 1993 and 1995). Government thinking with regard to Joint Future has also followed this line of thinking. A key aspect of user/outcome focus is the devolution of responsibility to managers and professionals proximate to the client. This has been a major development in the management of the school and college sectors, enterprise development and other public funded agencies and bodies.

To this user/consumer orientation has been added two complementary objectives of concern to central government thinking. First, the stress on articulated ("joined up") policy making in the White Paper, *Modernising Government* (Cabinet Office, 1999), and secondly (also part of the White Paper's thinking) the growing attention given to use of "outcomes" (*i.e.* the results of government actions, a measure of effectiveness) rather than "outputs" (Flynn, 2002). The strategic aim of "joined up government" is clearly at the core of Joint Future but so too is the attempt to address effectiveness and outcomes. There has also been recognition that pre-existing arrangements were not adequate for the purpose.

At one level the aim by the centre to drive integration has been successful. Local partners in all of Scotland 32 local authority areas have Local Partnership Agreements in place. These partnerships are all operational to a greater or lesser degree. In some areas this has been helped by stability of membership and prior ad hoc collaborative initiatives of local councils and NHS bodies; in other areas the initiative represents a completely new approach by the partners. There is, though, strongly held views, apparent both in interviews and in questionnaire responses that effective and real integrated working has been compromised by inappropriate (rushed) timescales. This has also been noted in research on integration initiatives elsewhere in the UK (Martin, 2000).

At operational level, considerable activity has taken place to attempt to integrate practices. Most fundamental is the single shared assessment where a client's needs are assessed by either a nurse or social worker in a single process rather than through a division of responsibility between health and social work—in fact, the drive for single shared assessment was an initial priority of the Joint Future Agenda articulated by the Joint Future Unit. Information sharing between local authority and health partners is widely recognised as vital for effective partnership and integrated working. Throughout Scotland as a whole, information sharing has been an acknowledged problem area for Joint Future:

> "Almost 50% of the Joint Future areas by 2005 are expected to have received specific funding from central government through the Modernising Government Fund to help develop electronic information sharing." (NHS/COSLA, 2003)

At strategic level, the implementation in each Joint Future area of joint resourcing and funding was fundamental to determining the effectiveness of integration and partnership working. Along with single shared assessment, joint resourcing and management was the focus of Scottish Executive priority with the issue of guidance frameworks. The Executive ensured that legislative barriers to the pooling of budgets were removed, though the earlier preference for pooled rather than aligned budgets appears to have diminished. According to recent information, there has been "significant progress" in all areas regarding joint resourcing and management (NHS/COSLA, 2003).

For effective and symmetrical partnership working, local authority managers at the appropriate level will require similar levels of "autonomy" and "empowerment". With regard to Joint Future, this is particularly apt, given that the approximate ratio of local authority to health expenditure is 2:1.

The Community Care and Health (Scotland) Act 2002 gave individuals greater control over home care services by giving the right to direct payments from June 1, 2003. The legislation also amended the Social Work (Scotland) Act 1968 to enable carers to ask local authorities for an assessment of their ability to care—previously, carers could only request such an assessment if the person they cared for was also being assessed. Understandably then, while a relatively small proportion of Joint Future resourcing is specified under the terms of local outcome agreements, the Scottish Executive wish to roll out these agreements to cover all local authorities by 2003, though with little indication of the per centage of total Joint Future spend represented by such agreements.

Community Health Partnerships (CHPs)

CHPs are key building blocks in the modernisation of the NHS and joint services, with a vital role in partnership, integration and service design. It is recognised that partnerships will evolve according to local circumstances, but that there are minimum requirements for devolving appropriate resources and responsibilities for decision-making to frontline staff which should be met everywhere.

The background to the development of CHPs is contained in the White Paper *Partnership for Care*, and reaffirmed in the *Partnership Agreement*. It stated that Local Healthcare Co-operatives (LHCCs) should evolve into CHPs, which would have a new, more consistent and enhanced role in service planning and delivery, working as part of decentralised but integrated health and social care systems.

The White Paper stated that CHPs would:

- ensure patients, carers and the full range of healthcare professionals are involved;
- establish a substantive partnership with local authority services (*e.g.* social work, housing, education and regeneration);
- have greater responsibility and influence in the deployment of Health Board resources;
- play a central role in service redesign locally;
- focus on integrating primary and specialist health services at local level; and
- play a pivotal role in delivering health improvement for their local communities.

The White Paper required health boards to work with local authorities to ensure more effective working with social care in appropriate locality arrangements. It also set the development of CHPs within the wider context of better integration of health services, more effective partnership working with local authorities and other local agencies and greater public, patient, carer and staff involvement. Greater partnership working is also underpinned by the continued development of community planning, the progressive application of Joint Future and the delivery of the strategic objectives of *For Scotland's Children* and *Improving Health in Scotland—The Challenge*.

It is intended that CHPs will create better results for the communities they serve by being aligned with local authority counterparts and by playing an effective role in planning and delivering local services. Their principal role is to work with others to deliver better results and their work will be driven by a focus on jointly agreed outcomes. As they develop and mature, and partners recognise their potential, they will play an increasingly central role in the integration of services locally. All of this is aimed at improving the health of local populations as part of an ongoing programme of development and modernisation in public services.

Public Private Partnerships and Public Finance Initiative

Public Private Partnerships (PPPs) are a key element in the Scottish Executive's strategy for delivering modern, high-quality public services. The Private Finance Initiative (PFI) is one form of PPP. PFI projects are long-term contracts for services that include the provision of associated facilities or properties. Under the contract, the private sector will have responsibility for designing and constructing the building or facility, and maintaining and servicing it throughout the contract term. The public sector retains accountability for the public services provided. The public sector organisations specifies its requirements in terms of outputs and this gives the private sector partner the scope to determine how best to deliver the services to the required quality and performance levels.

Projects are financed on a project finance basis, that is, lending is against the cash flows arising from the project. The recourse of the funders is limited to the project company and hence the cash flows, in most cases. This demands that the projects are commercially viable with robust cash flows. Funders will usually put covenants in place with the borrower to make the cash flows more secure and to secure their claim on them.

The private sector is responsible for financing the project up front and only receives payment from the public sector once the construction has been completed and the services have commenced. Payment takes the form of a unitary payment at regular intervals over the life of the contract. The objective of PFI is to allow the public sector to employ private sector capital and management expertise in the delivery of public services.

Community Safety Partnerships

Under the framework of community planning, community safety is the strategic priority for a range of key players (including the local authority, police, fire and health authority) who collectively can build safer, more inclusive, healthier and more vibrant, economically attractive communities. There is a Community Safety Partnership for each local authority area.

Conclusion

This chapter has considered a range of contemporary influences of local authorities and health boards. There are public policy themes permeating these developments as the Scottish Executive seeks to promote efficiency and integrated approaches to public service provision through community initiatives. These changes clearly represent Government strategic thinking at the highest level. There is a political commitment to retain the quality of public services while at the same time responding to the changing demands of our society. Scottish devolution has created the opportunity of responding to the particular requirements of Scottish society in a bespoke manner. The concern of Westminster government is that this should only be done within national public expenditure guidelines. If this cannot be achieved then Westminster may reluctantly allow the Scottish Executive to make use of its limited independent revenue raising powers. This would mean Scottish taxpayers paying more than their counterparts in other areas of the United Kingdom and this may prove to be politically unacceptable to the electorate. If devolution is to be meaningful then it must allow for such deviation should circumstances demand it. This will be the test for devolved government over the next five years.

CHAPTER 9

DELIVERING PUBLIC SERVICES: POLICY IMPLEMENTATION, PERFORMANCE MANAGEMENT AND QUALITY

INTRODUCTION

This chapter begins by considering the concept of public policy implementation before examining the component parts of the system of performance management found in Scottish local government and NHSScotland. Although systems of performance management differ between public services they tend to include strategic planning and management, performance measurement, performance indicators (PIs) and quality management.

The ways in which public services are delivered to client groups has radically changed over the past 20 years. The White Paper, *Modernising Government*, published in March 1999, identifies a challenging agenda for improving public services and commits the Scottish Executive to improvements in policy making, increasing service responsiveness, and enhancing service quality and to more effective use of new technology. In May 2003, the Scottish Executive set out in *A Partnership for a Better Scotland* its continued commitment to improving public services in Scotland.

It is against this background that the delivery of public services in Scotland is taking place.

POLICY IMPLEMENTATION

Governments have to ensure that their policy objectives are effectively achieved. For a period of time from 1979 to 1997, the emphasis in public management shifted from public administration to New Public Management, but since 1997 there has been a renewed interest in the public policy process and policy implementation. In Scottish local government and NHSScotland, there is a concern that policy implementation expertise has been lost in the search for economy and efficiency. Much of the existing literature on policy implementation is based on the analysis of case studies where the objectives of the policy were not fully realised. From these case studies academics have derived models for the analysis of public policy implementation. Elmore (1978, p.129) states that "No single model captures the full complexity of the implementation process."

This review utilises a framework for analysing which combines the Hogwood and Gunn (1984, p.4) model of the policy process with the Hicks and Gullett (1981, p.54) model of control phases. The policy process model of Hogwood and Gunn identifies 10 stages:

1. Issue search or agenda setting: pre-control (planning);
2. Issue filtration: pre-control (planning);
3. Issue definition: pre-control (planning);
4. Forecasting: pre-control (planning);
5. Setting objectives and priorities: pre-control (planning);
6. Options analysis and option selection: pre-control (planning)
7. Policy implementation: concurrent control;
8. Monitoring and checking: concurrent control;
9. Policy evaluation and review: post-control;
10. Policy maintenance, succession or termination: post-control.

Implementation is only one element of this model but successful implementation requires effectiveness at each and every stage of the policy process (Dunsire, 1978). Stages 1 to 6 concern policy formulation and, essentially, address the environmental circumstances affecting the issue and the appropriate policy to achieve particular objectives. These stages require a consideration of the past, sensitivity to present circumstances and a vision for the future. This is, in the terms of Hicks and Gullett (1981), a pre-control phase, which sets out a course of action to achieve a particular purpose.

Stages 7 and 8 are where the policy is actioned by public and private individuals (or groups) to achieve objectives set forth in prior policy decisions (Van Meter and Van Horn, 1977, p.447). This is the concurrent control phase. Stages 9 and 10 involve a backward look at the process and the consideration of performance achieved in relation to output and outcome at the end of the implementation activity. These stages are essentially therefore, post-controls in that they are summative assessments of policy outputs and impacts.

Top-down and bottom-up

The "top-down" perspective, according to Barrett and Fudge (1981, pp.3–32) falsely assumes that all initiative is from the top or centre along with the ability to control the periphery or subordinate actors. The "bottom-up" perspective considers policy makers and implementors as more equal and the interaction between them is crucial to the study of policy implementation. Individuals' and organisations' actions and reactions may determine policy as much as policy itself determines actions and responses. Successful implementation depends on achieving consensus in the policy process.

Marsh and Rhodes (1992) suggest that there is a choice between ways of looking at the policy process between the "top-down" and "bottom-up" approach. Hill (1997, p.377) acknowledges that in British public administration there has been substantial change, clearly initiated from the top (government). Dramatic value shifts through institutional changes have been promoted through public policies in areas such as further and higher education. According to Hill (1997, p.383), government in the period from 1979 has not demonstrated any great concern for consensus in the policy process. Hoggett (1996, pp.9–32) comments on the ways in which government has tried to combine "rowing" and "steering", intervening inconsistently, using controls—particularly output controls—that are susceptible to manipulation and undermine trust. Hill (1997, p.383) concludes that the analysis of policies does not require the prescription of a correct starting point at the top or the bottom.

Implementation literature and pre-control

Policy failures can be attributed to bad policy, bad execution or bad luck (Hogwood and Gunn, 1984). The formulation of policy stage is crucial to the likelihood of policy success. The implementation literature on issue search and agenda setting identifies problems associated with the quality of environmental scanning, environmental awareness and environmental analysis. Van Meter and Van Horn (1977) and Hood (1976) recognise the importance of environmental sensitivity. The term "macro-environment" is commonly used to describe the major forces which confront organisations, *i.e.* demography, politics, economics, sociological trends, technology, legislation and culture (Kotter, 1980). Fahey and Narayanan's model of the macro-environment (1986, pp.28–34) offers a framework of analysis for identifying, tracking, projecting and assessing environmental trends and patterns. This model encapsulates a range of public policy issue search and agenda problems, which result from inadequate environmental scanning.

Filtration and definition involves making decisions on those issues to be addressed by policies and the clarification of such issues. Hood (1976) refers to the political acceptability of issues and the extent to which issues are manageable. Mazmanian and Sabatier (1981 and 1983), in their framework for analysing implementation, see the tractability of the problem as the key issue. They identify four dimensions of this:

(a) availability of theory and technology;
(b) diversity of target group;
(c) target group as a percentage of population; and
(d) the extent of behavioural change required.

Van Meter and Van Horn (1977) consider the problems associated with the awareness on the part of the policy formulator of the amount of change required and the extent to which there is agreement on the goals among the participants in the implementation process. This clearly requires an awareness of the current position (position statement) and a vision of the desired future to enable a comparison to be made between the two (gap analysis). There is also a need for sensitivity and empathy to better understand the likely reaction of people to policy goals. Van Meter and Van Horn hypothesis that implementation will be more successful where only marginal change is required and goal consensus is high.

Problems arise when there is imperfect knowledge of the issue thus preventing its accurate definition (Fesler, 1980, pp.256–293). King (1976, pp.162–174) makes a similar point:

> "An organisation might fail to achieve its objectives because the decision-takers did not know or understand what they needed to know or understand."

There is clearly scope for this competency problem to manifest itself at both the level of the politician and at the level of the implementor.

Forecasting requires knowledge of techniques, their limitations and their value. Hogwood and Gunn (1984, pp.128–129) recognise that forecasts cannot predict the future but can assist decision-makers. Policies may be based on an inadequate understanding of the complexities of a problem. Pressman and Wildavsky (1973) describe any policy as a hypothesis, which contains initial conditions and predicted consequences. Thus, according to Gunn (1978, p.169), every policy incorporates a theory of cause and effect and, if the policy fails, it may be the underlying theory that is at fault rather than the execution of the policy. Pressman and Wildavsky (1973) recognise the importance of the links in the chain of causality. The greater the number of links in the chain between cause and effect, the more complex the implementation becomes.

Setting objectives and priorities as part of the pre-control phase involves considering the coherence and compatibility of the objectives and the extent to which there is consensus over the priorities identified in stated objectives (Ingram and Mann, 1980, pp.11–32). Management theory contains many references to objectives which should be Specific, Measurable, Achievable, Realistic and time limited (SMART objectives). Objectives, according to Gunn

(1978), should also be understood and agreed, mutually compatible and supportive, and provide guidance for concurrent controls which monitor the extent to which pre-determined objectives are being pursued and attained.

Hood (1976) uses the term "external conditions of perfect administration" to describe the "ideal" situation where there are unlimited material resources, unambiguous overall objectives and perfect political acceptability of the policies pursued. He also comments on the problems that arise when these external conditions of perfect administration are relaxed.

Stage 6 of the policy process concerns options analysis and option selection. In Dunsire's model (1978) he states that:

> "Assuming Government has arrived at a correct and appropriate policy objective, a failure of implementation might occur because: an inappropriate strategy was chosen; or within an appropriate strategy, inappropriate Government agencies or machinery were selected; or inappropriate options were selected."

Underpinning the policy planning (pre-control) elements is the support for the policy in the form of time and adequate resources. Hood (1976) identifies this as one of his five "internal" components of perfect administration. Gunn (1978), Van Meter and Van Horn (1977), Fesler (1980) and Mazmanian and Sabatier (1981 and 1983), all identify the critical need for financial, human and other resources, including time, to be allocated appropriately to support policy implementation.

The selection of an appropriate implementing agency was identified by Van Meter and Van Horn (1977), as essential for successful implementation. In addition, they identified a number of characteristics which may increase an organisation's capacity to implement policy. These are:

(a) quality and quantity of human resources;
(b) control capability over sub-units;
(c) political resources;
(d) organisational vitality;
(e) the degree of open communications; and
(f) the agency's formal and informal linkages with the policy-making or policy-enforcing body.

Implementation and concurrent control

At these stages in the policy process, the policy is actioned by organisations and individuals charged with this responsibility. The actioning includes the monitoring of progression achieved compared to desired progression. Hood (1976), identified five major conditions as the "internal" components of perfect administration:

(a) A unitary administrative system;
(b) Uniformity in norms and rules;
(c) No resistance to controls;
(d) Perfect co-ordination and perfect communication; and
(e) Adequate time to utilise resources.

Failure to achieve perfect administration in any area of the above five could lead to implementation problems. Ingram and Mann (1980) identify the need for a high-status initiator of implementation, what the organisational behaviour literature might call "an influential champion". Dunsire (1978) recognises the need for a competent project manager to oversee the stages of policy implementation. Linked to this are the need for technical project planning and the use of techniques such as network planning and critical path analysis to identify tasks, relationships between tasks and the logical sequence in which they should be performed (Gunn, 1978).

Peters (1996, p.112) notes the possibility of organisational disunity where implementors do not share the same values and goals as those responsible for policy formulation. Van Meter and Van Horn (1977) focus on dimensions of the disposition of implementors and identify three crucial elements affecting their willingness to carry out the policy:

(a) their cognition (comprehension and understanding) of the policy;
(b) the direction of their response towards it (acceptance, neutrality or rejection); and
(c) the intensity of that response.

Several writers identify timing as a factor affecting implementation. The basic argument is that, depending on the policy, some times are better than others for achieving successful implementation. The commitment to the policy may be at its highest in the early stages following formulation, if delays occur electoral changes and declining interest may adversely affect commitment and the likelihood of success (Gunn, 1978, Hood, 1976 and Ingram and Mann, 1980).

Hood (1976) recognised that implementation is far more likely when compliance is guaranteed. This requires the policy formulator to be in a position of power over the implementor to ensure compliance with policy directives. Fesler (1980) comments on the importance of effective leadership and problems often arise when leadership changes. Effective communication at this stage of the process is essential and failures at any point in the accurate transmission and receiving of information will result in delays and inappropriate action, leading to misunderstanding and errors. Management information systems provide data on the extent to which desired performance is being achieved and these should be effective (Fesler, 1980 and Dunsire, 1978).

Ingram and Mann (1980) make an interesting point on policy rejuvenation. Old policies, unless they have gone through a period of reform and rejuvenation, tend to be ineffective policies. Policies should therefore not be perceived as "old wine in new bottles" but must be substantially revised and appropriately contextualised to meet the stakeholders' expectations.

Implementation and post-control

Stages 9 and 10 in the policy process provide essential feedback on policy success. Patton and Sawicki (1986, p.38) identify that no policy process is complete without considering policy outputs and policy outcomes. There are often unintended consequences, difficulties in implementation or changes in circumstances, which lead to policy failure. Hughes (1998) considers the post-control stage of review and evaluation to be fundamental to any policy, no matter how it is derived. The conclusions from review and evaluation often lead to policy revision and further initiatives constituting issue search and agenda setting (stages 1 and 2). The policy process can only be cyclical if the post-control activities inform planning activities. Policy failures, according to Hogwood and Gunn (1984), may arise because of bad policy, bad execution or bad luck. Unless there is review and evaluation the policy stakeholders, including policy formulators, will not be in a position to reflect on the policy output and outcome and assess the next course of action whether it be policy maintenance, policy succession or policy termination.

Mazmanian and Sabatier (1981 and 1983) identify a number of key aspects of policy output such as compliance by target groups, actual impacts, perceived impacts and the evaluation of the policy by the political system. The term "stakeholder perceptions" covers the range of parties with direct and indirect interests in the results of the policy both in the short term and in the longer term. Ingram and Mann (1980) conclude that there are few hard and fast rules about what makes for successful implementation as what works in one setting often fails in another. Local factors and characteristics unique to specific implementation contexts have strong direct effects on outcomes. Dunsire (1978) comments on an ideal policy process that overcomes all of the problems associated with the formulation and implementation stages. But, though all of these dangers were surmounted, nevertheless something else can go wrong at the operational level including the response or reaction of those affected being other than had been calculated. This leads to the conclusion, that success and failure is unpredictable and luck has a part to play in policy implementation.

To conclude, Barratt and Fudge (1981) introduce an interesting aspect of review and evaluation. In some situations there need not be a policy output or outcome to consider as activity ceased at the policy formulation stages. The policy in such circumstances becomes a substitute for action and this may be sufficient to appease pressure groups. This approach may be useful when confronted by a problem, which is difficult to address (low tractability), and policy implementation activity may result in no tangible signs of improvement. The policy as a statement of intent is a substitute for action.

There has been concern for many years about the tendency to blame administrators for policy failure. The first major study of the implementation process was by Pressman and Wildavsky published in 1973 and since then many academics both in the United States and the United Kingdom have made interesting contributions to the body of literature on public policy implementation. This review has followed a structure based on a rational model of the policy process summarised by Hogwood and Gunn (1984) but, in addition, their process has been linked to an organisational control model. The literature generally fits this combined model and this review clearly concludes that the existing literature tends to concentrate on the pre-control or planning phase. Many writers advocate more rational and systematic policy planning where the potential implementation problems are addressed before they arise. There is less literature on the ways in which the policy is operationalised through implementation and on the stages addressing review and evaluation. The implementation literature is therefore targeted at policy formulation and policy planning.

Ramzek and Johnston (1999, pp. 107–139) recognise that implementation models tend to be relatively complex but common variables do emerge from the literature. The Gunn model of perfect implementation (1978) provides as comprehensive a model as exists (see Chapter 6 for policy models theory). It identifies ten pre-conditions of perfect implementation:

1. Circumstances external to the implementing agency do not impose crippling constraints.
2. Adequate time and sufficient resources are made available to the programme.
3. Not only are there no constraints in terms of overall resources but also that, at each stage of the implementation process, the required combination of resources is actually available.
4. The policy to be implemented is based on a valid theory of cause and effect.
5. The relationship between cause and effect is direct and there are few, if any, intervening links.
6. There is a single implementing agency, which need not depend upon other agencies for success, or, if other agencies must be involved, the dependency relationships are minimal in number and importance.

7. There is complete understanding of and agreement upon, the objectives to be achieved; and these conditions persist throughout the implementation process.
8. In moving towards agreed objectives it is possible to specify, in complete detail and perfect sequence, the tasks to be performed by each participant.
9. There is perfect communication among, and co-ordination of, the various elements or agencies involved.
10. Those in authority can demand and obtain perfect obedience.

This "ideal" model is a representation used by Professor Gunn as an aid to understanding where implementation can go wrong. If any of these pre-conditions of perfect implementation are not met then the policy may not be effectively implemented.

The consensus emerging from the literature is that by addressing potential implementation problems at the policy planning stages you create or formulate policies which are more likely to be effectively actioned. The logic of this cannot be disputed. However, from the analysis of the literature in this section it is apparent that there is insufficient attention given to the operationalisation of public policies. The question faced by administrators of "what to do with a policy?" remains largely unanswered by this literature. It appears to be based on the assumption that those responsible for implementation are (using Hood's terminology) "perfectly competent".

Hill (1997) comments on the downturn in the volume of empirical study and academic writing on policy implementation. This may be because many implementation problems are already known and, more importantly, because of the change from public administration to New Public Management (NPM). There is less concern amongst policy makers with "how?" the policy is implemented as long as it is implemented. The New Public Management (NPM) has shifted the onus of effective implementation from the public policy formulators to those organisations and individuals charged with responsibility for implementation. Such implementors have limited control over policy content and policy planning but must nevertheless operationalise implementation, often acting in a relatively autonomous manner. For example, colleges of further education, as a consequence of incorporation, act independently to promote the government's policies on lifelong learning. Such delegation of responsibility is part and parcel of the NPM and requires more people to possess policy implementation competences. This competency enhancement cannot be achieved without comprehensive training and development programmes, which address, as an essential component, policy implementation. There has been a tendency in recent years to replace public administration training and development with generic management training and development but this does not address the special nature of management in the public sector. Public policy implementation literature tends to reflect the public administration context of its heyday in the 1970s and early 1980s. The focus then was on improving policy formulation to take account of potential implementation problems and thus to counter the failures due to bad policy identified in the multiplicity of real case studies. However, there has clearly been insufficient attention given to policy failures due to bad execution and bad luck. This, coupled with the changing context of public policy and the advent of New Public Management, has shifted practitioners requirements. Public managers need theory from the academic literature to guide practice.

Policy implementors are public managers and, as such, need (and want) training in strategic and operational management to develop competences, including:

(a) public policy implementation;
(b) project management;
(c) operational planning, monitoring, review and evaluation;
(d) leadership and motivation;
(e) communication; and
(f) the management of change.

Academics should respond to these requirements by developing an underpinning body of literature, which examines public policy implementation in the context of the New Public Management. Further development of empirical research and subsequent academic literature should improve the existing knowledge of public policy implementation and thus reduce policy failure due to bad execution. Such a trend may also reduce failures due to bad luck provided the misfortune was actionable and not an "act of God". There will always be policy implementation failures due to unforeseen circumstances in the real world, but public policy implementation literature has tried to make all stakeholders more aware of those factors likely to contribute to such failures believing that being forewarned allows for forearming.

Performance management

Performance management in the private sector is often a system in which the organisation's business plan is thoroughly communicated to all staff and the contribution of each individual is expressed in a performance contract. The link between personal performance and financial reward is made increasingly explicit, often through performance related pay. The focus is on the integration of individual and organisational performance (Industrial Society, 1994, p.2).

Performance management in the public sector in the managerial activities is necessary to promote well-performing policy management and service delivery. A desire for improved performance in public sector organisations has resulted in a results-orientation and a cost consciousness in a range of OECD countries (OECD, 1997, p.8). Performance management requires a performance information system that can be audited and is related to financial management and policy cycles. Performance management requires performance measurement systems and PIs are part of a system of performance measurement (OU, B887, Block 3, p.79).

The management of organisational performance is the central activity of managers at all levels. This involves controlling organisational resources and activities to ensure that they are contributing to organisational effectiveness and to ensure that the organisation is not experiencing *strategic drift*. Strategic drift occurs when the reality of organisational performance is inconsistent with planned levels of performance. If there is a major deviation between planned and actual performance then the organisation must either adjust performance or modify plans.

The term performance management is commonly used today to describe a range of managerial activities designed to monitor, measure and adjust aspect of individual and organisational performance through management control of various types. Performance management integrates the management of organisational performance with the management of individual performance.

A performance management model

According to Audit Scotland (2002), public bodies are responsible for ensuring that suitable arrangements are in place to secure economy, efficiency and effectiveness in the use of resources, and that they work effectively. These include procedures for planning, appraisal, authorisation and control, accountability and evaluation of the use of resources, and for ensuring that performance targets and required outcomes are achieved. There is no fundamental imperative for an organisation to have a performance management system. However, there is compelling evidence to suggest that the discipline, clarity of accountability and challenge introduced by a system help organisations perform to ever-greater levels.

A common approach involves five "building blocks":

High-level aspiration

The first step is to define and relentlessly communicate a compelling aspiration for the future. It is critical that the aspirations are clear and consistent over time. Bold high-level aspirations serve as the rationale for aggressive objectives and targets.

Long- and short-term objectives, output measures and targets

The next step is to translate these aspirations into long- and short-term objectives, output measures and targets against which performance and progress can be measured:

- Long-term are three to five year objectives and targets derived from the aspirational objectives, priorities and targets. They must be quantifiable and measurable, or measure the completion of a specific task;
- Short-term objectives are annual (or more frequent as dictated by activity): again they should be derived from the aspirational objectives, priorities and targets and should be developed at an operational level. They must be quantifiable and measurable, or measure the completion of a specific task. The system must be integrated and related, so that the achievement of short-term objectives and targets contributes to the achievement of the long-term objectives and targets, and the achievement of long-term targets contributes to meeting the aspirational aims and objectives.

Ownership and accountability

Once the overall direction and targets have been set, organisational ownership needs to be established. Every target, both long- and short-term must be "owned". This can be done either individually or collectively (for example, by a team or other organisational unit) but must result in specific responsibilities for delivering each target. Ultimately, individuals must feel accountable for delivery.

Rigorous performance review

When accountability for delivering against individual long- and short-term targets has been clearly defined, a rigorous performance monitoring and review system is necessary. To be effective, performance reviews must exhibit the following characteristics:

- Personal involvement for all managers including the most senior managers in the organisation;
- Regularity;
- Structure and planning, with the inclusion of three layers of management at any one review;
- Constructive challenge and peer interaction.

Reinforcement and incentives

Reinforcing mechanisms must be in place, encompassing an appropriate set of positive and negative incentives. In other words, there is a requirement for a consequence management system, with positive consequences for success and negative consequences for under-performance against plan.

Holistic approach

For the model to work successfully, it is critical that all five of the system's building blocks are in place and applied in a systematic and consistent manner. If any of the blocks is not built into the management practices of the organisation, or is implemented in an ad hoc rather than a rigorous manner, the whole system will be ineffective.

Influences on Performance Management in Scottish Local Government

The Maud Report (1967) looked at management in local government. The importance of financial control was considered in relation to increasing levels of local authority expenditure:

> " . . . a local authority is hampered by having to deal with services to which the profits test can rarely be applied and to which accounting, costing or other numerical tests of success or failure are of only limited significance." (Maud, 1967)

The Maud Committee recognised the importance of value for money and mentioned financial measurement as an element in the process of obtaining value for money and the improvement of efficiency.

The Mallaby Committee (1967) was established to consider the recruitment and use of local government officers, and changes that might help to improve the services provided by local authorities. The Mallaby Report provided a particularly useful definition of local government management in the late 1960s:

> "Management involves the setting of objectives and planning how these objectives are to be achieved, the organisation and harmonisation of the work of various individuals and groups of people, the control of costs and the appraisal of results." (Mallaby, 1967)

Particularly significant are the references to controlling costs and appraising results.

The Hughes Committee (1968) was the Scottish equivalent of the Mallaby Committee and was established in June 1967. In relation to developments in organisation and management with a link to PIs, recommendations 53 and 54 address the effective use of staff. There is a specific reference to performance:

> "Above all it demands the ability to establish good communication with subordinates and to analyse their performance accurately and objectively." (Hughes, 1968, para.144)

Although the focus of Hughes, like Mallaby, was on staffing, there was recognition of the need for managerial competence and management development in Scottish local government.

The Wheatley Commission (1966–69) focused on local government structure in Scotland. In relation to financial control, the Wheatley Commission recognised that Government controls over local authorities had developed in a haphazard manner and the result was:

> "cumbersome, time wasting and oppressive, and does not respect the constitutional status of local government." (Wheatley, 1969)

The Commission formally stated that external controls should be replaced by internal control.

The Bains Report (1972) (England and Wales) and the Paterson Report (1973) (Scotland) advocated corporate management for the new local authorities, following local government reorganisation. A central tenet of both reports was the key role of the Policy and Resources Committee that would, among other responsibilities, monitor and review the performance of the authority (Bains 1972, p.32). Thus:

> " . . . greater attention must be paid to the development of methods of assessing the effectiveness of activities against which progress and performance can be measured. For too long the main criterion of success has been the amount of resources put into a particular service with but little regard for its output." (Bains, 1972, p.14)

This concern for output, progress and performance measurement indicated the growing concern with the extent to which local government outputs reflected the strategic objectives of the authorities.

Performance indicators

The literature on PIs over a 20-year period illustrates changing perceptions of their role and uses in public management. Focusing on recent studies and using the framework of performance governance, performance management and marketplace surrogate, comments are made on the changing focus of theory and practice over this period. Conclusions are derived from this analysis to inform the study of PIs and the performance agenda in public management today.

Ball and Monaghan (1993) conducted a survey of British local authorities on performance review and argue that many authorities have gone beyond the requirements of the Accounts Commission and the Audit Commission. They also note that the major implementation difficulties associated with performance review systems relate to behavioural problems relating to resistance from those responsible for reporting the performance information. Organisations should be sensitive to the human resources impacts of PIs. Ball (1998), from his survey and case studies, concludes that local authorities have tended to develop their own performance assessment systems to meet their own requirements. There is evidence of incremental changes over a period of time and the borrowing of ideas developed from good practice in particular authorities. The active support of the chief executive, chief officers and elected members is essential if the performance review system is to be successful. The main behavioural problems were lack of support from elected members and officers and problems with the organisational culture. The major technical difficulty has been the designing of appropriate PIs. Training and information management have been major resource issues.

The practices identified by Ball (1998) may be under threat as Best Value and the Citizen's Charter prescribe performance information requirements and this may reverse the trend of bespoke performance assessment systems and promote approaches which restore the performance governance thrust and the concern for consumerism, responsiveness and quality.

McKevitt and Lawton (1996, pp.49–54) looked at the human element in performance measurement and found that there exists quite widespread disillusion with performance measurement systems at middle management levels that may see them as underemphasising the traditional public sector values of equity and care. Systems seem to be driven from the top by senior managers and politicians with their own agendas. McKevitt and Lawton (1996) conclude that performance measurement will fail unless it is based on a participative approach designed to promote ownership at all levels.

Egan (1996, p.8) found good examples of local authorities using PIs constructively, incorporating published PIs into quality management systems, and seeing them as a position statement for subsequent improvement. The approach adopted by these authorities combined total quality management with the management of change.

Kravchuk and Schack (1996) developed a set of design principles, based on US experience, which incorporate good practice in managing change and a concern for clients and other stakeholders, these are as follows:

1. Formulate a clear, coherent mission, strategy and objectives.
2. Develop an explicit measurement strategy.

3. Involve key users in the design and development phase.
4. Rationalise operations as a prelude to measurement.
5. Develop multiple sets of measures for multiple users, as necessary.
6. Consider the clients, customers and stakeholders throughout the process.
7. Provide each user with sufficient detail for a clear picture of performance.
8. Periodically review and revise the measurement system.
9. Take account of past, current and potential future complexities.
10. Avoid excessive aggregation of information.

Key decision-takers should avoid using measures as a substitute for expert knowledge about, or direct management of programmes. Measure are better placed in a management by exception framework, where they are regarded as indicators that will serve to signal the need for further investigation. Such an approach promotes learning, adaptation and improvement.

Alford (1997, pp.49–58) considers the Australian experience of performance monitoring in the public sector and concludes that there are examples of effective performance monitoring systems and examples of where the system is less effective. He advocates a contingency approach where performance monitoring is contextualised for the particular circumstances faced by the public sector organisation. There are clearly difficulties in defining and measuring ends, and difficulties in relating means to ends. The effectiveness of performance monitoring is not solely a product of external environmental circumstances; there is a need for a managerial commitment to performance monitoring coupled with intelligent adaptation to organisational circumstances.

Talbot (1998, pp.4–5) comments that an interesting side effect of the move towards the production of performance information has been the difficulty of defining the purpose of central government departments. This difficulty has become more acute as government departments apply for "Investors in People" recognition. This IIP standard requires organisations to demonstrate the ways in which their employee development practices relate to their "business aims". Performance information could be used for a variety of purposes such as telling organisations what is really important about what they do. Performance information can promote continuous improvement and enhance accountability. There is very little evidence that performance information is actually used at all, let alone effectively. Some purposes of performance measurement pull performance measurement systems in contrary directions and this can have dysfunctional consequences.

Hyndman and Anderson (1998, pp.23–30) conclude that the focus on performance rather than on spending will lead to a more accountable public sector, and provide a stimulus for better management and performance improvement. Government agencies have a responsibility to account to those outside its management, and beyond to the directly responsible Minister.

Tichelar (1998, pp.29–35) identifies a number of developments in the use of PIs in local government. Local authorities are developing strategic management systems that incorporate performance review and PIs that reflect needs and priorities in their locality. Performance indicators are being introduced into community plans. Local government managers are increasingly concerned with qualitative assessment of service delivery and with service outcomes. Elected members are becoming more involved in performance management systems of which PIs are key components. The development of Best Value Regimes (BVR) is likely to stimulate local authorities further to define the key indicators which are relevant to their service and their authority. Statutory indicators are imposed on local authorities and have limited meaning to local government managers. Bespoke PI systems are developing as a product of interaction between local government managers, employees at different levels, elected members and clients. Best Value has provided an added impetus for the development of bespoke PIs that contribute to the assessment of the extent to which value for money is being achieved. Best Value guidelines imply PIs as planning tools which address quality and effectiveness as well as economy and efficiency.

Johnsen (1999, pp.41–66) examines performance management practices in the United Kingdom, the United States, Australia, the Netherlands, and Norway, and concludes that many academics and practitioners seem to unite in a recommendation of establishing close links between goals and PIs when implementing performance measurement systems. His research findings are congruent with the implementation advice in the performance measurement literature regarding emphasis on decision relevance in development of PIs, an incremental approach, bottom-up participation and management commitment. The main proposition is that separating PIs and organisational objectives may enhance implementation success and this is contrary to the advice given in management-by-objectives (MBO) literature and widespread governmental practice. Johnsen refers to this as de-coupling. The de-coupled implementation mode can provide management with buffers from the political processes of formulating organisational objectives and from resistance, allowing the organisation to measure performance, experiment with PIs, and then take satisfactory PIs into use over time to facilitate organisational learning and enhance efficiency, effectiveness and equity. Organisations that use the implementation mode of coupled PIs to organisational objectives may end up with low decision-relevant and unreliable PIs, dissatisfaction, and little usage of the system. Johnsen call for the need for more empirical research both about the implementation of performance assessment systems and their corresponding effects.

Some general comments can be made on trends in the use of PIs in public management. These comments are structured using three areas of potential use for PIs. These are:

(a) performance governance;
(b) performance management;
(c) and as a marketplace surrogate.

Performance indicators as performance governance emphasises accountability and control and is a "top down" perspective. Performance indicators as performance management, concentrates on the strategic and operational management use of performance data. Performance indicators as marketplace surrogates, focuses on consumerism, quality and responsiveness and requires the involvement of clients, customers and other stakeholders.

Performance indicators as performance governance

Many of the UK academic commentators in the 1980s were concerned that there was too much emphasis in the performance agenda on the "triumvirate of virtue': economy, effectiveness and efficiency" (Pollitt, 1986, pp.155–170). Economy, on its own, is a very limited concept for providing guidance to managers. Gray and Jenkins *et al.* (1988) suspected that there was a drive to minimise inputs almost regardless of outputs. In relation to efficiency, Mayston (1985) correctly identifies the distinction between efficiency and productivity in that a merely efficient organisation may not be more productive. Effectiveness is a measure of the achievement of targets or objectives (Flynn, 1986, pp.384–404). Pollitt (1986, pp.155–170) suggests that the subordination of outcomes to outputs (and the broader emphasis on economy and efficiency rather than effectiveness) may reflect the political objectives of a government that is primarily concerned with reducing public expenditure rather than performance evaluation. Pollitt called for a greater concern in performance indicator systems with the additional Es of *e*quality and *e*fficacy. Carter, Klein and Day (1992) found these criticisms of the domination of PI systems by the efficiency concerns of politicians and providers as unhelpful and suggested that the debate should move on to incorporate the diverse concerns of citizens and consumers.

Midwinter (1994, p.40) recognises that in order to improve assessment systems you would have to derive indicators that demonstrated how economical and efficient the organisation was in achieving effectiveness. Any such indicators, however, are representative only within the initial confines of a budget which is dictated by political choice and strategy. They do not represent economy and efficiency as dictated by an unconstrained environment. Caution must always be exercised in the use of performance indicator information by funders and other stakeholders as they are frequently "snap shots" of performance at a point in time. Interpretations of economy and efficiency are more credible in terms of internal comparisons over time and in relation to general trends, demographic changes, demand for services and value for money. Sizer (1991), in a five-country study of the development of PIs at the government-higher education interface, concluded that the identification of clearer institutional objectives was needed for evaluation, but governments should accept that complete goal congruence amongst similar service providers is not achievable.

Performance indicators as performance management

In the 1980s, academic writings contained substantial descriptive elements identifying the many ways in which (PIs) were used in public management. Much of the writing such as that of Pollitt (1986, 1990), was critical of the over-emphasis on performance governance whereby PIs were seen as tools of government designed to promote the government's economic objectives and exert greater control over the public sector. Concerns were expressed about the interpretations of the PIs data especially the data on schools and hospital performance. Flynn (1993, pp.115–125) commented that managers should only be expected to perform well by affecting the variables over which they can have some influence. It was not possible to compare "like with like" as particular organisations had to operate in unique locales with different resources and different clients.

Writers in the late 1980s and early 1990s began to add prescriptive comments aimed at improving the utility to enhance the contribution of PIs to public managers as tools of performance management. Kanter and Summers (1987, pp.98–110) identified the dilemmas of non-profit performance measurement as clients generally have limited influence over the service provider, the multiplicity of goals pursued, the concern for resources utilised (inputs), internal politics and goal displacement, and the inflexibility of professionals. Carter *et al.* (1991) argued that PIs needed to be taken away from a limited number of experts and integrated more into the democratic process at all levels. Commentators identified weaknesses in existing performance assessment systems in that indicators tended to be used as "dials" instead of using them as "tin openers" (Carter, 1991). There were deficiencies in the design, implementation and utilisation of information from the existing PI systems. Collectively, the academic writers were concerned that PIs had become tools of government and senior managers in that they were "top-down", prescriptive, value laden, input and process focused, and predominantly economy and efficiency-led.

Pollitt and Harrison (1992) were critical of the managerialist perspective which adopted the position that better management is the key to maximising the effectiveness and efficiency of government delivered services. This was a product of a concern within government for improving economic management coupled with a loss of confidence in professionals in the public sector. Stewart and Walsh (1994) commented on the difficulty of defining performance in the public sector; because it can never be finally defined, it can never be adequately measured. Similar criticisms were made by an array of academic writers, including Carter (1991), Flynn (1997), Jackson (1988) and Cave, Hanney and Kogan (1991). This trend in the literature is linked to a Tayloristic perception of management where managers are themselves efficiency-led and are largely concerned with ensuring compliance with government strategy directives. In order to promote these priorities, they rely on comprehensive control systems including controls over their own staff. This is a top-down perspective on the role of managers. It is a task-centred perspective that takes no account of the human element in management.

Caiden (1997) identified the managerialist trend in performance assessment whereby agencies produce a strategic plan with goals and outcomes, this is supported by performance plans which develop performance measures to monitor progress and these measures are based on data reports. Kanter and Summers (1987) nevertheless urged non-profit managers to try to set objectives and assess results to determine if they are indeed "doing well while doing good".

There is no doubt that introducing strategic management processes to public sector organisations is problematic, but the demand and need for performance assessment and measurement is unlikely to decline in the future. Factors contributing to this demand include the drive for "Best Value" and the reporting requirements of funding agencies. In response to the changing context of public management, many organisations are looking at the ways in which managerial staff are developed, and there is a trend towards generic management development which in turn must impact on the practice of public management. Carter *et al.* (1991) described a common evolutionary organisational learning cycle beginning with "perfunctory compliance" through reactive and critical resistance, to a broader appreciation of the potential value of PIs as weapons in the battle for resources.

Much of the writing guiding public managers on PIs as performance management has emerged from government agencies such as the Accounts Commission (Audit Scotland), the Scottish Office, the National Audit Office and the Audit Commission each advocating particular approaches to the management of PI systems. The Accounts Commission in *Planning for Success* (1998) created a five-point framework comprising: setting the direction; strategic analysis; making it happen; checking progress; and doing better. They also advocated the use of Kaplan and Norton's "Balanced Scorecard" approach (1996, pp.75–85) which links organisational vision with communication, business planning, feedback and learning (see Figure 9.3 below).

It may well be that more systematic systems of performance assessment linked to strategic management and underpinned by competent decision-takers will deliver enhanced organisational effectiveness.

Although the strongest stakeholders (government, funders and audit organisations) tended to shape the roles and content of PI systems in the 1980s and early 1990s, this trend is now changing as managers exert more influence on how their organisation and their individual performance is to be assessed.

Performance indicators as marketplace surrogates

Performance indicators as marketplace surrogates emerged in the late 1980s when writers, such as Pollitt (1986, pp.155–170), advocated the broadening of performance assessment to incorporate client perceptions. This continues to be a concern of academic writers who have gone beyond client perception to stakeholder and citizen perceptions of public service delivery. There was a need to change their emphasis to involve public managers, clients and other stakeholders in performance assessment systems that focus on output and outcome, effectiveness, client perceptions and quality.

This transition from performance governance and performance management to consumerism is reflected in academic writings of the latter part of the 1980s and into the 1990s. The literature tends to advocate a different approach to performance assessment and PIs with concerns for economy, efficiency, process and output being substantially replaced by advocacy for effectiveness, outcome, consumerism, equality and quality. In addition to academic literature, government agencies were also advocating a change, but their change tended to see the revised performance assessment system as retaining the performance governance focus and adding further elements of performance management with a concern for change management and human resources management; consumerism, quality and responsiveness.

Winkler (1987) questioned the extent to which quality and responsiveness were moving beyond the "supermarket model". Gaster (1995) critically evaluated the transferability of private sector quality management and marketing models to the public sector.

There is little evidence from the analysis of PIs in Scottish further education that would lead you to conclude that clients are exercising their rights as consumers of services to utilise performance information to inform choice. Therefore PIs appear to provide an input to internal quality systems but not to external responsiveness and do not act as a "marketplace surrogate". Much of the contemporary literature addresses the issue of improving the performance assessment systems through the use of participative approaches by managers both internally and externally. Ownership, quality and responsiveness are common themes in the literature.

Implementation studies focus on improving systems of performance assessment largely through the development of more people-centred systems which encourage participation and ownership. The environment of performance assessment has not radically changed since the mid-1980s and, despite changes in government, there remains a concern for accountability and value for money and thus an interest in performance assessment as performance governance remains a key item in the performance agenda. Tichelar (1998) identifies that many performance assessment systems still contain a substantial number of indicators that public sector organisations must utilise and consequently report. The audiences for such reports include: government; funding agencies; auditing agencies; client groups; stakeholders; and the general public. However, there is a discernible trend towards supplementing the required prescribed indicators by indicators that are much more focused on performance management and consumerism (Hatry, Gerhart and Marshall (1994) and Meekings (1995)). Tichelar (1998) and Ball (1998) note that Best Value Regimes (BVR) will require much more comprehensive reporting of performance to all stakeholders.

The themes emerging from the recent implementation studies are many and varied. These themes have changed over time to reflect the changing context of public management and developing experiences of PIs in action. Government agencies such as the Accounts Commission and the Audit Commission began, in the 1980s, with a clear focus on PIs as performance governance emphasising their accountability role. There was a concern for economy and efficiency with insufficient attention being paid to effectiveness and quality (Pollitt, 1986). However, these agencies and their contemporary counterparts are now recognising the need for PIs to become tools of managers (performance management) and tools of stakeholders (consumerism, quality and responsiveness) as well as tools of governance. To support these changes they are offering advice on the development of PI systems to embrace the changing focus. There remains a concern for input, process and output but there is a need to further develop a concern for outcome.

Academic studies of implementation in the 1980s focused on descriptive analysis followed by prescriptive conclusions and tended to emphasise the need to move away from efficiency-led PIs as performance governance to a greater emphasis on equity and consumerism. Several studies including Linkierman (1993) and

Smith (1995a) looked at implementation problems within public sector organisations and concluded that there are often dysfunctional consequences of implementing performance measurement systems. If organisations consider change management theory, they are less likely to encounter opposition from within the organisation. This requires a participative "bottom-up" approach where the system develops from within the organisation but is supported from the top and organisational members feel a sense of ownership of performance measures. Criticisms also relate to the over-emphasis on PIs as post-controls in that they are used for reporting past performance. There is insufficient use of PIs for concurrent controls and for planning purposes (pre-control).

Implementation studies reflect the problems identified in the public strategy implementation literature in that problems can arise for a variety of reasons. Sometimes the problem is the PI system; sometimes the problem is a result of the implementation strategy and difficulties in the management of change. Sometimes the problem is "bad luck".

The studies to date have not considered to any great extent stakeholder perceptions of PI systems. There has also been insufficient analysis of the managerial implications of PI systems.

Trends in the use of performance indicators

Mackie (2001) concludes that there are a number of discernable trends in the use of PIs in public management. These are as follows:

From performance governance to performance management

There is less emphasis on prescribed indicators from government, funding agencies and audit agencies and more emphasis on self-assessment and self-evaluation by public organisations.

From Post-control to concurrent and pre-control

There is much more use of PIs for monitoring organisational activity on a regular basis and to begin to use PIs as planning targets. There remains an interest in the summative assessment of annual performance through a prescribed suite of PIs.

Value for money to value added

There is a growing interest in the contribution of public sector organisations to the economy and to society. Government wants to know what the population gains from the use of public resources. If there is little or no tangible benefit then perhaps resources could be deployed elsewhere. This is a movement away from economy and efficiency to a concern for the quality of output and outcome.

From dials to tin openers

There is less emphasis on the annual "snap shot" of an organisations performance as seen through aggregated statutory PIs and more use of dis-aggregated PIs which prompt further investigation by operational and strategic managers.

Published "league" tables to confidential benchmarking

Less use of published "league" tables of performance achieved against prescribed indicators and more use of confidential benchmarking of processes and performance achieved in an effort to create awareness of existing performance standards to prompt action toward maintaining and improving relative performance.

Public administration to strategic and operational management

Less concern for the way in which in which strategy is implemented provided strategy objectives are being achieved. Performance indicators therefore need to be limited for the purposes of accountability and control but developed further for strategic and operational managers.

Use within a system to use by stakeholders

The original channel of communication for PIs was between government, funders and service providers. The publication of performance information to stakeholders was originally problematic as many stakeholders had difficulty in interpreting PIs. In recent years, the trend has been to make the PIs easier to understand but as yet there is little evidence of their use to inform clients and stakeholders.

Enhancing the competence of users

There is a growing recognition that benefits will only accrue to users of PIs if they develop competence in their use as management tools. This trend has been slow to develop and only in recent years has the need for training and development in the use of PIs been recognised. Unfortunately, there has been little evidence of support for such training and development from government, funders and audit agencies. The publication of guidance notes is an inadequate response to widespread gaps in competence.

Improving the management of performance indicators information

The trend in recent years has been to develop management information systems to promote more effective processing of performance data. In addition, there are concerns about the reliability and validity of performance data.

Accommodating diversity

Public sector organisations pursue a diverse range of missions in different environmental circumstances utilising a range of staff competencies in order to meet strategy and strategic objectives while satisfying discrete client and stakeholder expectations. The complexity of public organisations makes the use of a prescribed set of national PIs inappropriate as such a set cannot hope to accommodate such diversity. The trend here is to develop bespoke suites of indicators that are appropriate to the particular circumstances of each public sector organisation. For example, students with learning difficulties may never achieve all the modules required for attaining a named programme award and they may never gain employment, but they can have their lives enhanced by developing a range of competences which better helps them cope with life in our society. The performance of such students has a detrimental effect on current further education PIs, but their particular circumstances must be recognised and their learning requirements supported. Such programmes contribute to the needs of society and to the social inclusion agenda and therefore should be reflected somewhere in the measurement of an organisation's performance. Bespoke suites of indicators can do this and there is a high level of interest in this trend.

Performance Management in Local Government and NHS Scotland

Scotland is far from alone in designing a Performance Assessment Framework (PAF) to monitor and improve the performance of its healthcare system. Other governments around the world have introduced similar instruments, notably, in England but also in the United States and Canada. Their use is also apparent in other sectors in the United Kingdom through school league tables and through the introduction of the Comprehensive Performance Assessment of Local Authorities in England. The variety of settings in which performance assessment frameworks are used is indicative of the fact that they are not necessarily synonymous with a centrally planned healthcare system. A PAF is essentially a form of information and regulation which can be used within a market or non-market-based sector.

As one would expect given this variation in system setting, the production of such performance information is associated with a number of possible objectives:

1. To secure or enhance accountability to funders and other stakeholders;
2. To identify areas of poor/under-performance, and centres of excellence;

3. To help patients and purchasers of healthcare choose a provider;
4. To enable providers to focus on areas requiring improvement; and
5. To provide epidemiological and other public data.

The Scottish PAF has all of these at the heart of its objectives with the exception of the third, which is more applicable to market-orientated healthcare systems such as those of England and the United States. The Scottish system is also distinguishable from other systems by the lack of explicit financial or non-financial rewards and penalties attached to the performance assessment framework and the absence of published performance league tables.

The Scottish system is based on an annual production and assessment of data. The seven areas of performance covered by the data are:

1. Health improvement and reducing inequalities;
2. Fair access to healthcare services;
3. Clinical governance and effectiveness of healthcare;
4. Patients' experience, including service quality;
5. Involving the public and communities;
6. Staff governance; and
7. Organisational and financial performance and efficiency.

The Information and Statistics Division of the Scottish Executive provide the 15 NHS Boards with their own PAF data in February of each year. The data can be divided into quantitative data and qualitative data in the form of assessments. The quantitative data is presented showing comparisons with previous years and with other NHS Boards. Boards then have an opportunity to review and discuss this information prior to an updated version of the data being published at the end of May. The data are used to inform the NHS Board Accountability Reviews, which take place for each Board during the following June and July.

Clinical governance

Clinical governance is an overarching framework that demonstrates clinical quality and continuous improvement. It is a framework for clinical audit research and development, continuing professional development, critical incident review, and reflective practice.

Clinical governance, or safe and effective care, lies at the heart of all healthcare services, and over the last five years such governance has become embedded throughout NHSScotland. NHS Quality Improvement Scotland (NHS QIS) is committed to, and responsible for, supporting and developing clinical governance, and in a recent report the NHS QIS presents the first ever stocktake of NHSScotland's clinical governance arrangements since its introduction in April 1999 (NHS QIS, November 2004).

The extensive information and recommendations contained within this report will play a significant part in the development of the work programme for the newly established Clinical Governance and Patient Safety Support Unit. The findings will be used to develop a support framework that is based on identified needs. This work will also closely link with other NHS QIS clinical governance projects.

While this is a national report, each NHSScotland organisation involved has also received local feedback, which could be used to inform local development as well as informing the national picture.

Performance management in local government

The Performance Management and Planning Framework (Audit Scotland, 2004) is based on 10 criteria:

1. Clear leadership for a Best Value approach is provided by elected members, the service head and the senior management team.
2. We understand the needs, expectations and priorities of all our stakeholders.
3. We carry out effective Best Value reviews.
4. We have detailed and realistic plans for achieving our goals.
5. We make best use of our people.
6. We make best use of our assets.
7. We have sound financial control and reporting.
8. We actively support continuous improvement.
9. We monitor and control our overall performance.
10. We have an effective approach to public performance reporting.

Audit Scotland's provides guidance and this includes detailed advice on how authorities can assess themselves against these 10 criteria. Performance management and planning provides a practical management and accountability framework for local authorities to develop the policies arising from Best Value and community planning.

Quality and Quality Awards

Quality is best defined as "fitness for purpose" that is, the service provided to clients adequately meets the clients perceived requirements. Whilst each organisation is different in terms of the quality systems it already operates; the levels of awareness of quality issues among its staff, and the extent to which documentation is available, a generalised approach to implementation will involve the following process.

It is important that the organisation understands why it wishes to pursue a quality system. The lengthy time scale involved (up to two years) means that certification is a costly and time-consuming process. It must, therefore, be more than just a certificate to hang on the office wall—it must bring in work to the organisation or provide some other form of competitive advantage. Quality awards should be a means to an end and not an end in themselves. It will be necessary to provide considerable amounts of training for the staff who are to administer the system. Some of this training will concentrate on the specific task elements which will be required, including the correct completion of the documentation for each stage of the quality system. The other major element of training concerns the need to change attitudes; to educate people why it is important that the system is operated as laid down in the quality manual and that deviations or omissions from this process cannot be tolerated.

When the systems are in place and the training has been completed, it may be worthwhile to allow the system to run for a short period so that staff can become thoroughly familiar with the way in which the system operates and to become comfortable with the documentation on procedures. At this point, it is usual to carry out an internal audit of the procedures to assess their effectiveness; to provide the opportunity for the project team to review the systems; and to ensure that "drift" has not taken place in completing the procedures. This internal audit is usually carried out by someone from outside the immediate project team.

Finally, the systems will require to be audited by an external assessor. This assessment can take several days to complete and will lead to either the award of the quality assurance certificate or to the recommendation that certain areas within the quality system need to be amended in order to meet the audit requirements. Once these changes have been made then the system will be reassessed. Successful certification is, however, only the start of the external audit process, since a condition of award is that the organisation will permit regular repeat visits by the audit team (usually annually) and also spot checks (24 hours' notice).

EFQM Excellence Model

The EFQM Excellence Model is a comprehensive framework for assessing the strengths and areas for improvement of an organisation across all its activities. It is based on the practical experience of public, private and voluntary sector organisations across Europe including over half of all public sector organisations in the United Kingdom. It has been designed over 10 years with the active involvement and contributions of hundreds of organisations. Although the origins of this process lie in the private sector, the public and voluntary sector experience with the EFQM Excellence Model is significant.

The EFQM Excellence Model is promoted in Europe by the European Foundation for Quality Management (EFQM(R)) and in Scotland by their national partner organisation, Quality Scotland. The EFQM Excellence Model tells us that excellent customer results, people results and society results are achieved through leadership driving policy and strategy, management of people, partnership and resources, and processes, leading ultimately to excellence in key performance results (see Figure 9.1 below).

The EFQM Excellence Model consists of nine criteria, divided into Enablers (the how's) and Results (the what's). The Enabler criteria are concerned with how the organisation conducts itself, how it manages its staff and resources, how it plans its strategy and how it reviews and monitors key processes. The organisation's results are what it achieves. These encompass the level of satisfaction among the organisation's employees and customers, its impact on the wider community and key performance indicators.

Figure 9.1

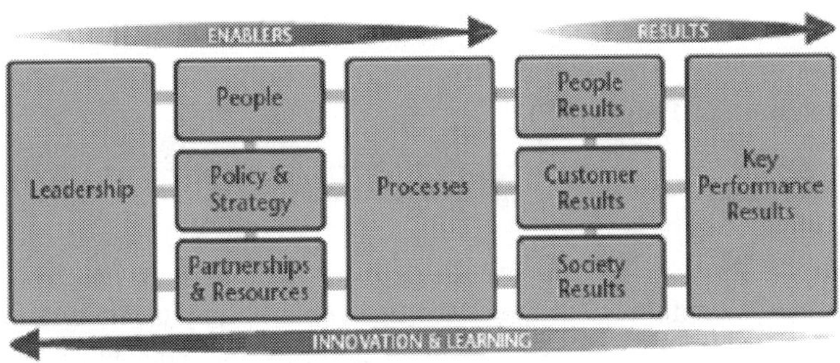

Figure 1 – The EFQM Excellence Model (©EFQM 1999).

Charter Mark

Charter Mark is the Government's quality improvement scheme for customer service. It is both a standard and a quality improvement tool to assist organisations in service delivery to customers.

Introduced in 1990, the scheme is now more relevant than ever to the new agenda for public service reform and service delivery. The Charter Mark criteria have been revised to reflect the main principles for improving the delivery of public services that have been developed by the Prime Minister's Office of Public Service

Reform. The new scheme was piloted during 2003 and became fully operational from the beginning of 2004.

Charter Mark continues to be unique in that it focuses on the experience of the customers and the service they receive. It provides applicants with a framework and a toolkit that can be used to drive customer-focused quality improvement programmes and a culture of continuous quality improvement, irrespective of the size or type of the service provided.

There is no quota for the number of organisations that can achieve the standard; all those who meet the criteria will achieve Charter Mark status. To date more than 9,000 organisations have applied for Charter Mark and there are currently more than 2,400 holders of the standard. The scheme was revised to make sure it reflects government priorities for public services, to reduce bureaucracy and make it easier for applicants to apply. This has been achieved by cutting out overlaps and duplication within the original criteria without diluting them in any way.

Charter Mark applicants are assessed against six criteria. These are:

- Setting standards and performing well;
- Actively engaging with your customers, partners and staff;
- Being fair and accessible to everyone and promoting choice;
- Continuously developing and improving;
- Using your resources effectively and imaginatively; and
- Contributing to improving opportunities and quality of life in the communities you serve.

Investors in People (IiP)

Investors in People is a national standard, which sets a level of good practice for improving an organisation's performance through its people.

The key principles are:

- Commitment: an Investor in People is fully committed to developing its people in order to achieve its aims and objectives;
- Planning: an Investor in People is clear about its aims and objectives and what its people need to do to achieve them;
- Action: an Investor in People develops its people effectively in order to improve its performance; and
- Evaluation: an Investor in People understands the impact of its investment in people on its performance.

Becoming an Investor in People involves a number of stages:

- Information gathering: including finding out more about the standard from others who have used it and talking to

Investors in People Scotland and the Local Enterprise Company (LEC);

- Initial diagnostic: to see how the organisation measures up against the national standard and to identify action to close any gaps;
- Develop people and processes as necessary;
- Further assessment to ascertain if the organisation meets the standard. Once it does, the organisation will be formally recognised as an Investor in People and can publicise this through use of the logo;
- Re-assessment: organisations will need to decide how often they wish to be reviewed against the standard. Recognition is for life subject to review at least once every three years. Organisations decide how often the review should take place, but the timing should ensure that continuous improvement becomes an integral part of retaining the standard.

ISO 9000:2000

The ISO 9000:2000 series are a set of tools to help organisations ensure that their processes are managed to enable them to meet customers' needs and expectations and any related statutory and regulatory requirements. The ISO 9000 family comprises:

- ISO 9000:2000 (Quality management systems—Fundamentals and vocabulary)
- ISO 9001:2000* (Quality management systems—Requirements)
- ISO 9004:2000 (Quality management systems—Guidelines for performance improvement)

To comply with ISO 9000, an organisation needs to review its processes in accordance with the standard's requirements. Organisations must:

- Have top management that are fully committed to the management system;
- Identify their processes and how they are applied;
- Determine what the sequence of the processes are, how the processes interact and how they will be managed;
- Ensure that the correct resources are available;
- Monitor, measure and analyse the processes; and
- Ensure that the processes and the effectiveness of the quality management system are continually improved.

Benchmarking

Benchmarking is defined as a continuous systematic process for evaluating products, services and processes within organisations that are recognised as representing best practices for the purpose of organisational improvement. In simple terms, benchmarking is a process of measuring and comparing specific aspects of performance between organisations. Benchmarking is used to establish processes of improvement to attain improved levels of performance.

The essence of benchmarking is the notion of comparison. It is all very well to know from your own point of reference how well you are doing but schools, teams or departments within schools should also take into account how well they are doing compared to similar schools, teams and departments or to other external standards. When you do such comparisons you are benchmarking.

A benchmark is a standard or point of reference against which one can measure or compare actual performance. Benchmarking is the process of comparison. Very often it will involve comparison of data, but it can also include comparing your practices or approaches with others or with what you have identified as best practice in the field. A useful formal definition would be:

> "Benchmarking is a structured and focused approach to comparing with others the performance levels achieved, and/or the practices used to achieve an outcome, so that one can identify and emulate best practice."

The Big Picture

The Big Picture is an organisational development framework with built-in practical tools (see Figure 9.2). It is designed to help people think about every aspect of their organisation and its work and to take action to improve it. The framework has been developed by people who work in and understand the voluntary sector. It recognises the unique qualities of voluntary organisations. At the same time, it draws on good practice from other sectors.

The Big Picture is based on the following principles:

Enabling results

Processes should lead to results. The Big Picture encourages people to satisfy their stakeholders and achieve positive impact in their work. This is done through effective steering by the board or management committee and effective management processes.

Continuous improvement

No matter where people are, they can still get better. There are acceptable standards that they all need to achieve but they should aspire to reach even higher levels. The act of questioning and learning through the use of the Big Picture will lead to a process of continuous improvement.

Non-prescriptive

Changes should relate to the needs of each organisation, not an external set of rules laid down by others. The Big Picture allows people to take a guided tour of self-discovery. They devise their own solutions based on their own experiences. This involves identifying their strengths and areas for improvement.

Non-judgmental

The Big Picture is non-judgmental in its approach. People are helped to identify the right questions, but it is up to them to determine the answers.

Figure 9.2

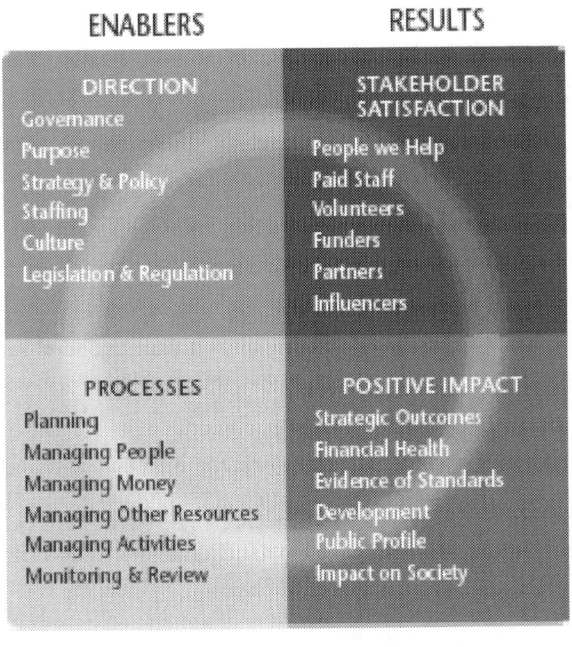

ENABLERS	RESULTS
DIRECTION Governance Purpose Strategy & Policy Staffing Culture Legislation & Regulation	STAKEHOLDER SATISFACTION People we Help Paid Staff Volunteers Funders Partners Influencers
PROCESSES Planning Managing People Managing Money Managing Other Resources Managing Activities Monitoring & Review	POSITIVE IMPACT Strategic Outcomes Financial Health Evidence of Standards Development Public Profile Impact on Society

Source: 'Promoting Excellence in Scotland 2004', Crown copyright.

The Big Picture has been designed to be used in a variety of different ways, by many different types of organisation (both large and small), at all levels within an organisation. It has also been designed around the development/planning cycle, which is an essential tool for all organisations wanting to improve.

It operates by:

- Identifying the needs to be met;

- Devising a plan to meet the needs;
- Doing something practical to meet the needs;
- Reviewing the extent of success in meeting these needs; and
- Identifying further needs to be met.

The Big Picture can be used in a variety of ways. Most commonly it is used at an away day to assess the need for change and to plan how this will take place. At a subsequent meeting the group can review the impact of this change using the framework. They can then go through the cycle again and identify the need for further changes. The Big Picture can also be used to assess the whole organisation and as a checklist for reports, plans, training needs analysis and induction sessions.

Balanced Scorecard

The Balanced Scorecard is a set of measures that are directly linked to the company's strategy. The scorecard allows managers to evaluate the company from four perspectives: financial performance, customer knowledge, internal business processes, and learning and growth.

Inside Balanced Scorecard is a concise definition of the company's vision and strategy. Surrounding the vision and strategy are four additional boxes; each box contains the objectives, measures, targets, and initiatives for one of the four perspectives. A properly constructed scorecard is balanced between short- and long-term measures; balanced between financial and non-financial measures; and balanced between internal and external performance perspectives. The scorecard is a management system that can be used as the central organising framework for key managerial process.

Balanced Scorecard is a framework for implementing and managing strategy at all levels of an enterprise by linking objectives, initiatives and measures of performance. The Scorecard provides a view of an organisation's overall performance by integrating financial measures with other key performance indicators around customer perspectives, internal business processes and organisational growth, learning and innovation.

Managers determine what is required to deliver and sustain the strategy and how to monitor progress in terms of the four dimensions:

(a) Finance
(b) Customer
(c) Process
(d) People

The respective measures within these dimensions are used to communicate the strategy, to allocate responsibilities and time frames and to monitor progress. The Balanced Scorecard focuses all parts of the enterprise on the critical success factors and shows how each part becomes a determinant of the eventual strategic outcome (refer to Figure 9.3 below).

Figure 9.3

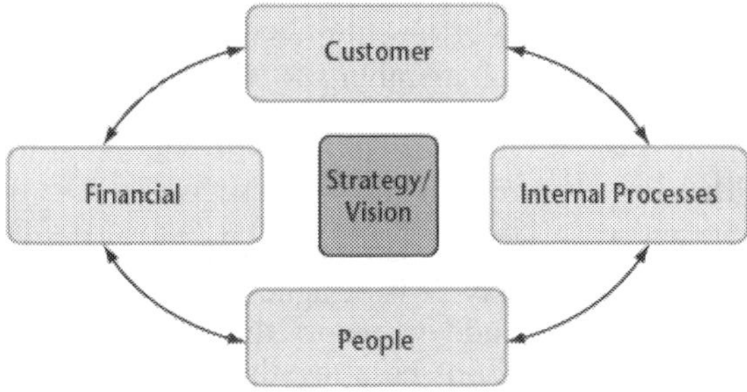

Source: 'Promoting Excellence in Scotland 2004', Crown copyright.

The Balanced Scorecard was originally designed for the private sector by Kaplan and Norton and it places financial results at the head of the strategic hierarchy. In the public and voluntary sector, there is a different focus, with the overarching mission or long-term objective of the organisation sitting at the head of the hierarchy. Within this context funders, or donors, represent the "finance" aspect of the framework. They are on an equal footing in the hierarchy with the people the organisation helps, *e.g.* service users or campaign beneficiaries, the "customer" element. The internal processes must be identified that will deliver the desired value propositions for both groups. The objectives within the scorecard can then be orientated towards the achievement of the high level mission.

The financial perspective differs from that in the private sector. In the private sector, the key financial objectives relate to profitability and returns on investment. In the public sector, financial considerations will have an enabling or restraining role but will not be the only criterion for assessing strategic options. Success for local authorities and health boards can be measured in terms of how effectively and efficiently they meet the requirements of their stakeholders.

The client/customer perspective focuses on the ability of the organisation to provide quality goods and services. It includes issues about the effectiveness of service delivery and overall client/customer service and satisfaction. In general, the customer perspective is the primary focus for a local authority. Local authorities are also more likely to have a stronger fiduciary care/stewardship perspective than private-sector organisations.

The internal business process perspective covers the internal business results that lead to financial success and satisfied customers. To meet their financial and customer requirements, local authorities and health boards must identify those internal processes that contribute to successful service outputs and outcomes. It is these key processes that are monitored to ensure that outcomes will be satisfactory.

The people perspective covers the competence of staff and the capacity of organisational members to develop individually and collectively to enhance effectiveness.

Kaizen Blitz

A Kaizen Blitz is a business improvement tool, which achieves "impossible" results quickly. It is designed to identify and strip out anything that does not add value to the critical process under examination. It is also about creating the right physical environment by removing obstacles that hinder the process. Facilitation by someone who is well versed in the Kaizen principles is essential to create and maintain the right environment. Their role is to train and guide the team members to develop and rapidly implement solutions to resolve critical business issues. The effect is immediate and the improvements in the process obvious. The key to the success of Kaizen is that it is the people who have hands-on knowledge of the existing process who explore and develop the new process, creating stronger ownership and sustainability.

Six Sigma

Six Sigma is a methodology for improvement. Six Sigma helps organisations manage and improve processes, both service and technical, in smarter ways. It is aimed at three main areas:

(a) Customer satisfaction;
(b) Reducing errors and defects; and
(c) Reducing cycle time.

The results of applying Six Sigma are measurable in hard financial and/or customer satisfaction terms. Although incremental change can be gained, Six Sigma is targeted to areas where "breakthrough" performance is required.

As with all major improvement programmes the involvement and leadership of the senior executive is an important element.

Conclusion

Many of the reforms of the Thatcher–Major era remain in place. Prior to the 1997 general election, the neo-liberal thinking which provided the impetus for reform under the Conservatives was under attack from "New Labour" with its concern for communitarianism and stakeholderism. Early targets for the Blair administration included the revamping of the NHS patient's charter to incorporate a greater range of quality of care indicators. Counterbalancing the acceptance of markets with policy interventions to strengthen social cohesion was very much in accordance with the notion of a "third way".

"Smarter" use of public money is to be achieved through the tighter monitoring and evaluation of the efficiency and effectiveness of public spending by a Cabinet Committee. The Blair Government and the Scottish Coalition Government are committed to both continuity and change in relation to NPM and therefore to the use of performance measurement, charging the new Cabinet Secretary with strengthening "the centre" of government to develop its strategic capacity, ability to progress-chase policies and promote greater organisational co-operation. All of these necessitate comprehensive performance monitoring systems (Painter, 1999, pp.94–112).

There is little doubt that the stimulus for the development of performance management came from the emergence of NPM as the dominant public management paradigm. The Efficiency Scrutinies, the FMI, "Next Steps", Charterism and "Network Governance" have all contributed to the logarithmic expansion in the use of performance indicators by governments, funders, public managers, clients and other stakeholders. Pollitt (2001, pp.183–184) identifies many of the perceived benefits of "reformed" public sector organisations. These include:

- Being close to clients/customers;
- Being performance-driven not rule-bound;
- Displaying a commitment to continuous quality improvement;
- Being structured in a "lean" and "flat" way highly decentralised, with street-level staff who are "empowered" to be flexible and to innovate;
- Practising tight cost control, with the help of modern, commercial-style accounting systems;
- Using performance-related systems for recruiting, posting, promoting and paying staff.

Pollitt goes on to identify the features of "reinvented" governments and these include:

- "Steering not rowing", *i.e.* become more concerned with strategy and less with operational implementation;
- Acting in anticipatory ways—pro-activity;

- Seeking to use market mechanisms wherever (possible, either in the form of quasi-markets or by contracting out);
- Seeking inter-organisational partnerships, both within the public sector ("joined-up government") and with the private and voluntary sectors.

Pollitt additionally comments (p.186) that there have been surprisingly few independent, broad scope evaluations of public management reforms.

Following the general movement towards performance measurement in the public sector promoted by central government, there was a need to operationalise the performance assessment and measurement demands of politicians and funders. Performance assessment was high on the Conservative Government's agenda in 1979 and its high profile, as a means of promoting performance governance, remained throughout the 1980s. Further pressure was placed on public managers by the drive to extend the scope of performance measures in response to the Next Steps initiative and the Citizen's Charter. Pollitt (1994, p.12) criticises the Charter initiatives for being " top down" from governors to people. The concept of citizen is based on individualism with little concern for the community. There remains widespread positive environmental support for performance assessment. The change of government in 1997 did not change the drive for improvements in the management of public services and there therefore remains a powerful lobby for performance assessment and performance indicators as tools of performance governance and performance management. There is an underpinning premise that competition and market mechanism will provide choice, ensure quality and enhance value. Accountability is not through the political process but through providing information and setting standards.

Public managers have had to respond to these influences by exerting greater managerial control over their range of responsibilities. This resulted in the development of performance assessment and performance indicators as tools of managers and the extension of managerialism in the public sector. Managerialism can be interpreted as the greater use of management theory and strategic management processes in an effort to enhance organisational performance. Performance indicators are the tools to underpin this measurement and assessment process. Performance in the public domain is, according to Stewart and Walsh (1994, p.45), an elusive concept and Carter (1991, p.99) sees it as a complex and contestable concept. Despite these concerns, public managers had to provide performance-related information to government, funding agencies and the general public. The consensus view of commentators is that if a performance system and its indicators are designed with specific objectives and a clear vision of how it will be used, then its overall purpose and its results will be more easily understood, despite the complexity of public sector performance. This view is qualified by Stewart and Walsh (1994, p.46) who state that performance assessment is a matter of judgment which can be informed by performance measures but which can never be determined by them.

Rogers (1990) and Carter (1988 and 1991) highlight three main areas of the wider context of public service delivery which are relevant to judgments of performance: stakeholder impacts; environmental pressures; and ownership of performance. In the public sector, the provision of services is undertaken for the benefit of society and, as such, has multiple constituencies and multiple stakeholders to address (Kanter and Summers, 1987, p.233). Differing political values and an imbalance in power relationships create a context of antagonism. The more the tasks in hand raise political issues, the more complex the performance assessment (Stewart and Walsh, 1994, p.49). Environmental pressures are dynamic and are often completely outwith the control of public managers (Carter, 1991, p.94). The ownership of decisions and accountability for their consequences has become blurred due to the increasing complexity of public services provision as a consequence of compulsory competitive tendering and public private partnerships. Given the complexity, interdependence and partnership functions now inherent in the public sector and the consequent emphasis on maximising joint inputs to action, clarity of purpose and performance assessment, there has to be clearly understood inter-relationships which are understood by all providers. Equity can be difficult to achieve in such circumstances, as it must involve balancing, sometimes conflicting, demands on resources from the multiplicity of stakeholders. This will inevitably result in a degree of insensitivity to the aspirations of some stakeholders in favour of others, especially those with the least resources, limited power and influence and most vulnerability (Carter, 1991, p.92).

NPM advocates the emergence of the post-bureaucratic organisation where there is less "hands-on" government, but neo-Taylorist arguments have been used to justify greater control over performance by funders and government. There has been a shift from input controls to output controls but this has not resulted in greater flexibility and looser control within organisations. UK public sector organisations appear to be overwhelmed by forms of performance monitoring including scrutinies, audits, performance review systems, peer assessments, appraisals, statistical returns, etc. (Hoggett, 1996). As a consequence of this there appears to be a contradiction in the role of performance indicators in public management. Performance indicators can be a tools of "hands -off" performance governance or they can support a rational-systems model of control that could be termed neo-Taylorist.

The Blair and McConnell administrations are committed to the extension of inter-agency collaboration. This concept of network governance, according to Painter (1999, pp. 94–112), lies somewhere in the grey intermediate area between the extremes of hierarchy and market.

Chapter 10

THE NEW PUBLIC MANAGEMENT OF SCOTLAND: RETROSPECT AND PROSPECT

Introduction

This chapter concludes our consideration of the contemporary context of Scottish local government and the NHS in Scotland by identifying a range of factors likely to influence their future.

The future of Scottish local government and the NHS in Scotland can only be partially determined by this analysis as the analysis remains incomplete and is, at best, an informed guess. The Scottish public sector is, in part, a product of its environment. This concluding chapter conducts a review of the New Public Management as it has impacted on local government and the NHS in Scotland before considering their future development.

Environmental influences and the Scottish Executive

Scottish local government has undergone radical change over the past 30 years and there is little likelihood of the pace of change abating in the foreseeable future. However, local government in Scotland still tries to promote the fundamental principles of local government embodied in the Wheatley Report of 1969, *Power, Effectiveness, Local Involvement and Local Democracy*. The conclusion of this chapter considers some of the key issues currently facing Scottish local government in relation to accountability and control.

The Scottish Executive is committed to implementing a new comprehensive ethical framework so that all will know with clarity the conduct expected of those in local government and will have confidence that any wrongdoing will be rapidly and effectively addressed.

The nature of the relationship between central and local government is not rigidly determined by the constitution. The history of these relations shows that the relative power, strength and influence of the two elements can vary over time.

There will always be a need for this local delivery of services and local government achieves this, while, at the same time, introducing aspects of local democracy and accountability. Local government is a means by which communities can make real decisions affecting the services to their area. There are, however, many critics of local government, some of whom question its usefulness and very existence.

There have always been two opposing views of local government: a centralist view and a localist one. Both were summarised by the Layfield Report (1976).

The centralist model

In this type of system, local authorities act as virtual agents for central government departments; the primary justification for their existence being their local awareness, knowledge and interest in the community. The contribution of local councils in such a system is to minimise any charges of remoteness and bureaucratic administration levelled at a centralised administration.

The localist model

In such a system, real political power is devolved to local councils who are best placed to act in the interests of local democracy and to exercise real authority and power in a manner relatively autonomous from central government.

The Layfield Report (1976) considered the implications of both types of government and concluded that the localist model was preferable. Few would disagree with this, at least in theory. Political and economic circumstances in the modern world, however, create a number of pressures towards centralism. These may have the effect of eroding or negating the attributes of local government to such an extent that it has no obvious advantage over a system of administration.

There are numerous valid arguments for central control, both economic and political. Local government in Scotland employs 260,000 people and the scale of its expenditure ensures that it cannot be insulated from the macro-economic policies of central government. Local authorities have to recognise that government, if it is to control the economy, must exert influence over public expenditure including local authority expenditure. Also, as local government becomes more "politicised", this inevitably extends the interest and influence of national politics and parties. The tendency is increased as local authorities come to provide more services which are central to the lives of their citizens.

The overall trend towards centralisation seems to be gathering momentum, helped by the internal weaknesses of local government. These relate to the legislative form and conduct of local government and hamper its performance as a provider of services.

Local government has found itself under increasing attack during the Thatcher administrations because of its perceived weaknesses and opposition to central policy. On the key issue of finance, the Conservative Government postulated three alternative strategies in its Green Paper, *Paying for Local Government*. These were:

(a) the fundamental restructuring of local government;
(b) the imposition of much greater central control over local authorities; and
(c) financial reform designed to improve local accountability.

The first two options were rejected, the former on the grounds of the upheaval that it would cause, and the latter because of the unacceptable demands on central government staffing that a centralist system would generate.

The Scottish Executive, in theory, sees the future in terms of increased local accountability, to guarantee the continued existence of a healthy, democratic system of local autonomy, which would also reduce the tension between central government and local authorities. In the longer term, increased accountability would lead to the improvement of services. This may be the Government's stated aim, but its actions so far have raised doubts about its commitment to real local autonomy. Many of the changes introduced by the Thatcher administration have weakened local government and further centralised power and the New Labour administrations have done little, so far, to change this. However, the 2003 Joint Statement by the Leaders of the Scottish Labour Party and the Scottish Liberal Democrats entitled *A Partnership for a Better Scotland* gives a clear commitment to change. In section 2 of the Joint Statement, entitled "Delivering excellent Public Services", the Coalition Government commit themselves to the setting of national standards for public services. In addition, the Joint Statement promotes devolved decision-making to the most local level wherever possible and sees community planning as one of the main methods through which the Scottish Government will promote and share best practice in the planning and delivery of public services. The Government will monitor progress by both regular and targeted independent inspection of performance and action against common standards, to ensure good performance is shared and to identify poor performance. The Government are promoting all modes of control instead of relying heavily on post-control modes of accountability.

Greater hands-on control from the centre must result in the reduction of Scottish local government autonomy. Some commentators argue that local government is but a shadow of its former self, because of the withdrawal of functions from local councils; the reduction of its financial independence; and the limitation of its political discretion. If this process of centralisation is to continue, then central government must consider the broad implications and decide whether the consequences are acceptable. There are signs that even the present Coalition Government recognises that there may be some dangers in total centralisation and there are calls for a revitalisation of the partnership between the two tiers of government. It may be that a new version of this partnership will emerge, in which local government; continues to deliver services; accepts that these services will increasingly be determined by national decisions on standards and expenditure; but would be part of a more formalised structure of consultation about these matters.

Clearly, the future of local government accountability depends on the composition of the government in power at Holyrood and its attitude towards the usefulness of local councils. The Conservatives under Mrs Thatcher and John Major tipped the balance heavily in favour of central government, but the devolved Government is pursuing a stated different policy for local government in relation to accountability and control. However, there may be significant drift between stated policy and actual policy as the Coalition Government seek to promote the attainment of "High Level Commitments". In order to do so, they must maintain and enhance their capability for performance governance and this requires comprehensive systems of accountability and control. The key to success in Partnership with local government must be to maintain appropriate levels of performance governance while encouraging devolved performance management at the level of the individual local authority.

Public expenditure in Scotland is about 50 per cent of gross domestic product. The Scottish Executive budget will rise to £255 billion by 2007–08 and the Government remains committed to ensuring that Scottish public services deliver the very best value for money. The Efficient Government Initiative, announced in 2004, is designed to deliver public sector savings of £500 million by 2007–08. Audit Scotland will continue to promote value for money in Scottish public services. The future of Scottish local government will be one in which the demands of Best Value continue to influence decision making in Scottish local authorities.

Scotland has a declining and ageing population. The population is around 5.05 million with 50 per cent of the population over the age of 30. The larger urban areas are declining in population with Glasgow declining by 8 per cent since 1991. Scottish local government has to respond to these trends by shifting resources from areas of declining need (education) to areas where there is a growing demand for services (care of the elderly).

Scottish local government is influenced by technological changes in its operations and by e-government initiatives. E-government is a term used to describe initiatives promoted by central and local government to deliver services using communication and information technologies (C and IT). In Scotland, the Scottish Executive is promoting the development of e-government projects through the

Modernising Government Fund. There will be a growth in the use of communication and information technologies in local government.

The key element of eco-environmental influence is undoubtedly the growing significance of sustainable development policies. The aim of sustainable development is to ensure that our actions today do not limit the quality of life in the future. In 2004, the Scottish Executive reiterated their commitment by publicising a progress report (*Indicators of Sustainable Development for Scotland, Progress Report 2004*) identifying progress across the range of indicators since 1999. Local government has a major role to play in contributing to sustainable development in areas such as waste management, energy consumption, transport, travel, education and social concern.

Local authorities and NHS Boards can only do that which they are empowered to do by legislation.

The Local Government in Scotland Act 2003 provides the best guidance on the future legislative influences on Scottish local government. This Act places a duty on local authorities to secure Best Value, to participate in the community planning process and it empowers local authorities to "advance well-being". It will be these three dimensions that will continue to require legislative support and guidance for the foreseeable future.

Current debate on constitutional status

Burrows *et al.* (2005) identified that the McIntosh Commission had recommended that, in addition to the Covenant, an agreement be reached between the Scottish Ministers and local authorities setting out the terms in which both would operate. The Partnership Framework, agreed between the Executive and local government, was adopted in 2001. This is a non-legally binding agreement which sets out the principles forming the foundation of partnership working. The key elements of which are the principle of respect, parity of esteem and the principle of subsidiarity.

The Partnership Framework has failed to achieve the desired parity of esteem between the Scottish Executive and Scottish local government. This has been highlighted by the failure on the part of the Scottish Executive to consult with COSLA or with local councils on key aspects of proposed policy; McFadden and Lazarowicz (2003) conclude that parity of esteem appears to be absent in the current relationship. Parity of esteem is clearly lacking in the enforcement mechanisms in the Local Government in Scotland Act 2003. That Act imposes a duty on local authorities to secure Best Value and to engage in community planning. This Act additionally empowers local authorities to enhance well-being in the communities that they serve. Scottish Ministers can use preliminary notices and enforcement directions to monitor and enforce the power of well-being where they believe that local authorities might act *ultra vires* (exceed their powers).

Retrospect

Using Hood's seven central tenets of NPM (1995) we can consider the experience of Scottish local government and the NHS in Scotland.

Disaggregation of public organisations

This implies each smaller scale organisation having its own corporate identity, greater autonomy in resource management, devolved strategic planning and operational management while retaining accountability and funding links to government and funding bodies. Some local government services have been taken away from local authorities and are now being provided by autonomous public service bodies such as further education services and water.

Competition

This implies the creation of competitive and quasi-competitive markets to replace monopolistic public service provision. This reached its peak with the introduction of CCT, the purchaser-provider split, the creation of Fundholding GPs and NHS Trusts. Best Value and the scrutiny of Performance Management Framework implementation by Audit Scotland have replaced many dimensions of competition.

Private sector styles of management

There was an exponential growth in managerialism in the local government and the NHS in the 1980s and 1990s, but there are signs that public sector values need to become a more integral part of public management development programmes.

Resource management

In reviewing the NPM developments over the past 25 years, it is clear that this central tenet has not gone away. There is more emphasis in public management today on Best Value and the need for efficiency gains than there ever has been. However, there is a firm belief that quality standards can be maintained and efficiency gains made.

'Hands-on management'

There is more direct involvement on the part of the Scottish Executive in the strategic management of public services mainly through processes of strategic plan approval, funding allocations, inspection and annual reporting. There remains a danger in public sector managers becoming too much like business managers. Public managers must operate in a business-like manner but they must not forget that they are providing public services and many decisions cannot be subject to the same criteria as a purely commercial decision.

Performance expectations

Devolved government has created opportunities for much more direct clarification of performance expectation by the Scottish Executive. Most public sector bodies are "target-driven" from their funding bodies and the Scottish Executive.

Performance results

There has also been growth in the use of statutory performance indicators which public bodies must disclose to Audit Scotland and the Scottish Executive. There is a danger of "paralysis by analysis" in this development whereby too much time and effort (and therefore resources) is dedicated to providing results information and there is an opportunity cost where direct public service provision loses out on additional resources.

The net effect

These environmental influences mean that Scottish local government is operating in turbulent times and therefore if it is to survive and succeed it has to have a capacity to be responsive and flexible. Gone are the days of rigid organisational structures with inward looking managers and administrators more concerned with status, maximising staffing levels and operating within the law and annual budget allocations.

Today's local authorities and health boards have to be much more dynamic; to be primarily outward looking to monitor changing environmental circumstances. The key influences remain central and developed government and the communities that are served. Councillors, health board members and managers have to be more strategic in their decision-making, ensuring that they act within the law and promote Best Value in everything that they do.

The Scottish Executive's vision for government in Scotland identifies four main themes:

(a) Growing Scotland's economy;
(b) Delivering excellent public services;
(c) Supporting stronger safer communities; and
(d) Developing a confident, democratic Scotland

Scottish local government has a key part to play in the promotion of all four elements of this vision for government. COSLA, in its

2004 Annual Report, reiterates its President's longer-term vision for local government in Scotland. The key elements of which are:

(a) Long-term constitutional protection for local government coupled with short-term guarantees of stability;
(b) Resources to be available in the right quantity and with maximum flexibility to use these in ways that are locally important;
(c) National rather than central priorities and trust in local government to use local discretion sensibly within a framework of national policy; and
(d) Recognition of local government's role as the lead player in local partnerships.

This is obviously a wish list and a negotiating position. The Scottish Executive has expressed a desire to exert greater control over local government expenditure while encouraging decentralised decision-making. The Efficient Government initiative launched in June 2004 by the Scottish Executive emphasises key principles of:

(a) Focusing on people;
(b) Ensuring excellence;
(c) Maximising choice; and
(d) Getting the best value for the public pound.

Efficient Government adopts an holistic approach to efficiency gain by considering the public sector as a whole and to promote better co-ordination and co-operation between different areas of the public sector in relation to purchasing, accommodation and support services.

The Scottish Executive is committed to improving the delivery of public services and will work in partnership with local government to ensure delivery. Scottish local authorities have received unprecedented rises in financial support since Devolution. In 2005–06, the average increase is 5.5 per cent and by 2008 the level of funding local authorities receive will have risen by a massive 55 per cent. Most local authorities have now set their council tax figures for 2005–06 in line with—or less than—their indicative figures. The average increase is therefore around 4 per cent.

The Scottish Executive expects the whole public sector to deliver on Efficient Government and ensure the best possible use of public money.

Prospect: The Future of Scottish Local Government and the NHS in Scotland

The Scottish Executive wishes to promote efficiency gains in local government and the NHS and have expressed in Efficient Government initial areas of focus "to promote better co-ordination and co-operation between different areas of the public sector in relation to purchasing, accommodation and support services". The Scottish Executive is currently operating with public sector structures that were substantially created by pre-devolution governments. In the case of the NHS, the current system was largely a product of the 1974 reorganisation and the local government system was created by a Conservative Government and took effect on April 1, 1996.

The Scottish Executive Minister, speaking at the COSLA Annual Conference in April 2005, stated that transforming Scotland's public services must be done in partnership to ensure the delivery of quality and efficiency. Public Service Reform Minister Tom McCabe said his agenda for better, more modern and more efficient public services was not about centralisation and that local government had a key role to play, in partnership with the Executive. Councils have much they can teach other public sector bodies about efficiency and Best Value—but they must be prepared to learn from others. This, according to McCabe, is the opposite of a centralisation agenda. It is about empowering local government, while recognising that we must work together. The Executive's view of local government is based on a belief that councils must be responsive to the needs of the communities they serve; accountable to the people they represent; committed to effective leadership and partnership with other local bodies in the best interest of their local communities, and providers of first class services.

According to McCabe, efficient government is key to delivering on the Scottish executive's goals. Efficient government is not about cuts. It is about getting more out of the money government spends both in the current spending review period and through longer-term service transformation. While the Minister made clear there were no plans for further council reorganisation planned before 2007, new approaches had to be considered to ensure continuous improvement in the delivery of public services.

The Scottish Executive are committed to improving the quality of life of the citizens of Scotland through better healthcare, greater economic opportunity, stronger communities and world class education. Therefore, if these goals are to be achieved then government policy and action must contribute to their attainment. The Scottish Executive want to see more co-operation between local authorities and more partnership working between local authorities and other providers of public services.

However, in the longer term, if the Scottish Executive has a desire to increase public services efficiency, they could amend current local government and NHS structures in some way to promote further opportunities to achieve the desired efficiency gains. Purchasing, accommodation and support services could be a starting point. Community Health Partnerships and the Joint Future initiative have highlighted a capability for joined-up community-based service provision.

One approach to further rationalisation could be to take the existing mainland Health Board (15) areas and use these as a basis for a local government re-structure. The geographic areas of the cities of Aberdeen, Dundee, Edinburgh and Glasgow could be expanded to take in the wealthier communities on the peripheries of these cities thus transferring the council tax revenue to the local authority that provides many of the services used by residents of these communities.

This could create the following structure for public authorities with responsibility for local government services, the NHS and other public services:

- Highland
- Grampian
- Aberdeen Metropolitan
- Tayside
- Dundee Metropolitan
- Fife
- Central (Forth Valley)
- Argyle and Dunbartonshire
- Edinburgh Metropolitan
- Lothian
- Renfrewshire
- Glasgow Metropolitan
- Lanarkshire
- Ayrshire
- Dumfries and Galloway
- Borders
- Western Isles
- Orkney
- Shetland

Nineteen public bodies would be providing the services currently provided by 32 local authorities and 15 NHS Boards. This is a much more rational approach to public policy than we have seen in the past and responds to concerns expressed by the cities and the Scottish Executive. If budgets for health and local government remained separate and if "front line" service delivery resourcing remained intact then service delivery would remain unaffected. Savings could be made across managerial levels and support services. Savings of £2.5 million per annum could be achieved from the reduction in the number of chief executives alone.

At this point in time (2005), the Scottish Executive is working in a situation where the implementation of their policies is constrained by public sector structures developed prior to devolution. Management theory recommends that structure supports strategy and therefore, in the public sector, it would be appropriate to develop structures that support public policy implementation. Scottish local government structures can be reorganised to better support Scottish Executive policy initiatives.

The timing of such fundamental changes is crucial to their success and it is the view of the author that, following the next local government elections in 2007, there is an opportunity to restructure Scottish local government. The introduction of the Single Transferable Vote (STV) system combined with the changes to the Westminster constituency boundaries (the number of Scottish MPs at Westminster has declined from 72 to 59) provide an opportunity for reflection and change in the Scottish public sector.

Conclusion

This book has considered the ways in which New Public Management (NPM) has impacted on Scottish local government and the NHS in Scotland over a 25–year period. NPM appears to have peaked in the late 1990s and since the election of a Labour Government at Westminster in 1997, there has been a general decline in the marketplace surrogate dimensions of NPM. NPM has not gone away and elements of it are retained in relation to Best Value and Performance Management Frameworks. The time may therefore be right to stop referring to the changes as New Public Management for there is a renewed interest in achieving an approach to management in the public sector that combines a public service ethos with more effective public management practices. This requires reflection on the NPM experiences and consideration of contemporary environmental influences (political, economic, social and technological) to inform the way ahead. There has to be a renewed interest in public policy analysis and policy implementation in combination with knowledge, skills and competency in management and its public sector adaptations.

The Scottish systems of local government and NHS are subject to a range of environmental influences as is the Scottish Executive. The implementation of the PI system over a 10–year period reveals a link between performance monitoring and management and the nature of the NPM. The Blair Governments have moved back from the "New Right" version of NPM and this is reflected, among other things, in the contemporary features of the local government and NHS systems. NPM in the United Kingdom today has changed in response to local, national and global influences. There is obviously a desire on the part on many governments to modify the NPM components to adjust to changing environmental circumstances. The "doctrinal components" of NPM have been modified in part by Scottish Executive policies and by the changing context of public policy and public management.

The fundamental message is that the public policy process should be more dynamic and responsive to the changing context of public management while retaining its distinctiveness. Public managers must accept that they are substantially mandated to provide specified public services. Beginning with the general recommendations, if public managers implement public policy, then policy makers and implementors must better understand each other. There is a need to integrate theory in public policy analysis with management theory, contextualised for public managers, to inform public policy and its effective implementation and to truly reflect the context of today's public management environment.

Knowledge of policy analysis is necessary but not sufficient. Knowledge of management theory is also necessary but not sufficient. Policy formulators (government and government agencies) and policy implementors (strategic and operational public managers) must have knowledge and understanding of public policy and management theory in the context of public management. What is needed is a public management development programme that integrates the two perspectives. Such a programme could draw on good practice from within and outwith the public sector to promote innovations and to reflect the changing nature of public management. Core elements of this proposed management development programme would be:

(a) public policy analysis;
(b) public management;
(c) strategic management in the public sector;
(d) public marketing;
(e) stakeholder analysis; and
(f) managing change.

In recent years policy analysis and the policy process have dropped out of public management development programmes and there has been an overwhelming movement towards generic management development. This movement ignores the unique elements that are central to public management and loses the underlying public service ethos. Policy analysis should be retained but it must also be updated to reflect the changing relationship that exists between government, government agencies and public service providers.

In the 1980s, management techniques associated with NPM should have carried a Government Health Warning as few public managers could see any benefit from their use. Today, more and more public sector organisations are making greater use of NPM management techniques and, although not without difficulties, this trend is becoming the norm. As competence in the use of these techniques grows, more public managers will regard them as essential to their managerial roles and will not be able to do without them.

The effort-reward relationship in public sector organisations has radically changed over the last 20 years and there must come a point when the priority of Government and Funders is to restore an appropriate balance in this relationship.

The NPM of the 1980s is not the NPM of today. The paradigm is dynamic and necessitates a changing approach to managing in the public sector to support its effective implementation. In the case of Scottish local government and the NHS in Scotland, the future will require more collaboration and partnerships and this again will require different management competencies. Devolved government presents an opportunity for delivering quality public services to meet the needs and wants of the people of Scotland and the Scottish Executive should take the opportunity to respond to this challenge by adapting NPM to current and future circumstances. This may mean doing this differently from the rest of the United Kingdom but surely that is what devolved government is about, "doing well (effective) while doing good (responsive to social requirements)".

References

Accounts Commission (1986), *Annual Report*, Edinburgh: Accounts Commission in Scotland.

Accounts Commission (1993), *Local Government Act 1992: Publication of Information,* Edinburgh: Accounts Commission in Scotland.

Accounts Commission (1994), *Local Government Act 1992: The Publication of Information (Standards of Performance) Direction 1994*, Edinburgh: Accounts Commission in Scotland.

Accounts Commission (1995), *Performance Information for Scottish Councils 1993/94,* Edinburgh: Accounts Commission in Scotland.

Accounts Commission (1998), *Performance Information for Scottish Councils 1993/94,* Edinburgh: Accounts Commission in Scotland.

Adonis, A. and Pollard, S. (1998), *A Class Act: The myth of British classless society,* London, Penguin.

Alford, J. (1997), 'Performance monitoring in the Australian Public Services: A government-wide analysis', *Public Money and Management,* April-June, Vol.17, No.2.

Alison, G.T. (1993), 'Public and private management: are they fundamentally alike in all unimportant respects? In Perry, J.L. and Kraemer, K. L. (eds.) *Public Management: Public and Private Perspectives,* California, Mayfield Publishing.

Allsop, J. (1984), *Health Policy and the National Health Service,* London, Longman.

Aucoin, P. (1990), 'Administrative Reform in Public Management: paradigms, principles and pendulums', *Governance,* Vol. 3, No. 2, pp.115–137.

Audit Commission (1985), *Obtaining Better Value from Further Education,* London: HMSO.

Audit Commission (1986), *Performance Review in Local Government: A Handbook for Auditors and Local Authorities: Education*, London: HMSO.

Audit Commission (1988), *Performance Review in Local Government: A Handbook for Auditors and Local Authorities: Education*, London: HMSO.

Audit Commission (1989), *Performance Review in Local Government: A Handbook for Auditors and Local Authorities: Education*, London: HMSO.

Audit Commission (1995), *Using Your Indicators : A Councillor's Guide to the Local Authority Performance Indicators,* Bristol: Audit Commission.

Audit Scotland (1998), *Planning for Success,* Edinburgh, Audit Scotland.

Audit Scotland (2002), *How Government Works in Scotland,* Edinburgh, Audit Scotland.

Audit Scotland (2004), *Performance Management and Planning audit: A manager's Guide*, Edinburgh, Audit Scotland.

Bains (1972), *The New Local Authorities: Management and Structure,* Report (The Bains Report), London: HMSO.

Ball, R. (1998), *Performance Review in Local Government,* Aldershot.

Ball, R. and Monaghan, C. (1993), 'Performance Review: Threats and Opportunities', *Public Policy and Administration,* Vol. 8, No. 8 Winter.

Barrett, S. and Fudge, C (eds) (1981), *Policy and Action,* London, Methuen.

Boyne, G. et al (2003), *Evaluating Public Management Reforms,* Buckingham, Open University Press.

Brech, E.F.L. (1975), *The Principles and Practise of Management,* 3rd edn, London, Longman.

Bryson, J.M. (1988), *Strategic Planning for Public and Nonprofit Organisations,* San Francisco, Jossey-Bass.

Burrows, N., Carter, C., Fletcher, M. and Scott, A. (2005), *Local Government in Scotland and the European Governance Agenda: A discussion Paper,* Edinburgh, Convention of Scottish Local Authorities (COSLA).

Butler, T and Savage, M. (eds.) (1995), *Social Change and the Middle Classes,* London, UCL Press.

Byrne, T. (2000), *Local Government in Britain* Harmondsworth, Penguin.

Cabinet Office (1970), *The Reorganisation of Central Government*, Cmnd. 4506, London: HMSO.

Caiden, N. (1997), 'Public services Professionalism for Performance Measurement and Evaluation', *Conference Paper on Public Services in Transition*, Thessalonika, Greece.

Carter, N. (1988), 'Measuring Government Performance', *Political Quarterly,* Vol. 59 No. 3, pp.369–375.

Carter, N. (1989), 'Performance Indicators: "Backseat Driving" or "Hands Off Control', *Policy and Politics*, Vol. 17 No. 2.

Carter, N. (1991), 'Learning to Measure Performance: the use of indicators in organisations', *Public Administration,* 69, pp.85–101.

Carter et al. (1991), 'Measuring Government Performance, *Political Quarterly,* Vol. 59 No. 3, pp.369–375.

Carter, N., Klein, R. and Day, P. (1992), *How Organisations Measure Success: the use of performance indicators in government,* London: Routledge.

Carter, N. (1998), 'On the Performance of Performance Indicators' in *Evaluation Des Politiques Publiques,* Paris, L'Harmattan.

Cathcart, (1936), *Report of the Committee on Scottish Health Services,* Cmnd. 5208. Edinburgh HMSO.

Cave, M., Hanney, S. and Kogan, M. (1991), *The Use of Performance Indicators in Higher Education: A Critical Analysis of Developing Practice*, 2nd. edn, London: Jessica Kingsley.

Cave, M., Hanney, S. and Henkel, M. (1995), 'Performance Measurement in Higher Education-Revisited', *Public Money and Management,* Vol. 15 No. 4 pp.17–24.

Citizens Charter (1991), *The Citizens Charter: Raising the Standard,* Cmnd 1599, London: HMSO.

Citizen's Charter (1992), First Report, Cm. 2101, London: HMSO.

Convention of Scottish Local Authorities (COSLA) (1995), *Future of the Convention,* Edinburgh: COSLA.

Convention of Scottish Local Authorities (COSLA) (2004), *Annual Report,* Edinburgh: COSLA.

Craft, N. (1998), *The Conservative Government's Economic Record: An End of Term Report,* Institute of Economic Affairs Occasional Paper 104, London, Institute of Economic Affairs.

Cuenin, S. (1986) *International Study of the Development of Performance Indicators in Higher Education: Paper Given to the OECD, IMHE Project, Special Topic Workshop*, Paris: OECD.

Dahrendorf, R. (1985), *Law and Order: The Hamlyn Lectures,* London, Stevens and Son.

Day, P. and Klein, R. (1987), *Accountabilities: five public services,* London: Tavistock.

Dror, Y. (1968) *Public Policy Re-examined,* San Francisco, Chandler.

Dunleavy, P.J. (1986), 'Explaining the Privatisation Boom: Public Choice versus Radical Approaches', *Public Administration,* pp.13–34.

Dunsire, A. (1975), *Administration: The Word and the Science,* London: Martin Robertson.

Dunsire, A. (1978), *The Execution Process Vol. 1 Implementation in a Bureaucracy,* London, Martin Robertson.

Dunsire, A. (1990), 'Holistic Governance', *Public Policy and Administration,* Issue 1, pp.3–18.

Egan, C. (1996), 'Fixing a course by flexible landmarks', *Local Government Chronicle Performance Indicators Supplement,* 22 March, 8.

Eglinton (1998), *Re-inventing Management: A study on the potential impact of the Scottish Parliament on the role and function of public managers,* Eglinton Management Centre, Edinburgh, 1998.

Elmore, R. (1978), 'Organisational models of social program implementation', *Public Policy,* 26(2), pp.185–228.

Etzioni, A. (1967), Mixed Scanning: A "Third" Approach To Decision Making, *Public Administration Review,* December, pp.385–392.

Fahey, L. and Narayanan, V.K. (1986), *Macroenvironmental Analysis for Strategic Management,* St. Paul, MN., West Publishing.
Falconer, P.K. (1999), *Better quality Services: Enhancing Public Service Quality through Partnership in the UK,* Paper presented at the Fifth International Conference on Public Private Sector Partnerships at the University of Cork, Sheffield, Sheffield Hallam University Press.
Fayol, H. (1949), *General and Industrial Management,* London: Pitman.
Ferlie, E. et al. (1996), *The New Public Management in Action,* Oxford, Oxford University Press.
Fesler, J.W. (1980), *Public Administration: Theory and Practice,* London, Prentice-Hall.
Flynn, N. (1986), 'Performance Measurement in Public Sector Services', *Policy and Politics,* Vol. 14 No. 3.
Flynn, N. (1993), *Public Sector Management,* London, Prentice-Hall Harvester Wheatsheaf, pp.170–185.
Flynn, N. (1997), *Public Sector Management,* 3rd edn, London, Prentice-Hall.
Fowler, A. (1975), *Personnel Management in Local Government,* London, Institute of Personnel Management.
Frederickson, H.G.(1980), *New Public Administration,* University of Alabama, University of Alabama Press.
Frederickson, H.G. (1996), 'Comparing the reinventing government movement with the New Public Administration', *Public administration Review*, Vol. 56, No. 3, pp.263–270.
Friedman, M. and Friedman, R. (1980), *Free to Choose,* Secker and Warburg.
Fulton (1968) *Committee on the Civil Service: Report,* Cmnd. 3638, London: HMSO.

Gamble, A. (1985), *The Political Economy of Freedom,* in Levitas, R. (ed.), *The ideology of the New Right,* Cambridge, Polity.
Gamble, A. (1994), *The Free Economy and the Strong State,* 2nd edn, Basingstoke, Macmillan.
Garrett, J. (1980), *Managing the Civil Service, London,* Heinemann.
Gaster, L. (1995), Quality in Public Services: Managers Choice, Milton Keynes, Open University Press.
Giddens, A. (1998), *The Third Way: the renewal of social democracy,* Cambridge, Blackwell
Goldthorpe, J., Lockwood, D., Bechhofer, F. and Platt, J. (1969), The Affluent Worker in the Class Structure, Cambridge, Cambridge University Press.
Goldthorpe, J. et al. (1987), *Social Mobility and Class Structure in Modern Britain,* 2nd edn, Oxford, Clarendon Press.
Gray, R. (1983), 'Problems of Accountability, *Public Finance and Accountancy*, November.
Gray, A. and Jenkins, W.I. (1985), *Administrative Politics in Britain,* London, Wheatsheaf.

Gray, A. and Jenkins, W.I. (1986), 'Accountable Management in British Central Government: Some Reflections on the Financial Management Initiative', *Financial Accountability in Management,* Autumn.

Gray, A. and Jenkins, W.I. with Flynn, A and Rutherford, B. (1991), 'The management of change in Whitehall: the experience of the FMI', *Public Administration,* 74, pp.41–59.

Gray, A. and Harrison, S. eds., (2004), *Governing Medicine: Theory and Practice*, Maidenhead, Open University Press.

Gray, R. (1983), 'Problems of Accountability', *Public Finance and Accountancy*, November.

Greenwood, J., Pyper, R. and Wilson, D. (2002), *New Public Administration in Britain,* 3rd edn, London, Routledge.

Gunn, L.A. (1978), 'Why is implementation so difficult ?', *Management Services in Government,* Vol. 33, pp.169–176.

Gunn, L.A. (1987), 'Perspectives on Public management', in Kooiman, J and Eliassen, K.A., eds. (1987) *Managing Public Organisations: Lessons from Contemporary European Experience,* London, Sage.

Gunn, L.A. (1994), *Public Management,* MBA Teaching Papers, Glasgow: University of Strathclyde.

Haddow (1934), *Committee on the Qualifications, R3ecruitment, Training and Promotion of Local Government Officers: Report of the Committee* London, HMSO.,

Halsey, A.H., Lauder, H., Brown, P. and Stuart-Wells, A. (1997), *Education: Culture, Economy and Society,* Oxford, Oxford University Press.

Harrison, A. and Gretton, J. (eds.) (1987), Reshaping Central Government, Bekshire: Policy Journals (Hermitage).

Hatry, H., Gerhardt, C., and Marshall, M. (1994), 'Eleven ways to make performance measurement more useful to public managers', *Public Management,* September, Vol. 76.

Hayek, F. (1949), Individualism and Economic Order, London, Routledge.

Heald, D. (1983), Public Expenditure: its defence and reform, Oxford: M. Robertson.

Hicks, H.G. and Gullett, C.R. (1981), *Management,* 4th edn, New York, McGraw-Hill.

Hill, M. (1997), *The Policy Process in the Modern State,* 3rd edn, London, Prentice-Hall.

Hirsch, W. (1973), 'Program Budgeting in the United Kingdom', *Public Administration Review,* March/April, pp.120–128.

Hirschman, A.O. (1970), *Exit, Voice and Loyalty: Response to decline in firms, organizations and states,* Cambridge, Mass., Harvard University Press.

Hitch, C.J. (1965) *Decision-Making for Defence,* Berkeley, University of California.

HM Treasury (1982), *Financial Management in Government Departments,* Cmd 9058 London: HMSO

HMSO (1970), *The Reorganisation of Central Government,* Cmnd. 4506, London: HMSO.

HMSO (1982), *Efficiency and Effectiveness in the Civil Service,* Cmnd. 8618, 1982, London: HMSO.

HMSO (1988), *Civil Service Management Reform: The Next Steps Session 1987–88 Eighth Report,* London: HMSO.

HMSO (1992), *The Next Steps Agencies Review*, Cm. 2101, London: HMSO.

Hoggett, P. (1996), 'New modes of control in the public service', *Public administration,* 74, pp.9–32.

Hogwood, B.W. and Gunn, L.A. (1984), *Policy Analysis for the Real World*, Oxford: Oxford University Press.

Hood, C.C. (1976), *The Limits of Administration,* London, Wiley.

Hood, C.C. (1991), 'A Public Management for All Seasons', *Public Administration,* Vol. 69 Spring 1991.

Hood, C.C. (1995), 'The "New Public Management" in the 1980s: Variations On A Theme', *Accounting, Organisations and Society,* Vol. 20, No. 2/3, pp.93–109.

Hood, C.C. (1996), 'Bureaucratic regulation and New Public Management in the United Kingdom: mirror image developments, *Journal of the Law Society,* Sept. Vol. 23, pp.321–345.

Hughes (1968) *Committee on the Staffing of Local Government in Scotland: Report* (The Hughes Report), Edinburgh: Scottish Development Department.

Hughes, O. (1998), *Public Management and Administration,* 2nd edn, New York, St. Martin's Press.

Hutton, W. (1996), *The State We're In,* London, Vintage.

Hutton, W. (1997), *The State To Come,* London, Vintage.

Hyndman and Anderson (1998), 'Performance information, accountability and executive agencies' *Public Money and Management,* Jul-Sep, Vol. 18, pp.23–30.

Industrial Society (1994), *Performance Management,* London: Industrial Society.

Ingram, H.M. and Mann, D.E. (1980), *Why policies succeed or fail,* London, Sage.

Jackson, P. and Terry, F. (1988), *Public Domain: The Public Sector Yearbook 1988,* London, Public Finance Foundation.

Jackson, P. (1988), 'The Management of Performance in the Public Sector', *Public Money and Management,* Winter, pp.11–16.

Jenkins, K., Caines, K. and Jackson, A. (1988), *Efficiency Unit: Improving Management in Government: The Next Steps,* London, HMSO.

Jenkinson, J. (2000) in Nottingham, C. ed., (2000), The NHS in Scotland: The legacy of the past and the prospect of the future, Aldershot, Ashgate.

Johnsen, A. (1999), 'Implementation mode and local government performance measurement: A Norwegian Experience', *Financial Accountability and Management,* Feb., Vol. 15, No. 1, pp.41–67.

Johnson, G. and Scholes, K. eds. (2001), *Exploring Public Sector Strategy, Harlow*, Pearson Education.

Johnson, G. and Scholes, K. (2002), *Exploring Corporate Strategy, 6th ed., Harlow*, Pearson Education.

Kanter, R.M. (1984), *The Change Masters: Corporate Entrepreneurs at Work,* Allen and Unwin.

Kanter, R.M. (1995), *World Class,* Simon and Schuster.

Kanter, R.M. and Summers, D.V. (1987), in Powell, W.W. (ed.), *The Non-Profit sector: A Research handbook,* New Haven, CT, Yale University Press.

Kaplan, R.S. and Norton, D.P. (1996), 'Using the balanced score-card as a strategic management system', *Harvard Business Review,* Vol.74, Issue 1, pp.75–85.

Keeling, D. (1973), *Management in Government,* London, George Allen and Unwin.

Keeting, M. (2005), *The Government of Scotland: Public Policy Making after Devolution,* Edinburgh, Edinburgh University Press.

Kerley, R. (2000), *The Report of the Renewing Local Democracy Working Group,* Edinburgh, Scottish Executive.

Keynes, J.M. (1936), *The General Theory of Employment Interest and Money,* London, Macmillan.

Klein, R. (2001), *The New Politics of the NHS,* Harlow, Prentice-Hall.

King, A. (ed.) (1976), *Why is Britain Becoming Harder to Govern?* London, BBC Publications.

Kooiman, J and Eliassen, K.A., eds. (1987) *Managing Public Organisations: Lessons from Contemporary European Experience,* London, Sage.

Kravchuk, R.S. and Schack, R.W. (1996), 'Designing Effective Performance Measurement Systems under the Government Performance and Results act of 1993', *Public Administration Review,* July/August 1996, pp.348–358.

Lane, J. (2000), *The Public Sector: Control, Models and Approaches,* London, Sage.

Layfield (1976), *Committee on Local Government Finance:* Report (The Layfield Committee), London: HMSO.

Lindblom, C.E. (1959), 'The Science of Muddling Through', *Public Administration Review,* 19, pp.78–88.

Linkierman, A. (1993), 'Performance Indicators: 20 early lessons from managerial use', *Public Money and Management,* Vol. 13 No. 4.

McCrae. M. (2003), *The National Health Service in Scotland: Origins and Ideals 1900–1950,* East Linton, Tuckwell Press.

McFadden, J. and Lazarowicz, M. (2003), *The Scottish Parliament*, 3rd edn, Edinburgh, LexisNexis UK.

McIntosh (1999), *The Commission on Local Government and the Scottish Parliament Report* (The McIntosh Commission): Edinburgh: HMSO.

McKevitt, D. and Lawton, A. (1994), *Public Sector Management: Theory, Critique and Practice*, London: Sage.

McKevitt, D. and Lawton, A. (1996), 'The Manager, the Citizen, the Politician and Performance Measures', *Public Money and Management,* Vol. 16, No. 3, pp.49–54.

McTavish, D. and Mackie, R. (2003), 'The Joint Future Initiative in Scotland: The Development and Early Implementation Experience of an Integrated Care Policy', *Public Policy and Administration,* Vol. 18 No. 3, Autumn pp.39–56.

Mackie (2001), Paper for the Centre for Public Policy and Management (CPPM) at Glasgow Caledonian University (unpublished).

Mackie, R. (1999), *Management Development in Scottish Local Government*, Paper Presented at COSLA Training and Development Conference (unpublished).

Mackie, R. (2004), 'Local Government Management Development in Scotland: A Study of Public Policy and its Implementation, 1967–2002', *Local Government Studies,* Vol. 30 No. 3, Autumn pp.345–359.

Mallaby (1967), *Committee on the Staffing of Local Government: Report* (The Mallaby Report), London: HMSO.

March, S. and Simon, H.A. (1958) *Organisations,* New York, John Wiley.

Marsh, D. and Rhodes, R.A.W. (1992), *Implementing Thatcherite Policies,* Buckingham, Open University Press.

Maud (1967), *Committee on the Management of Local Government: Report* (The Maud Report), London: HMSO.

Mayston, D.J. (1985), 'Non-profit Performance Indicators in the Public Sector', *Financial Accountability and Management,* Vol. 1 No. 1 Summer.

Mayston, D.J. (1991). 'Educational Performance Assessment—A New Framework of Analysis, *Policy and Politics,* April, Vol. 19, No. 2, pp.99–108.

Mayston, D.J. (1992), 'Capital Accounting User Needs and the Foundations of A Conceptual Framework for Public Sector Financial Reporting', *Financial Accounting and Management,* Vol. 8, Issue 4, pp.227–249.

Mazmanian, D. and Sabatier. P (1981), *Effective Policy Implementation,* Lexington Mass., Lexington Books.

Meekings, A. (1995), 'Unlocking the Potential of Performance Measurement: a Practical Implementation Guide', *Public Money and Management,* 15 (4), pp.5–12.

Metcalfe, L. and Richards, S. (1987), *Improving Public Management,* London: Sage.

Midwinter, A. (1994), 'Developing Performance Indicators for Local Government: the Scottish experience', *Public Money and Management,* Vol. 14 No. 2 April-June pp.37–43.

Midwinter, A. (1995), *Local Government in Scotland: Reform or Decline?* Basingstoke, Macmillan.

Midwinter, A. and McGarvey, N. (1995), 'Organising the new Scottish Local Authorities—some problems with the new management agenda', *Local Government Policy Making,* Vol. 22 No. 1 July, pp.3–15.

Mintzberg, H. (1975), 'The manager's Job—Folklore or Fact', *Harvard Business Review,* Jul-Aug, Vol. 53 Issue 4.

Mintzberg, H. (1989), *Mintzberg on Management: Inside Our Strange World of Organizations,* New York, Free Press.

Monies, G. (1996), *Local Government in Scotland,* Edinburgh, W. Green.

Montgomery Report (1984), *Committee of Inquiry on the Islands Councils,* Cmnd 9216, Edinburgh: HMSO.

Niskanen, W. (1971), *Bureaucracy and Representative Government,* Chicago, Aldine-Atherton.

Nottingham, C. ed., (2000), The NHS in Scotland: The legacy of the past and the prospect of the future, Aldershot, Ashgate.

O'Donnell, A. (1996) in Pyper, R. (ed.) (1996), *Aspects of Accountability in the British System of Government,* Wirral: Tudor Business Publishing.

Onslow (1929), *Third Report of the Royal Commission on Local Government,* London HMSO.

Open University (1993), B887 *Managing Public Services*, Milton Keynes: Open University.

Organisation for Economic Co-operation and Development (OECD) (1997), *In Search of Results: Performance Management Practices,* Paris: OECD.

Osborne, A. and Gaebler, T. (1992), *Reinventing Government: How the Entrepreneurial Spirit is Transforming the Public Sector,* Reading MA, Addison-Wesley.

Painter, C. (1999), 'Public Service Reform from Thatcher to Blair: A Third Way', *Parliamentary Affairs,* Vol. 52, Issue 1, pp.94–112.

Paterson (1973), *The New Scottish Local Authorities: Organisation and Management Structures: Report* (The Paterson Report), Edinburgh: HMSO.

Perry, J. and Kraemer, K.L. (eds.) (1986), *Public Management: Public and Private Perspective,* California, Mayfield.

Peters, B.G. and Savoie, D.J. (1994), 'Civil Service Reform: Misdiagnosing the Patient', *Public Administration Review,* Vol. 54, Issue 5, pp.418–426.

Peters, T.J. and Waterman, R.H. (1982), *In Search of Excellence: Lessons from America's Best Run Companies,* New York: Harper and Row.

Piore, M. and Sable, C (1984), *The Second Industrial Divide: Possibilities for Prosperity,* New York, Basic Books.

Plowden (1961), *Control of Public Expenditure: Report (The Plowden Report)*, Cmnd. 1432, London: HMSO.

Pollitt, C (1986), 'Beyond the Managerial Model: The Case for Broadening Performance assessment in Government and the Public Services', *Financial Accountability and Management,* Autumn, pp.155–169.

Pollitt, C. (1987), Performance Measurement and the Consumer, London: National Consumer Council.

Pollitt, C. (1990), Managerialism and the Public Services: The Anglo-American Experience, Oxford, Basil Blackwell.

Pollitt. C and Harrison, S. (1992), *Handbook of Public Services Management,* Oxford, Basil Blackwell

Pollitt, C. (1993), Managerialism and the Public Services: The Anglo-American Experience, 2nd edn, Oxford, Blackwell.

Pollitt, C. (1994), 'The Citizen's Charter: a preliminary analysis', *Public Money and Management,* Vol. 14 No. 2 April-June, pp.9–14.

Pollitt, C. (2001), 'Is The Emperor In His Underwear? An analysis of the impacts of public management reform', *Public Management,* Vol. 2, No. 2, pp.181–199.

Potter, J. (1988) 'Consumerism and the Public Sector: how well does the coat fit?', *Public Administration*, Summer Vol. 66 No. 2.

Pressman, J. and Wildavsky, A. (1973), *Implementation,* Berkeley, Calf., University of California Press.

Prime Minister (1991), *The Citizen's Charter. Raising The Standard,* Cm. 1599 London: HMSO.

Pyper, R. (ed.) (1996*), Aspects of Accountability in the British System of Government*, Wirral: Tudor Business Publishing.

Pyper, R. and Robins, L. (ed.) (2000), *United Kingdom Governance,* Macmillan.

Rainey, H. Backoff, R. and Levine, C. (1976), 'Comparing Public and Private Organisations', *Public Administration Review,* Vol. 36 pp.233–246.

Rainey, H.G. (1990), *Public Management: recent developments and current prospects,* New Jersey, Chatham House.

Ranson, S. and Stewart, J. (1994), *Management for the Public Domain: enabling a learning society,* London, St. Martin's Press.

Redcliffe-Maud (1969), *Royal Commission on Local Government in England and Wales: Report* Cmnd. 4040, London: HMSO.

Rogers, S. (1990), *Performance Management in Local Government,* Harlow, Longman.

Rowe, C. and Thompson, J. (1996), *The Human Implications of Information Technology,* London, McGraw-Hill.

Scotland, J. (1969), *The History of Scottish Education,* London: University of London.

Scott, W.R. (2003), *Organizations: Rational, Natural and Open systems*, 5th edn, Upper Saddle River, Prentice-Hall.

Scottish Leadership Foundation (2002), Scottish Leadership Foundation Website.

Scottish Office (1963), *The Modernisation of Local Government in Scotland*, Cmnd. 2067, Edinburgh: HMSO.

Scottish Office (1971), *Reform of Local Government in Scotland*, Cmnd. 4583, Edinburgh: HMSO.

Scottish Office (1992), *The Structure of Local Government in Scotland: Shaping the New Councils*, Edinburgh: HMSO.

Shaw, J. E. (1942), *Local Government in Scotland*, Edinburgh, Oliver and Boyd.

Simon H.A. (1947), *Administrative Behaviour,* London, Macmillan.

Sizer, J., Spee, A. and Bormans, R. (1992), 'The Role of Performance Indicators in Higher Education', *Higher Education,* Vol. 24 pp.133–155.

Spurgeon, P. ed. (1998), *The New Face of the NHS*, London, Royal Society of Medicine.

Smith, P. (1995), 'Performance indicators and outcome in the public sector', *Public Money and Management,* Oct/Dec. Vol. 15, No. 4, pp.13–16.

Smith, P. (1995b), 'On the Unintended Consequences of Publishing Performance Data in the Public Sector', *International Journal of Public Administration,* Vol. 18 2/3 pp.277–310.

Smith, P. (1996), *Outcome Measurement in the Public Sector,* London: Taylor and Francis.

Stephens, A. and Bowerman, M. (1997), 'Benchmarking for Best Value in Local Authorities', *Management Accounting,* Vol. 75, No. 10, pp.76–77.

Stewart, J and Walsh, K. (1994), 'Performance Measurement: When performance can never be finally defined', *Public Money and Management,* Vol. 14 No. 2 April-June, pp.45–50.

Stodart Report (1981), *Committee of Inquiry into Local Government in Scotland: Report*, (The Stodart Report), Edinburgh: HMSO.

Stoker, G. and Wilson, D. (ed.) (2004), *British Local Government into the 21st Century,* Basingstoke, Palgrave Macmillan.

Talbot, C. (1998), 'Output and Performance Analysis—Time to Open up the Debate?' *Public Money and Management,* Apr-June, Vol. 18, No. 2, pp.4–5.

Taylor, J. and Williams, H. (1991), 'From Public Administration to the Information Polity', *Public Administration* Vol. 69 No. 2.

Tichelar, M. (1998), 'Evaluating performance indicators: current trends in local government', *Local Government Studies,* Autumn, Vol. 24, No. 3, pp.29–35.

Van Meter, D.S. and Van Horn, C.E. (1977), 'The Policy Implementation Process: A Conceptual Framework', *administration and Science,* 6(4), February.

Vickers, G. (1964) 'The Psychology of Policy Making and Social Change', *British Journal of Psychiatry.*

Wheatley (1969) *Royal Commission on Local Government in Scotland: Report* (The Wheatley Report) Cmnd. 4150, Edinburgh: HMSO.

Widdicombe, D. (Chairman), *The Conduct of Local Authority Business: Report of the Committee of Inquiry into the Conduct of Local Authority Business,* Cmnd 9797, London, HMSO.

Wildavsky, A. (1966) 'The Political Economy of Efficiency: Benefit analysis, Systems analysis and Program Budgeting', *Public Administration Review,* Vol. 26, No. 4.

Wilson, D. and Game,C. (1998), *Local Government in the United Kingdom,* London, Macmillan.

Wilson, J. ed. (1998), *Financial Management for the Public Services,* Buckingham, Open University Press.

Wilson, J. and Hinton, P. (1993), *Public Services & The 1990s,* Wirral: Tudor Business Publishing.

Winkler, F. (1987), 'Consumerism in Health Care—Beyond the Supermarket Model', *Policy and Politics,* Jan. Vol. 15, No. 1, pp.1–8.

Woods, K. and Carter, D. eds. (2003), *Scotland's Health and Health Services,* London, Nuffield Trust.

Websites

Extensive use was made throughout this text of the websites of the following organisations:

Audit Scotland:	*www.audit-scotland.gov.uk*
COSLA:	*www.cosla.gov.uk*
NHS Scotland:	*www.show.scot.nhs.uk*
Scottish Executive:	*www.scotland.gov.uk*
Scottish Parliament:	*www.scottish.parliament.uk*
Management Standards:	*www.management-standards.org.uk*

INDEX

[all references are to page number]